Sexy Beast

STAN CATTERMOLE
THE INTIMATE ADVENTURES OF AN UGLY MAN

Collins

Paperback edition published in 2010 by Collins

HarperCollins Publishers
77-85 Fulham Palace Road
London W6 8JB

www.harpercollins.co.uk

First published by Collins in 2009 as *Bête de Jour*

13 12 11 10
7 6 5 4 3 2 1

646.
77

ISBN: 978-0-00-731964-0

Design template by seagulls.net. Typeset by www.TheOakStudio.co.uk
Printed and bound in Great Britain by Clays Ltd, St Ives plc

Mixed Sources
Product group from well-managed
forests and other controlled sources
www.fsc.org Cert no. SW-COC-001806
© 1996 Forest Stewardship Council

FSC is a non-profit international organisation established to promote the
responsible management of the world's forests. Products carrying the FSC
label are independently certified to assure consumers that they come
from forests that are managed to meet the social, economic and
ecological needs of present and future generations.

Find out more about HarperCollins and the environment at
www.harpercollins.co.uk/green

For Melanie, with love,
and for Ange, with boundless optimism.

A WORD ABOUT THIS BOOK

This book was born of a blog. The blog was born of a dream. The dream was born of a desperation to change things. And the good news is, it worked. Things have changed. My life is now wholly positive and I will never frown, curse, spit, swear, scream, or suffer an overwhelming urge to go on a murderous rampage through South London ever again.

This, then, is the story of my life: the ups, the downs, the sickness, the health, the good, the bad, and the ugly. As it was and as it is. All the names of the people in my life have been changed because, for various reasons, they don't deserve otherwise. The dialogue has also been polished for purposes of heightened readability. A few of the locations have been changed too, as well as one or two absolutely crucial facts. But the rest is pretty much verbatim. I hope it pleases you. If it doesn't please you, I am genuinely sorry, and I hope you find what you're looking for elsewhere. Before you get stuck in, however, be warned ...

This book has a happy ending.

... I, that am not shaped for sportive tricks,
Nor made to court an amorous looking-glass;
I, that am rudely stamp'd, and want love's majesty
To strut before a wanton ambling nymph;
I, that am curtail'd of this fair proportion,
Cheated of feature by dissembling nature,
Deformed, unfinish'd, sent before my time
Into this breathing world, scarce half made up,
And that so lamely and unfashionable
That dogs bark at me as I halt by them;
Why, I, in this weak piping time of peace,
Have no delight to pass away the time,
Unless to spy my shadow in the sun
And descant on mine own deformity:
And therefore, since I cannot prove a lover,
To entertain these fair well-spoken days,
I am determined to prove a villain
And hate the idle pleasures of these days ....

Richard III, William Shakespeare

CHAPTER ONE

NOBODY, NOT EVEN THE RAIN

I have been led to believe that when I was first presented to my mother, her face collapsed in on itself like a failed soufflé. All of the joy and lust for motherhood leaked from her body, face first, like she'd just been handed a baby with little more than blunt stumps for limbs, or a baby with its heart on the outside of its skin, clinging to its chest like a silver bell on a kitten's bib, beating and bleeding and raw for all to see.

But really there was nothing wrong with me. I was just a bit ugly.

It was often said, by my father, to his friends, that I had the kind of face only a mother could love. Just not *my* mother. How Father would laugh.

Mother wanted to know. 'What's wrong with it?'

'Nothing's wrong with him,' she was told. 'He's a perfectly healthy baby boy.' As it happens, this was true only to a certain extent. I was healthy, yes, but I had a couple of conditions which would in time necessitate medical intervention.

'But,' Mother insisted, scandalised, unable to stem the flow of fat, affronted tears, 'but he's so ugly! How can he be so ugly?'

Father was there too, sweating pale ale and chip fat. It is to him that I owe this account of Mother's reaction. Although Mother did later confirm it.

I was born with a large face, shaped not unlike a lozenge, or even – if one were feeling particularly cruel – like a gravestone in a rough part of the cemetery, defaced, vandalised, and overgrown. I had the dark patches of skin – intrinsic atopic dermatitis – which were later to become my trademark. Added to which, my eyes were further apart than was strictly necessary and, irritatingly, they were staring out in opposite directions. This was rather unpleasantly pronounced strabismus, which I am ecstatic to say was later corrected with surgery. When I first opened my eyes, however, it was apparently something of a shock. Oh, and also – for a baby – I did have rather a large nose.

In short, I was a beast.

I was, however – if anyone was interested – in predominantly very good health.

Unfortunately, my health was not at the front of my parents' concerns. They were rather superficial people who apparently had their hearts set on a beautiful baby, a beautiful baby boy more specifically, of the bouncing variety. I didn't bounce. They were disappointed, and for reasons best known to themselves, they never attempted to conceal their disappointment. Rather they muttered and cursed, mocked and sneered, shook their heads and prayed to their malevolent God that my ugly face would prove ephemeral as puppy fat, and that in no time at all I would grow out of that and into great, unutterable loveliness. Tragically, their prayers remained not only unanswered, but also cruelly ridiculed, as rather than gradually transforming me into a handsome swan as they'd requested, their malevolent God had me bound through my childhood like a kangaroo in a minefield, exploding into one physical aberration after the other.

My parents were embarrassed and ashamed, and it didn't seem to mitigate their shame at all that as I got older I began to excel at school. On the contrary, I think it may have made things worse.

In time I came to realise that when they were schoolchildren themselves, my parents were most probably vicious, vindictive bullies, for whom kids who had the temerity to actually enjoy reading were alien and fearful. Having one such child under their very own roof was, I suspect, an unpleasant reminder of their own cerebral and parental shortcomings, and yet another reason for them to despise me. They seemed to think that because I read books and they did not, I presumed I was better than them. They were right. I did. So they would deride me, cruelly. They would call me 'smart arse', 'clever shit', and 'Little Lord Fauntleroy', an adaptation of which they had seen on television, but not really understood.

For my own part, I had no choice but to take refuge in other people's words. Time spent reading was an escape from my parents, from the persecution of schoolfriends and, of course, from myself. It was the only time when I began to see that life had the potential to be a thing of beauty, and so I did my absolute best to immerse myself in the lives of fictional people as often as I possibly could. Indeed, for a very long time, fictional people and fabulous, anthropomorphic beasts were my only real friends.

I had no brothers and no sisters, and although it was alleged that extended family members did exist, I rarely saw them. There was an uncle, who posed for photographs with his penis hanging outside of his flies, and a paternal grandfather, from whom I inherited not only my clumsy name, but also my uncomely face. I saw an ancient cracked photo or two of my grandfather and it's true that, as far as appearances are concerned, the man was a monster. Apparently, the one thing that made him an attractive enough proposition to eventually snag a female and procreate was the fact that he owned a farm. In those days, of course, farms were all the rage. Owning a farm back in the day was like driving round in a gold-plated Ferrari today, pissing pearls.

I don't have a farm.

I don't even have a window box.

All I have is this unfancy face, full of terrible fortune, half-resignation, and the fading scars of dead eczema. So I suppose it's not really surprising that people are intrigued by the idea of me having sex. I'm intrigued myself.

I've had sex with two women in my life. And the fact that I've had it before must surely mean that I can have it again. The first time came out of nowhere – like a spear of frozen urine from an overhead toilet facility – when I was twenty-four years old.

Her name was Avril, and she was my Diana Adams.

Diana Adams is Rocky Dennis's salvation in the film *Mask*, a film which had a profoundly salubrious effect on me and helped me through many a low ebb during my teens. When I was desperately down, excruciatingly alone, weeping and wishing I'd never been born, *Mask* came to me, like a deformed genie wrapped in a daydream, and it gave me a good old kick up the arse, in much the same way as Jesus does, for many otherwise rational people. Before *Mask* it was *The Elephant Man*. But *Mask* was much more important because, not only was it set in a world with which I could much more readily identify, but also, it had kissing, and I had always been inordinately fond of the idea of someone kissing me.

No one kissed the Elephant Man.

Poor Elephant Man.

Rocky Dennis was born with craniodiaphyseal dysplasia, an extremely rare bone disorder which causes a calcium build-up in the skull. Instead of a head, imagine a giant cough sweet in a ginger wig. That was Rocky Dennis. And *Mask* is the true story of how he overcame the daily torture of physical deformity and lived as ordinary and fulfilling a life as he possibly could. At least, until he was sixteen, when he died.

For all his physical misfortune, however, Rocky had two things which I never had when I was growing up (three if you count a great porn name): he had a supportive circle of family and friends; and he had Diana Adams, played in the film by Laura Dern.

Diana Adams was – believe it or not – a blind girl. Which makes you think. Firstly, it makes you think, yes, that makes sense. For only a blind girl could see beyond the cough-sweet skull and discover the worth in such a shocking-looking young man. But then, secondly, hold on just a minute – surely, when she got round to touching his face, wouldn't she have pretty much the same reaction that other people have when clapping eyes on him for the first time? Well, I guess the theory is that by the time she'd touched his face, Diana had got to know him, without the impediment of having judged his freakishness with her eyes, and to know Rocky was to love him.

I identified with Rocky Dennis an awful lot and, particularly at that time in my life, I felt that my face was not that far removed from his. So, naturally, from the moment I saw *Mask* for the first time, I was on permanent look-out for a sexy blonde blind girl who would tousle my hair, press her soft lips against mine and not give a damn about my big, ugly face. I actually went as far as to enquire at a college for the visually impaired, but that's not something we need dwell on.

Then, quite by chance, I met Avril.

Avril was thirty-three. She was not what you'd call good-looking in the traditional sense, but she did have astonishingly striking eyes and a large, quite perfect chest. Furthermore, she was bright, articulate, and often viciously funny. On the downside, however, she also had phocomelia.

Phocomelia is the congenital disorder which afflicted many of the children of thalidomide mothers. Apparently the word itself comes from the Greek for 'seal limbs', a reference to the flipper-type hands which are a common symptom.

Avril was severely physically disabled and spent most of her time in a wheelchair. She had two tiny legs and a tiny left arm, which she labelled 'fun-size', and occasionally 'fin-size'. Her right arm was slightly twisted but otherwise OK, except for the hand, which again, was a little on the small side.

The first time I laid eyes on Avril, I must admit, I thought, 'Now there's someone who might be desperate enough to have sex with me.' She later confessed that she'd thought pretty much exactly the same thing about me.

I became friends with Avril through her brother, Stu, who I'd worked with very briefly on an aborted radio show. Feeling bad and beholden because I'd ended up working and not getting paid, Stu invited me over to dinner one night. At his place. With him and his wife.

In truth, I didn't actually relish the idea of spending the evening with a happy couple in their happy home with their happy, well-adjusted baby gurgling happily close by, jerking its tiny fists and having happy, well-adjusted baby dreams. But I did relish the idea of a free meal, so I graciously accepted.

And, as it happens, it was disgustingly pleasant. Stu's wife, Carolyn, was lovely, Stu was charming alongside her, and – OK, I'll say it – even the baby was inoffensive enough. I was enjoying myself.

Then the house telephone began to squeal. It was Stu's sister. She was outside in a taxi, fuming angry. She'd had a big row with their parents. Stu huffed and puffed, apologised, excused himself, then went outside.

While he was out of the room, Carolyn said, 'I don't know if Stu's mentioned Avril before ....' He hadn't. 'Well, just so you know, she's in a wheelchair.'

'Oh,' I said. 'That's um ... that's great. Well, not great obviously. I mean, that's fine. Which is to say, I've not got a problem with that. Obviously. I mean, why would I?'

Carolyn smirked at me and briefly limpened a wrist as if to put me at my ease.

I smirked back.

Avril was still in feisty mood when she whirred up to the table. Stu introduced us. Avril immediately picked up on my dithering over whether or not to shake her hand – she was used to it. I had already stood up and was wondering whether even that might be construed as a rather insensitive move. She held out her right arm. 'Here,' she said. 'Shake my tiny hand.' I laughed and did so, and even then it crossed my mind, the old adage about men liking women with small hands. But I thought better of sharing it. Instead I said,

'Pleased to meet you. That reminds me of the E. E. Cummings poem.' Then I immediately felt like such an obnoxious, idiotic, ham-fisted oaf. I blushed. But I'd started, so I had to finish. 'Nobody,' I quoted, 'not even the rain,' I continued, 'has such small hands.'

Avril pulled a face. 'What are you saying?'

I blushed some more. 'I don't know really. It's a poem.'

'I've got absolutely no idea what that means,' she said.

'Now play nice,' said Carolyn.

Avril laughed. 'No, I'm not being mean. I genuinely don't understand. The rain doesn't have hands. Or am I missing something?' She looked at Stu, who shrugged unhelpfully. I wondered whether 'Am I missing something?' was a joke.

'I don't think it was meant to be taken literally,' I offered.

'You don't think he wrote the poem about a deformed girl then?' asked Avril.

I shook my head, then changed my mind. 'Actually I think he did,' I replied. 'Yeah, I remember now. He definitely did. He wrote it about a girl with really tiny hands.'

Avril laughed again. 'Marvellous,' she said. 'That's marvellous.' I drank some more wine, relieved.

At the end of the evening Avril and I were left alone. Stu and Carolyn were tidying up in the kitchen and making coffee.

'You know the worst thing about my disability?' Avril asked me, apropos of nothing.

'Hold on a minute,' I said. 'Let me think.'

I thought. The answer that occurred to me was 'Not getting enough sex?', but I didn't voice it, because I didn't want to offend. So instead I said, 'Swimming in circles?', which was just unbelievably, unconscionably, excruciatingly dumb. But she laughed anyway, which was nice of her. 'No,' she said. 'The worst thing about being in this chair, and having these fucked-up limbs ...' – she had quite a fruity vocabulary, Avril – '... is that most men tend not to think of me in terms of someone they might like to fuck.'

Perhaps over-enthusiastically I responded, 'I know! That's what

I thought, I just didn't like to say! But I do know exactly what you mean. I don't know whether you've noticed, but I'm – well, I'm quite an ugly bloke.'

'Oh, I dunno,' she replied. 'You're no Tom Cruise, but you know, you're not ...' She ran out.

'That was a valiant effort,' I said. 'And it's appreciated, really it is. But the fact is, I am a frighteningly ugly bloke, and I don't mean to demean your condition when I say this, but ugliness, to this extent, is actually a kind of disability.'

'Oh, *come on*,' she said.

'It is!' I squeaked.

'How so?' she asked.

'In a way,' I continued, 'it's actually worse. Because at least you have an excuse.' She raised an eyebrow. Perhaps 'excuse' wasn't the right word. Well, too late now. I moved on. 'Let me explain. People look at me and their reaction is probably similar to the reaction they have when they look at you. They think, you're just not in the running. No pun intended. You're not someone they'd consider – whether for sex, for a job or, nine times out of ten, even for conversation ... One of the reasons I work as a copywriter is because I can get a lot of work without having to turn up for an interview. Most of the jobs I get are on the strength of my writing. I don't have to impress in person.' I was getting into my stride now, the alcohol filling my mouth with words. 'I'm pretty much good at everything I do – no arrogance intended – but I've never got a job I had to interview in person for. Even if I've been perfect for the job. And this is because I'm butt-fuck ugly.'

Avril laughed.

'Yeah, laugh it up. At least you've got rights groups and laws looking out for you. Do you know it's not even illegal to discriminate against ugly people?'

'That's a disgrace,' she said. 'Maybe you should start a campaign,' she said.

'Maybe I should,' I said. 'Maybe I will.'

I didn't.

'It'd be a complete waste of time though,' she countered. 'You'd still be discriminated against. Trust me. So where did you say you lived?'

The question took me by surprise. I hadn't said any such thing. 'Herne Hill,' I told her. 'Why?'

'Just making conversation,' she said. 'Do you live alone?' When I said that I did, she said, 'Maybe you should invite me round for dinner this weekend then? I promise I won't discriminate against you.'

'OK,' I said. 'Maybe I will.'

I did.

So. That weekend, in an act of mutual desperation, I lost my virginity. Actually, that sounds terrible. It was an act of mutual attraction as much as anything. And, as I found out later, Avril wasn't remotely desperate. It was just me. I had waited an awful long time for this moment, and when it finally happened, it was fun, and it was passionate, and although I didn't realise it at the time, it was actually rather kinky. We got up to all kinds of shenanigans, and I'm not just talking flipper-play. Then, at half past midnight, she asked me to call her a cab.

'Don't you want to stay?' I asked. 'You're welcome to stay.'

'I'd like to,' she said, 'but my husband likes me home.'

'Your ... You're married?'

'Did I not mention that? I thought you knew.'

I didn't know.

Avril had been married for six years. She and her husband had an open relationship. He was also, as she put it, 'a spaz', and he liked her to go off and have sex with other men. They would relive it together. It turned them both on. He knew she loved him. She knew he loved her.

Avril asked me if she thought it was weird, but before I could answer, she told me, 'It's not as weird as able-bodied men getting off on sleeping with disabled women, or blokes who can only get an erection if a woman has a stump or a flipper. Or wheels.'

I ended up seeing Avril once every couple of months or so for around two and a half years. Then I started to want more. I wanted a proper relationship. Not that a long-term affair with a lady in a wheelchair is somehow improper, but rather, I wanted to be in love.

Five years later, that's still what I want. Now, however – thanks in part to my faithful companion, Pablo – I'm finally determined to do something about it.

CHAPTER TWO

WHISKERS OF IMMORALITY

Pablo's ears prick irritably as, across the street from my house, a woman screams. It's not an ugly scream, however, but a scream with laughter oozing out of the cracks. It's like she senses something, something magnificent and formidable stirring nearby. I drag myself to my feet and limp magnificently to the window, twitching back the curtain like a man twice my age.

It's New Year's Eve, and a few minutes to midnight. The Festive Season is almost at an end. Thank God for that.

I've never been a fan of the Festive Season. Especially as a child. It started well enough, with the slightly forced excitement of the last school day, but it was all pretty much downhill from there. The Festive Season was like dead air. It was slow, tense time between the predictable uproar of the special days, when the banks were closed and television was relentless. I spent this time in my bedroom, in hiding, or else playing darts at my best friend's house, and if there was a rumpus of some description at home, I kept out of it as much as I possibly could, blocking out the bickering to the best of my ability, ignoring the tantrums, and suffering whatever contact sports Father was mad enough to insist upon with mute disdain and very occasional outbursts of my own.

The Festive Season was fraught.

Christmas was hateful enough, charged as it was with instinctive, seasonal self-pity, but New Year's Eve always had something particularly ominous and dreadful about it. Unlike

Christmas, New Year's Eve was neither a time for family, nor for God. Rather, New Year's Eve was a time for drinking heavily, going berserk and breaking things.

By the age of six or seven, I had already begun to associate the end of the year with scenes of extraordinary domestic ugliness. Many of these scenes came to me in eavesdroppings as I lay plastered to my bedroom floor with my ear cupped to the carpet, or else crouched at the top of the stairs like a cat, coiled and holding my breath. Others I witnessed firsthand as I was summoned to make an appearance and coerced into shaking the nicotined hands of the drove of drunken buffoons whom Father had corralled home from the pub. Inevitably, one or more of these soused strangers would leave a pool of urine on the canvas floor of the toilet, awaiting my bare feet in the early hours of the morning.

From the age of eight or nine, if I was at home, Father made a point of pestering me to join him and his friends in 'drinking in the New Year'. The first time it happened I knew no better. He called me over and bent down beside me with a beaker of cheap whiskey. I was afraid, but warmed by the gesture. I sipped at the lip of the warm glass slowly, excited and grateful. Then the whiskey hit my tongue and I felt like I'd been poisoned. Worse still, I felt tricked and humiliated. Instinctively, I spat out the poison and fled from the kitchen, coughing and wheezing, pushing through bodies and heading for the stairs, where Mother grabbed hold of my arm and laughed smoke and Bucks Fizz into my burning face. I wriggled free and made a dash for it, slamming my bedroom door behind me. Father was laughing and shouting something up the stairs. I never accepted a drink from him again.

During our last New Year together, Father grabbed me as I was sneaking home from a friend's house. 'You come and have a drink!' he demanded, staggering through the house half full of the usual drunken jumble of strangers. 'It's New Year's Eve, for fuck's sake.' He led me to the heart of an inebriated throng, half-filled a plastic cup with neat whiskey and fumbled it into my hands. 'Drink up,' he said. 'Happy New Year!' He knocked back his whiskey and cheered. A few of the strangers knocked back their drinks too, and a short chain of cheers spread throughout the mob and died. Someone turned the music up. It was 'You Can't Hurry Love'. The Phil Collins version.

'Happy New Year,' I said quietly, raising my glass but not drinking.

Father was silent for a moment. Then he knocked back more whiskey and started shouting over the music. He wanted to know who the hell I thought I was. I didn't know. He wanted to know why he'd sacrificed the best years of his life putting food on the table for an ungrateful little bastard like me. I didn't know. He wanted to know if I thought I was better than him. This one I did know.

I thought I was better than him because I didn't spend my entire life trying to belittle and humiliate the people I was meant to love and nurture.

I didn't say anything. I tried to walk away, but Father put his hand against my chest and insisted. 'Do you think you're better than me?'

I looked into my father's eyes. They were grey and wet, bulging like infected oysters. I was fifteen years old, full of cider and nihilistic dread. My face was hot, but my eyes were cold, and I assume my father could see something in them that made him slightly afraid. 'I'm going to bed,' I said. I tossed the whiskey in the sink behind him and he let me pass, scowling and grumbling.

Later that night Mother fell on top of the television and cracked a rib.

This kind of nonsense went on all year round, of course, but New Year's Eve always came with a special tension. All that forced introspection; all that vain expectation; all that shame.

Meanwhile, feeling no shame whatsoever, the woman across the street laughs uncontrollably as her boyfriend holds her against a wall and kisses her roughly. One of his hands disappears inside her skirt, which is, it has to be said, little more than a belt. My right hand caresses my left eyebrow instinctively, and my breath clouds up the window. She must be jolly cold. She pulls away from the man and trots off, dragging him behind. 'Let's go!' she tweets. 'It's ten to!'

They disappear into a party to see in the New Year. I hobble back to the settee, pull the duvet over my body and unmute the TV with the remote.

I'm limping not because of nascent arousal, but because I have a severely bruised coccyx from a fall yesterday morning. I was inching down the metal staircase outside my house when I slipped on an icy step and fell like a sack of cement on to the small of my spine. I am still in considerable agony.

Pablo hops into my lap and regards me with a certain disdain.

'What?' I ask. 'What's your problem?'

He says nothing, just blinks softly as if to say, 'What kind of loser sits home alone on New Year's Eve talking to his cat?'

'Oh, piss off,' I snap. 'You're no better.'

Again, his eyes do the talking. 'Ah, but cats don't celebrate the passage of time,' they say. 'We have better things to do.' And, as if to prove his point, Pablo pads three tight circles, then curls up and closes his eyes.

On television, this year's celebrities are prancing and gurning, all shrill glibness and crass, forced jollity. There is less than a minute to go. Thirty seconds. Ten. Nine. Eight. And so on, till another exhausted year takes off its timeworn hat and with a wildly over-theatrical gesture, replaces it with another, identical hat. Which is not to say that this year will not be different, because this year most certainly will. Recent events have brought change, and the course of True Love is one on which I am suddenly very eager to enrol. I know what must be done, and it shall be done, but not just yet. Tomorrow is another year, but for now I make myself comfortable and listlessly pleasure myself to the familiar grunts and slaps of online pornography.

After which, as I'm removing the sock I have used as a cotton catcher's mitt, I inadvertently knock Pablo awake with a loose knee. As he eyes me with thinly disguised contempt, I flash back, with shame and confusion furrowing my brow, to my sweaty adolescence, and a sweet little kitten called Mavis.

Mavis was no more than six months old at the time, and one afternoon I was home alone, much as I am now, watching TV in my room and eating toast with Dairylea triangles and too much Marmite. Inadvertently, some of the Marmite found its way on to the back of my hand. Rather than wash it off thoroughly, I merely licked it off lazily with a Marmitey mouth. Then, later that afternoon, still in my room, Mavis began licking the back of my hand with unusual attentiveness. One might even say passion. 'Hmmm,' I thought. 'Interesting.'

A few days later – hours, minutes, whatever – I decided to conduct a little research. I popped down to the kitchen, returning moments later with the lidless Marmite jar. I undressed myself, lay on the bed and smeared a tiny trail of Marmite on – at first – my nipples, which are particularly sensitive, then later, when that proved an enormous success, on the end of my burgeoning boyhood. I'm not proud. But I'm not ashamed.

When I imagine the scene objectively – a teenage boy with a bulbous head lying naked on an unmade bed in a rank and rancid bedroom, the dying summer sun trying and failing to squeeze its fingers through permanently closed curtains – I feel bewildered and amused by what I regard as innocent, albeit slightly bizarre experimentation. Much like the time I pranced in front of the bathroom mirror wearing nothing but my mother's brassiere and lipstick, or the time I tore my dead uncle's penis from a photograph and carried it around in my jeans pocket for weeks.

At the time, as I lay on my side, holding myself in my right hand, a tiny black kitten lapping at the tip of my youthful johnson with its tiny, sandpapery tongue, I remember suddenly feeling baffled and incredulous.

As it happens, the experiment didn't last very long. Not

because I discharged myself in poor Mavis's tiny, startled eyes, but because at some stage – more or less exactly the same time that she began to get a little bitey – I guess I saw what I was doing, objectively, as if watching a documentary about bestial teens, and I felt alarmed, and not a little dismayed. So I stopped. Then I went and washed myself, took Mavis downstairs and gave her some proper food. We said no more about it. Least said, soonest mended.

I remember all this as I pull up my pants, with Pablo curled up close by. I remember it every time I pleasure myself when Pablo's in the room, and I always feel just a little bit guilty. But not ashamed.

Pablo cocks his head and looks at me now as if he knows all about Mavis. But he doesn't. I never told him and I never will. This is why he relents at my touch, closing his eyes and purring when I scratch his neck, rather than hissing at me and calling the Cat Protection People. There is, however, a note of distrust in his eyes. As far as he's concerned, I'm still on probation after the distressing behaviour he witnessed only weeks ago, when I flapped around the dark flat helplessly, shamelessly flailing in the jaws of a giant, inertia-induced doldrum.

After not leaving the house for eight or ten days, maybe more, I'd reached a legendarily low ebb. Pablo had enough food to last him a few more days, but I was completely out. The last thing I wanted to do was leave the house, but I was becoming painfully hungry. My gut was screeching like dolphins. Which is when it happened.

I was feeding Pablo, spooning fish-flavoured meat from a tin to his bowl, when I wondered, 'How bad would this taste if I heated it up?'

Minutes later, I stood with a single chunk of meat before me on a spoon. It was every bit as succulent, I'm sure, as meat one might find in the guts of a Goblin Meat and Gravy Pudding, for example, but that didn't stop me retching slightly as I moved it closer to my open mouth.

Pablo was watching me. His head was hovering above his bowl, his eyes focused on mine as if to say, 'What the hell do you think you're doing?'

I turned away, stuffed the meat into my mouth and gobbled it down. It wasn't so bad, but still my face was twisted with disgust. Suddenly I saw myself objectively, and I despaired. I felt the kind of despair that only a man spooning cat food into his mouth can truly feel. Thankfully the despair seeped into disgust, and the disgust slapped me hard across the face and prompted action.

I apologised to Pablo and immediately went upstairs to get dressed. Then I left the solitude and hopelessness of the sanctuary of my home, because they were making me unwell, and I forced myself on to the street which marched me swiftly, slightly too swiftly, into bustling Brixton.

Brixton is generally a fairly easy place to feel anonymous, but on that day I was feeling unusually conspicuous. I felt that people were staring, more so than usual. There was disapproval in the air. Condemnation. Despite the cold, which I felt intensely, my skin was clammy with sweat. I was feeling paranoid. Then someone offered to sell me a skunk called Charlie and I freaked out and ran into the Ritzy Cinema, where a young lady with a sleepy face let me hide in the bathroom for ten minutes.

I hadn't had a panic attack in over ten years. Not like that.

When I got home that afternoon, I sat myself down and gave myself a good, stiff talking-to, if not more of a shouting-at.

My life was a mess. I was spending most of every day smeared across the futon like a rash, like bed-sores, propped up in front of bad TV and Tony Hawk's *Pro Skater 4* on unruly piles of pillows and cushions, incapable of finding the impetus to move. The curtains were permanently closed to keep the day at bay, and my waking hours, mostly at night, were filled up with DVDs and packet after packet of Sugar Puffs, Jaffa Cakes and chocolate HobNobs. I rarely left the house. My weight was inching up to the 20-stone mark. My flesh was the colour and consistency of yesterday's gruel, and although I was pretending to be dead to the fact, I was well aware that I was about to turn thirty. And I had never had a girlfriend.

In the conventional sense of the word.

I had even stopped self-pleasuring, which is a very, very bad sign. When you can no longer take even the most fleeting physical pleasure from your own body, and your own brain, that's when you know you're in trouble.

I realised that, unless I acted, by the time I was thirty-two I'd be one of those tragic souls who has to have the walls of their house removed so they can be lifted by crane to the nearest hospital for gastric-bypass surgery. Libido would be a thing of the past and I would neither remember nor care. I would survive on a diet of puffed wheat, sugar and cat food. Pablo would long ago have left home.

I had to do something. There had to be change.

And on the night of my thirtieth birthday, there was.

CHAPTER THREE

BAG OF ELBOWS

I was afraid. It was a cloudless night, ice hanging in the air. My breath was bright like broken glass and my skin was colder than Christmas. I shivered. The fear I felt had nothing to do with the fact that I was expanding into middle age like a dirty great stain, destined to spend the rest of my life with only my cat for company. No. Rather it concerned the fact that I was trudging towards a pub in Dartford where a gang of my childhood peers was lying in wait, doubtless preparing to relive our schooldays by taunting me with a cruel concoction of harsh words, drawing pins, and spittle, until I'd have no option but to leave the room, walk slowly to the nearest lavatory, lock myself in a cubicle and sob, silently.

But it had to be done. I was in recovery.

All my life I'd been terrified of what people thought of me. I went back to Dartford on the night of my thirtieth birthday because, finally, that had changed; because, finally, I didn't care any more; and because, finally, I refused to be terrified. Now I was merely afraid, and the verbal slings and arrows which previously I'd allowed to reduce me to a whimpering, bleating, petrified feedbag, would from that point forth bounce off my broad back like ducks off a diving board.

Plus, I'd been invited to a school reunion via Friends Reunited, which I'd joined on a whim a mere matter of months before. It seemed like fate.

Keith, my lifelong friend and schoolmate, had refused to

accompany me. We'd been in mostly different classes at school and many of the people I knew, he didn't. Nor did he particularly want to. The idea of going alone was dreadful to me, but I had to get out of the house or there was a very real danger I was going to lose my mind.

So there I was. Out of the house and consumed with good old healthy fear.

Resisting the ever-present temptation to turn round and go home, I soldiered on, on the path to recovery, all dressed up and taking the bull by the horns.

The last thing I want, incidentally, is to come across as bigoted in any way, or discriminatory, or supercilious – but it's important that I'm honest about this perhaps slightly controversial fact: people from Dartford are subnormal. If you've ever spent any time in Dartford, you will know this to be true. I don't know what went wrong in the gene pool, but I suspect that, at some stage in Dartford's history, some malevolent swine shat in it. I swear, the people of Dartford possess less human kindness, less discernment, less decency, and fewer IQ points than the inhabitants of any other inner-city conurbation anywhere else on planet Earth … with the one single exception of Orpington. Maybe. It's a close-run thing.

I hadn't been back to Dartford since my mother's funeral some years previously, and I felt sick, like I was about to jump out of an aeroplane or dive from the top of a giant building in the name of sporting glory.

I caught sight of myself in the window of a stationary car and sighed. Apart from my face, which was an abomination, and my body, which was bursting at the seams, I looked good. Which is to say – with all thanks due to Leonard Cohen – I was dressed well.

While I was studying for 'A' levels I would never achieve, mooning after Marie Meeks in her well-filled duffel coat, with her shiny black hair and dazzling mouth, Leonard Cohen came to me with the following words: 'An ugly man needs good clothes.' These words struck me in the gut and left a mark that would endure. Until then I'd dressed like a slob, like your average, miserable teenager who gave no thought to matters sartorial. I knew I looked bad as a whole and so assumed – stupidly – that the clothes I wore would make no difference whatsoever. But I trusted Leonard Cohen, and the time and care I began to invest in my attire paid dividends. I felt better about myself and, at least to a certain extent, it showed.

So when I walked into the not especially charming and not especially friendly bar of the Hufflers Arms public house at precisely 8 p.m. – an hour after some of my former classmates had promised to arrive – I may have looked fat and afraid and ugly, I may have been sweating preternaturally, like a pig in a steam room but, at the very least, I was dressed like a prince. And that counted for something.

I made for the bar and ordered myself a pint of Guinness. When it finally arrived, I glugged at it like an overexcited man kissing a beautiful woman for the first time.

The pub was busy. As I sipped at the second half of my drink and glanced around, I recognised no one. I knew that, sooner or later, I'd have to wander through to the other rooms. The thought pained me considerably. Who would be the first person to recognise me, I wondered, and what would they shout out? Which of the hideous, heart-wrenching barbs that passed for nicknames would I first be forced to relive?

'Stan?'

I turned, and there it was. The smiling face of the first woman to whom I never dared offer my unreciprocable love.

Angela Charlton. Ange.

To my credit, I didn't stutter. Well, maybe a little. A slight cha-cha-cha on her surname, but nothing to tango to.

When she leaned forward to hug me, something inside me leapt. It was the Christmas-themed sandwich I'd scoffed in Charing Cross station an hour ago. I managed to keep a lid on it as she pecked me on the cheek and cried, 'Wow!' Her hand still on my arm, she said, 'You look good, man. How are you?'

Bless her. Bless you, Angela cha-cha-cha-Charlton, for that small but much appreciated kindness. She was never so kind at school, but I loved her anyway.

I looked at her, felt for a moment that I might be holding back tears, then pulled myself together. 'I'm fine,' I told her. 'I'm OK. You know?' I added. 'I'm all right.'

I wanted to say, 'I survived. I survived the five years of torture that was my comprehensive education.' But instead I just smiled inanely, suddenly happy to be there.

'How are you?' I managed. 'You look ...' I stopped. How did she look, this woman whose face had filled dozens of socks with my plump, ungainly seed? Actually she looked old and tired and sad. 'You look fantastic!' I cried. It was true. She still had an achingly sexy face, with limpid blue eyes, a perky, some might say haughty nose and a lusty, pornographic mouth. Plus she was still stunningly put together, her breathtaking body still lofty, proud and pneumatic. She looked remarkable. I gazed into her eyes and the love I used to feel coursed back through my being.

She rolled her eyes. 'Right,' she said. 'I look like my grandmother is how I look. I'm all right though. It's good to see you.'

'Can I get you a drink?' I asked.

'Yes,' she answered. 'Please. That'd be great.'

While I was being served, Angela Charlton's phone made a noise. She picked it up and put it to her ear. 'Oh, hi,' she said. 'Yeah, I'm here .... No, not yet, I just arrived, but you'll never guess who's here .... No, no, don't be silly. No ....' Then she said my name. No nicknames. Just my name. Again it was appreciated. 'Yeah! Yeah, I'm standing right next to him actually ....' I sensed that the person on the other side of the conversation had not been so kind.

Indeed, the person on the other side of the conversation, whoever it was, had shrieked it after the mention of my name.

'*Bag of Elbows?!*'

I had a lot of nicknames at school, but 'Bag of Elbows' – along with its variations – was without doubt the most popular. Variations included 'Elbows', 'Elliot Elbow' and – sadly only once – 'Edgar Allan Elbow'. Also, when I was fourteen, overnight – thanks to a Sunday-night screening of *The Elephant Man* on BBC2 – I became 'Merrick'.

The elbow theme kicked off in the first week of secondary school. I was eleven years old, and Gary Butler said to his friend Simon Figgins that I, sitting at an adjacent desk, had 'a face like a bag of elbows'. Despite the fact that it made my first year absolutely unbearable, I can still see that it was quite a perceptive and well-crafted observation. There's truth in it. I do have a face like a bag of elbows.

So, naturally, when Gary Butler said those words on that fateful day, they stuck. Bag of Elbows. That's what I became, and to a certain extent, certainly in the minds of people who know me from school, that's what I still am. A voluminous bag, fashioned from thick human skin and filled to bursting with the bones of a thousand elbows.

'You'll never guess who that was,' said Ange, sipping at her drink. 'It was Karen Walsh.'

'Ah.' Yes, I remembered Karen Walsh. 'Oh, joy,' I said.

Ange laughed. 'Don't worry,' she said, 'everyone's grown up a bit since school. Even Karen.'

'Just a bit?' I tried to affect a sophisticated expression, but I think I may just have managed mean. 'So you two are still friends then?'

She said yes; they had drifted apart after school, then met at an earlier reunion.

Ange then spent five or ten minutes filling me in on her life since school – the bad exam results and time served at McDonald's, the subsequent promotions and wasted years; the Pole she loved and lived with, long before Poles were *de rigueur*; the baby she lost when the Pole got drunk and jealous and punched her in the kidneys; the six-month trip around the world with her younger sister; her new life as a teacher in Hackney, retrained, revitalised and, despite the frustration and laughably long hours, daily rewarded.

'We should go and find the others,' she said. My stomach turned. I was enjoying talking to her, listening to her, looking into her eyes and remembering. I really didn't want to find the others at all. 'Let me just get another drink,' she said, knocking back the rest of her rum. 'Do you want another Guinness?'

'*ELBOWS!!!*'

And so it began.

Suddenly a fist of faces reared up at me from the past. There was Neil 'Bucky' Buckley, who had a reputation for violence at school he appeared not to have outgrown. He was in tip-top physical condition, with some unpleasant tattoos, including a small blue teardrop high on his left eyelid. When he came towards me laughing, I flinched, but he was friendly. 'Look at the size of you,' he laughed, and shook my hand vigorously. He seemed pleased to see me. He asked me what I do now. I told him I write stuff for junk mail. Looking slightly impressed, he said, 'That figures.' He said, 'You was well into all that shit.' I resisted the urge to correct his grammar.

The best story I heard about Bucky all night was that he might be about to lose his job as a security guard for smoking a joint at work. The detail that made the story golden was that he was filmed smoking the joint on the same security cameras he was being paid to monitor. Bucky had a copy of *Nuts* in his coat pocket and a rash of tiny white scars on the knuckles of his left hand. He was a travesty and, like me, he was the polar opposite of Deborah Hutton.

Deborah Hutton was almost as unpopular as I was at school, but for entirely different reasons. She managed to irritate almost everybody with whom she came into contact simply by being perfect. Well spoken, beautifully turned out, very bright and sweetly pretty, she always gave the impression that she was in entirely the wrong school. Other girls hated her because they sensed in her a superiority which they suspected was well founded; boys hated her because she wouldn't let them taste her unnaturally bright lips or put their grubby, nicotine-stained fingers up her skirt. I always liked her myself, but from a distance of light years. We were amusingly dissimilar, and I was very surprised to see her at the Hufflers Arms. She seemed surprised to see herself there. It was her first reunion too, and the only reason she was there at all was because her father was dying and she was desperate to escape the cloying stench of rotting flesh and ylang ylang, even for just a couple of hours.

Age had not withered Deborah Hutton. She was still bright and beautiful and beaming. Also, transformed by impending grief, she was caustic and careless and dangerous. When she smiled at me, I ached. I wished I were eight stone lighter and had Jake Gyllenhaal's face. Sadly, I do not. Happily, neither does Darren McLaren.

Fifteen years have not been kind to Mac. Indeed, time has transformed a boy with quite a pleasant face and a sprightly form into a man with a pot belly and a comb-over. On the upside, he no longer seems to be under the impression that spitting phlegm at people's backs is the height of sophisticated repartee. On the downside, nothing seems to have taken the place of this odious habit. Mac is a sophistication vacuum, and a charm void to boot. He's also a Business Manager at a branch of the NatWest bank in Dartford. Hearing this made me smile. It made me really happy to think that, although I may, in my time, have stooped devilishly low – so low, in fact, that neither stealing and defacing a bible nor ripping the genitalia from a dead man's memories were beneath me – I have never, *never* worked in a bank.

If we'd had US-style year-books at our school, Georgina Bentley would have been voted 'Girl most likely to end up in the sex industry'. Georgina apparently thought nothing of orally pleasuring any boy brave enough to ask her. Such was the reputation she never denied. Now she's a secretary for an insurance company in Maidstone.

Georgina – George – is a big, bouncy girl with a square face, eyes that are slightly too far apart, and a passion for Arthurian legend. She met her current boyfriend playing World of Warcraft. George isn't exactly the sharpest chisel in the toolbox, but she is fun and funny and extremely likeable.

Then there was Karen Walsh, sporting a sensible brown bob and a not unpleasant smile on her eager, open face. Walshy was an absolute shit to me at school. Now she's a social worker in Lewisham. She hadn't said a lot to me since arriving at the pub, but she definitely seemed to have changed. It was early though. The jury was still out.

The strangest thing was standing there actively harbouring a grudge for at least two of those people. After all these years. As if nothing had changed. As if we were still teenagers.

Things, however, had definitely changed. I'd changed. Apart from ballooning in size, the main difference was that I was no longer crippled by shyness and shame. I used to let the likes of Bucky and Mac make me feel inferior. Now I looked at them and I felt pretty damned good about myself. They both looked so spent, and defeated, and neither of them had anything of any consequence to say. I felt good.

Realising they no longer had the power to make me feel bad, I felt less pressure. I relaxed. And the grudge fell away, like a cloak of dead skin, and a new me emerged, unashamed, unafraid, and confident. Suddenly I was glad to be there. Back where I belonged, among people. However, there was still plenty of time for things to go horribly wrong.

But for now I was mingling magnificently and speaking to everyone. Alfie Mussett had turned up too, as had Liam McDowell and Julie Moore. I caught up with them all, and reminisced like Gulliver, excited and freshly returned from his travels. Sadly, none of us – except Deborah Hutton and Angela Charlton – had done anything particularly exciting with our lives. At least Deb and Ange had each travelled a bit, more than the odd fortnight in a hotel here and there. Bucky, I discovered, had never once set foot outside the

UK. And neither did he seem particularly perturbed by this fact.

'But there's so much going on,' I pointed out. 'There are, like, two hundred countries in the world, and nearly seven billion people. Don't you want to maybe, experience a bit of it?'

He scowled at me, and half laughed, but not in a mean way. 'You don't get it, do you? The thing is, I really couldn't give a fuck about all that. I'm happy where I am, with what I've got. I couldn't give a monkey's about the rest of the world, if I'm honest.' His face had softened. He was genuinely trying to explain himself. I felt quite touched and privileged in a distinctly patronising way.

I held my hands up in resignation. 'That's fine. I'm happy you're happy. I just can't help thinking, you know ...'

'Yeah, you always thought too much,' he interrupted. 'That was your problem, mate.'

'What does that even mean? And what the fuck else was I supposed to do?' I realised I'd kind of snapped this. And I swore. And I don't often swear. Not out loud. 'There was nothing else for me to do. I was hardly the most popular kid in school.' I'd snapped that too. I smiled at him, deliberately. I could feel myself getting emotional. That really wasn't supposed to happen. The grudge had gone. I tried to remember that. It was all in the past. Calm. Calm. 'What do you want to drink, Bucky? Let me buy you a drink.'

A couple more drinks down the line and I found myself talking with Ange, Deb, and George. I was drunk, they were drunk, we all were drunk, and the conversation turned to physical appearance. Not mine, but it was only a matter of time.

George was lavishing praise upon Deb Hutton. And rightly so. Then she extended her praise to Ange, congratulating them both on managing to keep their figures.

I interrupted. 'Oh, God, George. Don't you know it's seriously bad form to start talking about weight in the presence of someone who's morbidly obese?'

They laughed.

'You're not morbidly obese,' chirped George and Deb

predictably.

'You are definitely obese though,' said Ange.

George gasped. 'Don't be mean!' she cried.

'It's OK,' I said. 'As it happens, she's right.' Ange gave me a playful punch on the arm. I scrunched up my face at her adoringly, but I'm not really sure how it went across.

The conversation remained cosmetic. George was talking about her sunbed addiction. 'It's just about the only time I ever leave the house,' she said, 'apart from work. I even do it in the summer.' Deb was the opposite. With her white, flammable body, she was obsessed by skin cancer and terrified of the sun.

'I went to a tanning salon once,' I said, 'but I think I was allergic.' They laughed. 'It's far from funny,' I insisted. 'I came out in a rash. But it's good that it gets a laugh. It's good that my suffering brings a little happiness into the world.'

'Oh, poor you,' said Ange.

I laughed. I love Ange. 'No, but it's a nightmare,' I persisted. 'It's like there's nothing I can do to even pretend that I'm healthy ...'

'You could lose weight,' said Ange, flatly. Followed by the disapproval of George and Deb. George actually blushed on my behalf.

I smiled. 'No, she's absolutely right,' I said. 'Losing weight would be a good place to start.'

'No, but I think it's really good.' This was George continuing to shy away from the truth. 'You know, everyone is so vain these days, and I include myself in that, although you might not think so to look at me. I'm a complete slave to vanity and I hate it. I think it's really good that you're not ... you know, that you haven't give in to the pressures ...'

'What makes you think I haven't given in to the pressures of vanity, George?'

She stopped talking, unsure of whether or not I was joking. She searched my expression. Her drunken eyes bobbed across my many-elbowed face, like wooden hoops down cobbled streets. 'No, I just mean ...' She was lost.

I put her out of her misery. 'I know what you mean,' I chuckled. 'And I know there's a compliment in there somewhere desperately trying to fight its way through to the surface and I really appreciate it, honest I do. But you're going to have to give me a blow job to make up for it.'

I was drunk. Part of me strived to feel embarrassed and apologetic for what I'd just said but it was getting laughs and it *was* only a joke, for God's sake – kind of – and the new me was a little bit more loose-lipped than the old me. And I liked him for that.

Ange was patting George on the back, really quite firmly. George was choking, having laughed some of her wine up through the roof of her mouth into her nose. At one stage, she was bent double, a piece of grit in the very eye of a coughing fit. 'Seriously though,' I continued, 'it was very difficult for me at school, being the only boy in the third, fourth, and fifth year that you never went down on.'

Eventually George recovered enough to say, between loud sniffs and mutterings of 'Oh dear', 'Well, you never asked, did you? Everybody else asked.'

'You're in there, Stan,' Ange declared bawdily. 'She's just a girl who can't say no.'

To which George replied, 'Hold your horses, Ange love, that was fifteen years ago.'

'A leopard never changes its spots,' Deb piped up.

'So what, you're the same prissy bitch you were when you were at school, are you?' George retorted.

'Now this is more like it.' Ange laughed. 'This is what I come to these things for!'

'If you thought I was a prissy bitch then, then yeah, you probably still will now, but that might say more about you than it does about me,' came Deb's decidedly prissy reply.

'Yeah, no change there,' George snapped back, and they both laughed drunkenly, all talk of my oral pleasure washed away on this exultant wave of slightly bitter nostalgia.

Then Bucky appeared with a tray which was positively

overwhelmed by drinks. 'Here you go, peeps,' he said. 'Peeps!' I repeated, grabbing hold of what I guessed was my fifth, but it could have been my eighth Guinness. 'Cheers!' I shouted. Suddenly everyone was standing around in a rough circle, maniacally clinking one another's glasses.

'Look in the *eyes!*' cried Karen, as she clinked each in turn. '*The eyes!*' cried Ange. Cries of '*Eyes!*' reverberated round the pub, and people clinked and reclinked while drunkenly staring avidly into the windows of one another's souls.

'Here's to the *past!*' I cried, to still more clinks, and there it went – '*the past!*' – bouncing clumsily but merrily round a ring of rubbery wet mouths.

When last orders were called, I found myself drinking vodka, which I knew to be a very stupid idea right then as I was pouring it into my fat neck. The conversation had turned to Christmas, the conversational curse of the season.

Bucky, Ange, Kaz, and George reminisced about some Christmas party where Graham Uren (whose surname made his life a misery) got so drunk that he believed he was possessed by the devil. Complete breakdown. Oh, the hilarity.

Well, I wasn't at that party, because I wasn't invited, but I do remember that Christmas. The Christmas of 1992. I remember the last day of term particularly well, because it was the day I was suspended from a goalpost on the school football field, wrists tied over the crossbar with a length of rope, me stretched on to my tiptoes, and my trousers pulled down around my ankles. It was the day thirty or so fellow pupils came to look and laugh and point and I had to wait for twenty-five minutes, in mute terror and fierce, boiling humiliation, before anyone had the decency to let me down.

'It was funny though,' Mac pointed out.

He'd been one of the five or six of my schoolmates responsible for tying me up.

'No.' I looked at him, really trying to stop my eyes from tearing up. 'No, it really wasn't funny,' I repeated. 'It totally fucked me up for a long time and it really wasn't funny.'

Mac eventually became aware that there was a situation. He glanced back and forth at other faces, his grin fading.

'Darren, have you ever been publicly humiliated, or bullied?'

He squirmed and nodded his head. 'All right, mate, I'm sorry. It was a long time ago, you know what I mean ...'

I was about to continue to argue with him, when Karen stepped forward and grabbed my arm, gestured for me to follow her and walked me away from the group towards the door and out on to the street, where she took hold of my wrists, looked up at my face and into my eyes and said, 'Stan, I just wanted to say, I'm really, really sorry for the part I know I played in the torture that you had to put up with day in and day out for years in that ... horrible fucking school. I'm honestly, genuinely *so* sorry.'

And that's all it took. I burst into tears. My hands flew up to my face and I began to bawl. Karen tried to put her arms around me. I resisted at first, blocking her with my arms. Then I forced myself to stop weeping, and gradually lowered my guard. Karen's face was wet too. She smiled at me, put her arms around my neck and squeezed.

Off I went again.

I don't believe I'd cried this hard since I was at school. Maybe not since recovering from the goalpost incident. I held on to her like I could have squeezed the life out of her if I wasn't careful and I cried like a giant baby with a face that not even its mother could love. And if you think I'm ugly in the cold light of day, you should see me with a skinful of Guinness and vodka on a cold winter's night with my mad face sobbing and snot dangling from my nose.

'It's all right,' said Karen. 'It's OK. Everything's OK now. Come on. Come on, let's get your face dried up.'

Gradually my sobs subsided. Karen gave me tissues. 'I'm really glad you came tonight. For selfish reasons, I mean. It's really made me confront some things that I'd been pushing to the back of my mind, you know?'

I blew my nose. 'This is not *Oprah*,' I said, and Karen laughed. She looked at me, all smiles. 'You know what?' she said. 'You turned out really fucking well.' And that was that. I was off again.

Back in the pub a little while later, there were more drinks from somewhere, loud music and erratic loose-limbed dancing. Then time was called. It was over. We were being moved on.

'But I was just getting going,' I told the barman.

'Just get going,' the barman replied, wittily.

'We're going clubbing, mate, come on!'

'Mac!' I yelled.

'We're going to Air & Breathe!'

'Breathe!' I yelled. 'Breathe!'

Then I remember choking, trying to breathe, trying desperately to catch my breath, fighting the feeling that I was drowning. Then I remember movement, falling and tumbling. Then I remember waking up, parched and gasping, my throat like a rusty cheese-grater. Then waking again with my legs and arms held hostage by a giant, sweet-smelling duvet. Light filtering through half-closed curtains. I had absolutely no idea where I was. I was alone. I was naked. I felt horrendous and frightened and lost. I closed my eyes and crawled away from the pain of consciousness, back into the sanctuary of sleep.

I was woken again at 10.15 a.m. By Ange. She knocked and popped her head round the bedroom door. 'Wakey wakey,' she chimed. I groaned, believing this to be the appropriate response at moments such as this. I pulled the duvet instinctively over my face, which was somehow covered in bits. 'Where am I?' I whimpered.

'You're at Ange's house in Hackney,' Ange replied. I was in Ange's spare room. I breathed it in. 'You had a bit too much to drink last night and got sick on George, so we brought you home in a cab. Karen's here too and we're all about to eat breakfast together and have a good old laugh about last night.'

Minutes later I shuffled through the living room and into the kitchen. My clothes were still drying so I was squeezed into Ange's dressing gown, which I was trying not to feel too closely or smell too keenly for fear of inappropriate arousal, and which just about covered my shameful amplitude but was in truth a tad too pink and flowery for my taste; much pinker, in fact, and a great deal more flowery than I was feeling. '*Goooood* morning!' cried Karen, bright as a bag of buttons on Cardigan Day. 'Don't you look good enough to eat!' She laughed, amused by herself.

Apparently, we never made it to the club. Outside the pub I had an attack of best frienditis and began hugging everyone and telling them that I had learned a lot and that I considered them all very dear friends, while someone tried to organise taxis. I ended up with Georgina, shambling, falling into her, my body slurring. Ange witnessed this and shouted, helpfully, 'What about that blow job, George?' At which point George laughed and licked her lips at me.

Apparently, my blacking out and my vomiting occurred simultaneously, so I was already on my way down to the ground when George's legs got between my puke and the pub car park.

I cringed into my coffee. I felt ill all over again. My head began to spin and bruises I'd just been reminded of began to breathe and throb in my arms and legs.

Ange and Karen were still very amused by the whole episode. 'There was loads of it,' said Karen.

'It ran down her tights and into her boots,' added Ange.

'Gallons of it,' insisted Karen.

'God,' I moaned. 'I was aiming for Mac.'

'I find that difficult to believe,' said Karen. 'You'd just told him you loved him.'

Apparently – if any of this nonsense is to be believed – I'd also professed my love to both Ange and Karen while drifting in and out of consciousness in the cab home. Also, by all accounts, I even made a coarse proposition or two. But I was assured my advances were 'hilarious' rather than 'ugly'. So that was something.

I felt bad. But I felt wonderful too. Suddenly it seemed that I was part of the gang, that I'd been accepted. And all it took was for me to get drunk and be sick on someone.

'Poor George,' I said. 'That's terrible.'

'She was definitely going to blow you too,' added Ange. Then suddenly my penis was the topic of conversation and both Ange and Karen were laughing and passing conspiratorial looks back and forth.

'What?' I said, worried.

They looked at me, mock-suggestively, and I felt the blood rising in my face.

'You don't remember anything about how you got from the cab, covered in your own vomit, into my bed, naked and clean, do you?'

My mouth fell open.

'You're hung like a horse, my lad,' said Ange.

I was embarrassed, but in a good way. They explained that they'd dragged me upstairs, undressed me and sponged me down. 'I swear you were awake,' said Karen. 'Go on, you can admit it now.'

I wasn't awake. At least, not fully. I remembered climbing stairs and heat on my legs but I think I thought I was dreaming. A brilliant dream, befitting of a birthday.

I started laughing.

'Part of him was certainly awake,' said Ange. 'Know what I mean?' she added, in the voice of Marsha from *Spaced*.

I laughed for a while longer, slightly maniacally. Then I was wiping my eyes. 'Do you know, that was the best birthday I've had for years.'

'What?'

'Probably ever, if I'm honest.'

'Did you know it was his birthday?'

'It was your fucking birthday?!'

Blimey. They suddenly seemed really annoyed. 'How could you not say anything?' they wanted to know.

I shrugged. 'I dunno. It didn't seem important.'

On the contrary, they explained, it was actually very important indeed. Then, in order to show me just exactly how important it was, they made immediate arrangements to take me out to lunch.

Lunch, in time, turned into drinks, drinks turned into cocktails and cocktails turned into a wonderful long day becoming firm friends with two women who in very different ways had made my schooldays a living hell.

We finished it all off with a meal in a Korean restaurant, one of those where they cook your meat in front of you, on grills built into the table. 'I'm going to change my life,' I said, as we tucked in. 'I'm going to sort myself out. Lose weight and start, you know, putting myself out there. Yesterday was the first time I've been out to a pub, or out of the house in any social situation, in about six months.'

Ange and Karen were both shocked by this, and full of encouragement for my plans.

'I'm thinking of starting a blog too,' I said.

'What's a blog?' said Karen.

'Do it,' said Ange, after berating Karen for her ignorance. 'If you think it'll help. I'll be happy to cook you a healthy meal once in a while too,' she added. 'And I must say, I'm loving your PMA.'

'I *love* your PMA,' I corrected. 'What's my PMA?'

'Positive Mental Attitude,' she said. 'I'm loving it.'

Ange stuck out her tongue and clamped it between her front teeth. It was something she did when she thought she'd said something funny.

'Put your tongue away,' I said, adoringly.

It was a wonderful day. They wouldn't even let me pay. And when finally I returned home, I was a changed man, more than ready and one hundred per cent willing to face the challenges of a new year and, if it wasn't a tad too pretentious, a new life.

I felt like dynamite. In fact, for the first time in thirty years, I no longer felt afraid.

Or at least, not cripplingly so.

CHAPTER FOUR

LIKE A LEOPARD ON A DOVE

Crippled by withdrawal, I ache, itch, shiver and whine. I'm beginning to think that stopping both smoking *and* eating, at the same time, was asking maybe just a little too much of my central nervous system. I think I may – ironically enough – have bitten off more than I can chew. It's almost 11 a.m. Ordinarily by this time, I would have polished off three bacon sandwiches, a bowl of Sugar Puffs and at least two cups of coffee. Plus biscuits. And right about now, looking forward to my third or fourth cigarette, I'd be heading to the kitchen for another pint of coffee and a pair of chocolate croissants. No wonder I'm such a bloater. I'm lucky to be alive.

The lack of nicotine is beginning to make me edgy. I'd kill for a cigarette. I'd maim and torture for a joint. But they're right when they say it's a gateway drug. If I had a joint now, by bedtime I'd be out of my mind on Maryland Cookies and Häagen-Dazs.

In response to the nicotine withdrawal, my fingers are twitching and I'm coughing like a consumptive, spitting up phlegm till I'm retching and short of breath. When my breath does come, it's bad like a butcher's latrine, and as I belch away heartburn, my mouth *actually* tastes *brown*. I feel awful. My mouth didn't taste brown when I smoked. What's going on? Nothing is right. I feel unhealthy, thick screams welling up in my head. I belch more brown and recoil from myself, shaking my wretched face and shivering.

'*Enough!*' I yell.

Pablo jerks his head and looks at me as if to say, 'How many times have I told you not to do that? Jesus.'

'Sorry, Pablo.'

But balls to January. I'm better than January. I'm better than one measly month, and I can beat these cravings. I made a promise to myself. I know I make promises to myself at a rate of two or three a week, and I know I really mean it every time, especially in January, but this time – I swear by St Münchhausen – it's different.

This year I have eschewed New Year's Resolutions in favour of the infinitely more grandiose 'New Life Resolutions', which are as follows:

1. *Lose 8 Stone in Excess Body Fat and Become Fit and Healthy*

2. *Stop Smoking Cigarettes Completely and For Ever*

3. *Meet and Fall in Fully Reciprocated Love with the Woman of My Dreams*

Furthermore, I have enlisted the help of the internet to keep me on the straight and narrow.

I have, as threatened, started a blog. As well as keeping track of my progress with the above resolutions – which I feel fall foul of neither trifling nor unfeasible – I hope that the blog will add monster strength to my convictions. Thus, I have confided in it in much the same way as one might confide in one's harshest, most mean-spirited friends – friends you inform that you've given up smoking, *just like that* (you may click your fingers for emphasis), making a really big deal of it, shaking your head when they doubt your willpower, smiling all smug and wholly self-satisfied. You are Jesus. 'O ye of little faith,' you say, maybe even making a bet or two for good measure. You do all this knowing full well that if you fall from the wagon and fail, they will mock you and sneer at you and publicly humiliate you with a venom that will bring tears to your eyes. They will poke you mercilessly with verbal sticks of shame and cruelty until you weep openly, destroyed by their *schadenfreude*. Of course, this is exactly why you tell them in the first place. The fear you feel of your friends' bitching and barbs spurs you on, perhaps even more than your fear of being eaten away by cancer.

So this is why I have started a blog. The blog will take the place of the mean-spirited friends I do not have. I have made grand claims on this blog. I am Jesus, smiling smug and self-satisfied, and fear of the potential opprobrium of feisty strangers is already keeping me focused and incentivised.

What this means, of course, is that I have to find readers. Apparently, the thing to do is to visit other people's blogs, link and leave comments, create a trail of virtual breadcrumbs and 'establish a presence'. So this is what I've been doing and, so far, I think it's going quite well. People are coming. Also, interestingly, those that have come – so far, at least – are predominantly female. Which leads me to confront the very real possibility that if I blog well, which I fully intend to, there's no reason that the Woman of My Dreams won't happen upon my words and fall instantly, eternally in love with me.

No reason at all.

We shall see.

Of course, blogging is just one way in which the internet can aid me in my search for True Love. There are others. Which is why a few days ago I signed up to Love and Friends, 'the online dating site for thinking people'. This sounds perfect. Not only does the term 'thinking people' describe me to a T, but also, almost certainly, the Woman of My Dreams.

Filling in the profile took me most of a long Sunday evening, but you can't rush these things. Also, I think it's essential to be honest, and if at all possible, brutally so. Asked to give my thoughts on the subject of 'Sports and Exercise', I wrote: 'I'm a big man, but I'm out of shape. Horribly out of shape. In a word, I'm fat. In fact, I worked out my body mass index recently and I'm ashamed to report that

I'm actually "severely obese". But before you start sending me your salacious winks, you chubby-chasers, you should know that all this is about to change, just as soon as my coccyx is healed. Indeed, by the end of this year, my body will have become my temple, and I want you – yes, you! – to be first through the doors on worship day. (Friday.) And you don't even have to take off your shoes. Although it would be the polite thing to do.'

I was, and remain, disproportionately pleased with that.

Asked to describe an 'Enjoyable Evening Out', I plumped for the following: 'Buckets and buckets of dim sum followed by a film premiere in a swish Soho screening room, accompanied by the woman I love. Oh, and she's in love with me too – I'm fed up with all that unreciprocated nonsense. Incidentally, I wrote the screenplay for the film we're watching – I may even have directed it – and when it ends, the whole audience jumps to its feet and starts cheering. We can't hear them, however, because we're too busy doing it.'

Seriously, what thinking woman in her right mind would fail to fall for that kind of pizzazz? Well – as it turns out – all of them. In the four days since I 'established my presence', I've received precisely no interest. Neither an unsubscribe nor an ironic poke. I don't really know why I was anticipating some interest, but I was. I guess I'm really not as amusing as I think I am.

Or, of course, it could just be the fact that I didn't put up a picture of myself on my profile. I did consider it, but then I thought that doing so would be rather like praying to be picked for the school football team while sitting at the edge of the pitch in a wheelchair. So instead I put up a photo of the Elephant Man. Which, thinking about it, is rather like praying to be picked for the school football team while sitting at the edge of the pitch in a wheelchair, dressed as the Elephant Man.

I know it's potentially counter-productive – although not necessarily – but I'm really not ready to put my face on the internet yet. Actually, there's more to it than that.

In a nutshell, it's a reaction to the fact that all my life I've been judged and persecuted because of the way that I look, because of the way my face is put together. The magnificent thing about the internet, and establishing a presence thereon, is that, robbed of the physical fact of my appearance, people are finally forced to react to what lies beneath the surface. They are forced to react – if you will – to the real me.

I'm fed up with being a freak show. Done with it. I'm done with the titters and the comments and the endless *opinions*. I'm done hearing, 'Oh, you're not that bad,' and I'm especially done hearing, 'Yeah, actually, I see what you mean.' I'm done with all of that.

Now I exist in a place separate from my unpleasantly misshapen face, and that's how I like it.

However, what's good for the blog may not necessarily be good for the dating site. After all, I know that when I search for the Woman of My Dreams, I always tick the box that says 'Photos Only'. I suppose my hoping that the Woman of My Dreams is not quite as superficial as I am – as well as wickedly beautiful – is probably a tad unfair.

Oh well. Balls then, to dating sites.

Thankfully, the internet is not yet out of ideas.

Last week I began frequenting chat rooms in earnest. In case you've never dabbled in such things, let me explain. Chat rooms are basically online spaces packed out with young people, the vast majority of whom – if my intuition holds water – are wasted teenage boys pretending they're unusually attractive, sexually active, lexically unsophisticated, and incredibly non-discriminating women. However, I am convinced that there are genuine women in there too, and if you happen to have your wits about you, you can sometimes track one down.

After a few hours on my first night on chat patrol, I tracked one down.

For the next few days, we chatted intermittently, and after a couple of hour-long sessions, I'd say we knew one another fairly well. It was only in the early hours of this morning that the conversation began to take a turn towards the spicy. Her name was Grace. Or, quite possibly, his name was Grace. No matter. Although if he was a teenage boy pretending, then kudos to him. He was good.

So here, with permission, is my virtual cherry, all popped and pulsating ...

wicked.grace: *So do you want to 'cyber', as I believe the kids call it?*

elbows: *But I'm eating my banana and peanut butter sandwich.*

wicked.grace: *Well hurry up. I'm feeling sexy.*

elbows: *Oh my.*

wicked.grace: *What are you wearing?*

elbows: *Oh god, lots of clothes. It's freezing in here at the moment. I think the heating's busted. I keep meaning to have a word with the landlord but there just aren't enough hours in the day. And he's not the easiest person to get hold of at the best of times, let alone when I want something doing. You still feeling sexy?*

wicked.grace: *You're not taking this seriously are you?*

elbows: *I'm sorry. Am I supposed to? Are you?*

wicked.grace: *A bit. Well, I was going to try and give it a try.*

elbows: *OK, hold on. Right. Sandwich finished. Now I just need to establish a couple of ground rules here – I've never done this before you see and I really don't know how it works. So – am I supposed to tell the truth? Or just tell you what I think you want to hear?*

wicked.grace: *I'm not sure. The truth I guess. Maybe with a couple of sexy lies thrown in.*

elbows: *Really? OK, here we go. I'm wearing a large T-shirt with an amusing slogan on it ('Warning: this T-shirt may contain tits' – hilarious), plus a big fisherman's jumper, plus a woolly hat pulled down over my ears. On my bottom half, however, I'm wearing skin-tight sexy rubber pants, and no underwear. Woof!*

wicked.grace: *Hmmm.*

elbows: *What are you wearing?*

wicked.grace: *I'm wearing leather boots and tight blue jeans. On* *my top half I'm wearing a green shirt and a green scarf around my neck.*

elbows: *Long or short sleeves?*

wicked.grace: *Long sleeves, pulled up to the elbows.*

elbows: *Please don't say 'elbows'.*

wicked.grace: *Sorry. Long sleeves. I'm also wearing red lipstick and my hair is tied back in a pony tail.*

elbows: *Gosh, I'm becoming aroused already. It really works!*

wicked.grace: *Would you like me to take off some clothes?*

elbows: *I'm not sure. Is your heating working OK?*

wicked.grace: *Tip top, yeah. I'm actually quite warm.*

elbows: *OK then. Maybe you could slip something off.*

wicked.grace: *Will you join me?*

elbows: *OK then.*

wicked.grace: *I've loosened the scarf around my neck first. I've slipped it off and let it drop to the living room floor.*

elbows: *I've taken off my hat. And thrown it at the cat.*

wicked.grace: *I've undone the top button of my shirt. And the next.*

elbows: *You'll be here all night at that rate. Hold on .... There. I'm naked.*

wicked.grace: *Hmmm.*

elbows: *Nnngh! Nurk!*

wicked.grace: *?*

elbows: *I came.*

wicked.grace: *I don't think you're very good at cybersex. I'm sorry to have to say that to you. I don't mean to hurt your feelings, but you should know. In fact, you're the worst I've ever had.*

elbows: *I'm sorry.*

wicked.grace: *Meh.*

elbows: *No I really am sorry. I wish I could make it up to you.*

wicked.grace: *Maybe you're better in real life.*

elbows: *Much better, yes.*

wicked.grace: *I bet you're not as repulsive as you say you are.*

elbows: *Honestly, I'm worse.*

wicked.grace: *I kind of wish you were here anyway, so I could see for myself.*

elbows: *I am here.*

wicked.grace: *I mean here.*

elbows: *So do I. I'm standing behind you right now. Can't you hear me breathing?*

wicked.grace: *Oooh, hello.*

elbows: *You're sitting at your desk in the living room. I'm standing behind you. I reach my hand out and run my fingers over your neck, over the hair at the back of your neck.*

wicked.grace: *That's nice. Would you kiss it maybe?*

elbows: *Kissing's later. First I pinch your ear lobes with my fingers, then lean forward and smell your hair.*

wicked.grace: *You're making me slightly moist.*

elbows: *It smells nice. Your hair I mean. Not your moistness. I can't smell your moistness. Not yet.*

wicked.grace: *You're making murmuring noises into my ear.*

elbows: *Yes, I kiss the top of your left ear, slowly, murmuring.*

wicked.grace: *Mmmmm.*

elbows: *You are a little tense though – I think I need to apply some pressure to your back. My hands move down and my thumbs burrow into your flesh.*

wicked.grace: *I groan and reach around to you.*

elbows: *I kiss your neck.*

wicked.grace: *I can feel how hard you are.*

elbows: *Lightly. I groan.*

wicked.grace: *I start to touch you.*

elbows: *Where?*

wicked.grace: *Gently rubbing the top of you. You're poking out of your trousers.*

elbows: *I've moved my hands round to your breasts – I can't resist.*

wicked.grace: *I'm loosening your belt and reaching in to hold all of you in my hand.*

elbows: *I'm caressing your breasts with my hands. I want to kiss you.*

wicked.grace: *I want to turn around and take you in my mouth.*

elbows: *I really need to kiss you.*

wicked.grace: *I'm turning around and looking up at you.*

elbows: *I stroke your face.*

wicked.grace: *I offer you my tongue.*

elbows: *I bend towards you.*

wicked.grace: *I lick your hand.*

elbows: *I move your face to mine.*

wicked.grace: *I look into your eyes.*

elbows: *I kiss you lightly on the top lip.*

wicked.grace: *My lips are throbbing with desire.*

elbows: *I lick them, lightly.*

wicked.grace: *Mmm, you tease.*

elbows: *With the tip of my tongue.*

wicked.grace: *I intake breath, sharply.*

elbows: *My hands are on you. My hands are all over you. I unbutton your shirt.*

wicked.grace: *Please ...*

elbows: *I unbutton you quickly and pull your shirt over your shoulders while I'm kissing your cheeks, the corners of your mouth.*

wicked.grace: *I lick you every time you come near me.*

elbows: *I pull away a little, teasing you ...*

wicked.grace: *I'm still offering you my tongue and I'm still holding your cock, lightly. I start to move my hand.*

elbows: *I need to feel you.*

wicked.grace: *It's throbbing, moving on its own.*

I unzip you.

I turn to get close to you.

I pause to lick your stomach and breathe hot air on the part I've just licked.

I move down, slowly, peppering your body with kisses until I reach your man-hair!

And I feel your cock, throbbing, pulsating against my cheek.

I rub my cheek against it for a moment. It responds, nudging me back.

elbows: *I need to remove, I need you to remove – pull my pants down! please!*

wicked.grace: *I slowly tug at your pants.*

They fall down around your ankles.

elbows: *I feel like I'm about to lose control. It's all too much.*

wicked.grace: *Keys and change in the pockets clinking.*

I take you in my mouth, your hot hardness, and I take my tongue and offer it to your cock instead.

elbows: *My cock accepts your tongue.*

wicked.grace: *I'm feeling your every movement inside my mouth.*

elbows: *I put my hand on the back of your head and push it on to me.*

My cock is deep inside your mouth.

wicked.grace: *I take you as deep as I can.*

My throat opens up too.

elbows: *nnngh*

wicked.grace: *And I move back and forth, tickling the underneath of you with my tongue.*

elbows: *This is too much for me. I lift your head from my cock and kiss you passionately. Then I drag you to the bed and leap on top of you, like a leopard on to a dove. My tongue is deep in your mouth.*

wicked.grace: *I'm trembling with lust.*

elbows: *I am kissing you hard.*

And my left hand has moved down to your crotch.

wicked.grace: *I'm scratching your back with my nails.*

elbows: *I am rubbing you violently.*

wicked.grace: *And moaning.*

elbows: *I undo your belt.*

Your top button.

Scratching at your zip.

I undo it.

I use my other hand and start to pull at your jeans.

wicked.grace: *I am very wet now.*

I let you.

elbows: *I move down your body quickly and pull off your jeans – down your legs – off!*

wicked.grace: *I raise my ass off the bed to help you a bit.*

elbows: *Don't say 'ass'.*

Then I remove your knickers in one swift movement and while your bum is raised I flip you over on to your stomach.

Then I move up between your legs and thwap my cock against your buttocks.

wicked.grace: *Mmm, I love being face down.*

elbows: *thwap thwap*

I push my hand into the small of your back.

My thumb finds its way into your bum.

wicked.grace: *Mmmm, it slides in because you've licked it.*

elbows: *My fingers are in your vagina too.*

Of course I've licked it. It's dripping.

wicked.grace: *That gets wetter as you play with my ass.*

elbows: *sigh*

My hand is in you like a bowling ball.

(Sorry for the bowling ball analogy.)

wicked.grace: *Dirty. I like it.*

elbows: *OK then. I bowl you across the room and the furniture goes flying.*

I follow you.

wicked.grace: *erm*

elbows: *And launch myself at your rectum. Then I'm in you like a light sabre through a knob of butter. fffshoom.*

wicked.grace: *No no no*

elbows: *fffshoom. shhhhhvummm. fffshoom. fffshoom.*

wicked.grace: *Stop with the analogies. Keep the butter, lose the light sabre.*

elbows: *What about the knob?*

wicked.grace: *So, you're buttering me up.*

And slipping in.

Yeah, the knob can stay.

elbows: *I slide in slowly ...*

... like, real slow.

wicked.grace: *In and then out and then in again, ever so slowly.*

I can feel myself opening up to you.

Bit by bit.

elbows: *I can feel myself throbbing inside you.*

wicked.grace: *I can feel that too, inch by inch, you're filling me up*

I'm wriggling away a bit, as it's so intense, and then coming back for more.

Pushing myself back on to you.

Enjoying the impalement.

elbows: *I push myself into you a little harder as you try and inch away.*

I'm not letting you get away.

I pull you on to me.

Grabbing your hips.

Pulling.

I grunt involuntarily.

wicked.grace: *I'm clawing at the bedsheets and the pillows.*

I'm grunting too.

elbows: *I scratch your back and slap you hard on the right buttock.*

Slap!

wicked.grace: *I'm almost there, you're almost all in.*

The last part is the most fulfilling.

elbows: *slap! slap! slap!*

wicked.grace: *Then everything opens up like a flower, and I feel the whole of you.*

elbows: *My right hand snakes around your hips to your frontal flower and slips and slides and rubs and gently pinches.*

wicked.grace: *I feel your front against my back, and your hand on my petals ... or should that be my stamen?*

elbows: *My hand is sticky with your love pollen.*

wicked.grace: *I'm moaning with agony and ecstasy. Mostly ecstasy.*

elbows: I'm pumping into you quite hard now.

wicked.grace: Yes, I'm so wet, I'm leaving a wet patch on the bed.

elbows: And squeezing you.

Slapping your buttocks.

Scratching your back.

Pulling your hair.

It's like I have twelve hands.

wicked.grace: I'm moving against you, pushing when you pull.

elbows: And three cocks.

wicked.grace: You feel huge. And hard.

elbows: The bed is juddering.

wicked.grace: I'm biting my lip, biting the pillow, anything in reach.

elbows: I'm bellowing.

Someone starts banging on the ceiling from upstairs.

I carry on bellowing …

wicked.grace: The rhythm quickens.

elbows: … like a mad fuck-wizard.

I pull back your head by your hair and lift your legs.

wicked.grace: I'm moaning loudly.

elbows: You're floating.

We're both floating!

wicked.grace: I'm calling your name.

elbows: A frantic floating fuck!

I'm calling yours!

I can't hold out much longer!

wicked.grace: I'm going to come with you.

I'm going to judder as hard as the bed.

elbows: You'd better be quick then – I … I ….

wicked.grace: I reach down and touch myself to quicken my orgasm.

I'm coming with you.

elbows: aaaaaaaaaaaaaaahhhhhh

I am screaming.

Weeping.

Coming from every orifice.

wicked.grace: *I'm speechless.*

Just breathless.

Still shuddering, weak-kneed.

elbows: *I'm blind.*

And deaf.

There are lights behind my eyes.

I cannot breathe.

Where am I? I feel your breath.

I open my eyes.

wicked.grace: *I feel your cum pumping into me, like foam from a fireman's hose.*

elbows: *Nice analogy. I look at you. You are the most beautiful woman I have ever seen in my life.*

I kiss you tenderly.

wicked.grace: *I'm pink-cheeked and sticky.*

I kiss you back.

Softly.

elbows: *I hold you.*

wicked.grace: *I run my hands through your hair.*

elbows: *I pinch your cheeks and punch you on the shoulder, like the Fonz. Eeeeeyyyyyyyyyy.*

wicked.grace: *Eeeeeyyyyyyyyyy.*

elbows: *Heh. You know what? That was fun.*

wicked.grace: *Did you come?*

elbows: *What, really? No, I wasn't even touching myself. Were you? Did you come?*

wicked.grace: *No, not quite. I'm going to go and finish myself off now. You should send a photo.*

elbows: *I'll try.*

wicked.grace: *Try hard. x*

So this morning I wrote an email to Grace. I attached a photo.

At the time of writing, I've yet to hear back. I'll give her till the end of January, then that's it. She's dumped.

CHAPTER FIVE

BEING IS OTHER PEOPLE

I hate January. It's such a dark and dreary downer of a month. Perpetually cold, dully predictable, a constant reminder that life is all just little bits of history repeating.

Perhaps unsurprisingly, the last couple of weeks have been marked by great swathes of languorous self-pity. After an exciting start, things have slowed down, dramatically.

I'm currently working on a website for a city council in the north of England writing words about Local Finance, Multiple-Occupancy Homes, Sheltered Housing, and Health & Social Care. I wish I could say it's as interesting as it sounds, but it really isn't. Not by a long chalk. This month is going so s l o w l y . . .

The last couple of weeks have staggered by like a frozen hare tied to a dispirited tortoise, and my coccyx steadfastly refuses to heal. I want to run! Stretch! Play tennis! Dance! – but all I can manage is to sit here on a large disc made out of sponge, the kind favoured by old men with haemorrhoids. I think I might be getting haemorrhoids. The ailment of stretched mothers and desiccated old men. I have an itch. A terrible itch. Added to which, this dieting lark is deeply, shockingly tedious. I miss the quick-fix fun of fat, sugar, and cholesterol. I miss eating whenever I feel like it, blithe as a billygoat.

I bought a set of digital scales and now, every morning when I rise, every evening when I set, and seven or eight times in between, I hoist myself upon this instrument of despair and stare at the pithy display. Invariably I shake my head. My weight has started to fluctuate wildly, up and down like the lift in a kangaroo's whorehouse. Last week I ate nothing but carrots, peas, apples, bananas, and wine, and on Friday I was seven pounds lighter than at the start of the week. Then at the weekend I pigged out on pizza, beer, and exotically flavoured crisps, and as a direct consequence, five of those seven pounds are right back where they started. What can it all mean?

And what's it all about? Why am I making my life so much harder? I ask myself that question and for a moment I do not know the answer. Then it comes flooding back. I am pursuing a healthy lifestyle, so that I can transform myself into a healthier human being, and somewhere along the way, find myself a lady. A lovely lady at that. One with silken skin and leathery skirts. Or vice versa. One who would make me giddy with adoration and fill my nether regions with hot sticky blood and fizz-gristle. A lady to laugh with and love with, to have and to hold, to tickle and tether from this day forth, as long as we both shall live. Or at least for a couple of months, till the inevitable withering and/or betrayal. A lady, in fact, like Ange. Ange is my inspiration. My first love. They never die, you know. And Ange is making great efforts to keep in touch. She has pledged to help me all she can to stick to my various regimes. She has pledged her support. 'Day or night,' she said, 'if you need to talk to someone, I'm here for you. Don't ... why are you looking at me like that?'

I blushed, smiling. 'Like what? I just ...'

'I'm not going to have sex with you, Stan. Sorry if that's not what you were thinking, but that's what it looked like.'

That was what I was thinking.

'That's not what I was thinking,' I said. 'I'm just glad we could finally be friends is all.'

I once wrote a poem about Ange's breasts. It was called 'Two-Headed Love God'.

Ange is adorable and vivacious and dangerous and, I'm hoping, just mad enough to get really drunk one night and sleep with me. She was mad enough, after all, to lick her lips at me, moaning that she wanted me, that time after assembly, while her friends screeched their ghastly passerine approval and I let out an audible cry of terror.

Aaah, how many times have I permitted my hands to seduce myself to generous, wilfully erotic adaptations of that painful memory? I don't know. Twelve or so.

The last time was on Sunday night, when I bottomed out after having spent the day before with Keith, boozing and smoking weed like know-nothing losers with nothing but time. Then I'd fallen into a feeding frenzy. Most of Sunday I'd spent in bed, beached and buried in shame. Then I got up, weighed myself, and fell face first into a bubbling well of despair. I would like to blame Keith, but I can't bring myself to do it. In truth, Keith is blameless. Perennially so.

Keith is my oldest friend, my dearest friend. I'm not so sure how mature it sounds to still cling to the concept of a 'best friend', but maybe that's because most adults are not so sure if they have them any more. I am sure. Keith is my best friend.

I've known him since I was just a few months old. Our parents' back gardens bordered for a while and Keith and I became fast friends and grew up together. Because I was a hideous eczematic little freak, I was often picked on and bullied by clear-skinned Nazi kids, and I have lost count of the number of times that Keith stepped in and stopped the violence. Or tried to. He did take the occasional beating alongside me too, which produced in me such profound feelings of love that I suppose it's fair to say that over the years I developed a bit of a crush on him. But it passed, it passed.

When we were about twelve or thirteen, Keith and I were enjoying a day out on the beach at Southend with a couple of distant schoolfriends, 'Dirty' Dean Curtis and Kevin 'Hodge' Hodge. Hodge found a giant flatfish washed up on the sand, dead. When he picked it up and threatened me with it, I ran. Hodge ran after me. I got away, though, because somehow I was faster than him. Then, in the same way that gunmen in films shoot at cars speeding off in the distance, more last-ditch desperation than genuine attempt to find their target, Hodge threw the fish after me, and by utter fluke, it landed with a slap on my bare back, where it stuck fast, suckered to my skin. It was funny. I can see now that it was funny, but at the time it was a) humiliating, as my friends all fell about laughing, and b) somehow terrifying. I started screaming and flapping about trying to get it off my back, but it was properly stuck. This was probably the nearest I'd ever come at the time to a panic attack.

Despite my shrieks and shouts and tears, Hodge and Dirty Curty found it increasingly hilarious. Keith, however, seeing that I was genuinely upset, came up to me, peeled the fish off my back and calmed me down. I was embarrassed and I had to go off to be alone, but I was touched too, and I've never forgotten it.

When I was fifteen, there was violence at home. Tempers were lost and blood was spilt and suddenly there was the possibility that I was going to be taken into care. Keith at this point persuaded his parents to take me in and look after me, essentially to foster me. Again, it brings tears to my eyes to think how much that meant to me and what a selfless, genuinely heartfelt gesture it was.

A year and a bit later, Keith and I moved into a flat together in Dartford, and without putting too fine a point on it, Keith basically mothered me for the next two years. I was in and out of college, in and out of work and often struggling to pay the rent, but Keith never failed to help me out, even when it meant leaving himself short. I wouldn't say he always did so uncomplainingly, but that's because he wasn't a feckless pussy. On occasion I needed nothing more than a healthy, hefty kick in the pants, and Keith was always on hand to give it.

For my eighteenth birthday, Keith drew me a card. He had always been a very talented artist, and up until his early twenties, he drew a lot. Then he fell into a career in art direction, via set design, and kind of stopped. Which is a shame. The card he made for my eighteenth was an ink and watercolour depiction of the front cover of a novel I talked about a lot but would never write. The novel, called *Irresistible*, was about an ugly man who one day wakes up and – against all odds – finds that he is utterly irresistible to all women. I did manage to write a couple of chapters, and they were filled with the most hideously embarrassing teenage wish-fulfilment imaginable.

The cover on my card, however, was a thing of great beauty. It featured a brooding, saturnine version of me surrounded by what can only be described as a bevy of buxom beauties, fawning all over me, groping me, licking me, breathing me in. It was magnificent. Scantily clad they were. All adoring, imploring, and swooning. I was blown away by it, and I showed my gratitude by a) never writing the novel, and b) eventually ruining the card entirely with half a bottle of red wine. What an unbelievable klutz I am. Stupid clumsy sausage-fingered motherfucker. I hated myself for some time for that. But Keith forgave me.

Five weeks ago, he bought me a bunch of sex toys and condoms and various other sexual accessories for my birthday. He knew about my quest to change my life and find the Woman of My Dreams, and this was his way of wishing me luck. In an accompanying card, he wrote: 'You'll notice there is no fleshlight here. That's because you won't be needing one. Go get 'em, tiger.' I was actually very pleased at the lack of a fleshlight, because if there'd been one, I would have had to try it, and the idea of making sweet love to what is essentially a synthetic vagina in a plastic tube is singularly depressing.

A week after that, Keith invited me to spend Christmas with him at his girlfriend Patricia's house – just him, her, and – stopping me feeling like a giant Christmas gooseberry – her two kids, Ben and Dina. I'm sure Patricia had a hand in the invitation too, of course, but the point is, in these and in countless other ways, Keith has shown me consistently that he cares for me, that he loves me, more than any other person I've ever known. This is why, at the weekend, it was a pleasure for me to help him paint the walls of the house he's just moved into. Actually, 'pleasure' is maybe gilding the lily somewhat, but I was happy to do it.

Keith's new place is in Peckham, which I've always rather imagined as the armpit of London, if not the scrotum or even the anus of London, and for most of my life studiously avoided. The time I have spent there recently has done little to disabuse me of this, but yes, OK, I suppose I must confess – despite the gobbing teens, the astonishing amount of crap in the streets and the intoxicating, God-awful stench – it does have a certain charm of which I was hitherto unaware. Exotic fruit and veg stalls, for example, a preponderance of large African men singing religious songs in the street, and yesterday I saw a Christian steel-drum trio, just playing outside a mobile-phone shop seemingly for the sheer hell of it. I guess Peckham is kind of like Brixton, but without the overweening drugginess and concomitant sense of impending violence. Oh, and without the nice places to eat and drink.

Keith's new flat is in a state of some squalor and disrepair, a little like the entire area. It needs a lot of work, which is why we spent the weekend repainting his living room. Occasionally Keith would have to stop because of pins and needles in his right hand. Every twenty minutes or so, in fact. 'Look,' he'd say. I'd look but see nothing. Just a hand, not working. 'It's spazzing out,' he'd say. 'Something's wrong with it.' I'd shake my head. It would pass. He'd roll another joint.

I tried to make the painting into a fitness thing, so that I'd feel less bad about the tobacco intake that came hand in hand with the joints, but I failed. I felt worse still on Sunday afternoon when I woke up with a cough like a canary in a coal mine. In order to assuage some of the guilt, I fell back on childhood rituals and for old time's sake said half a dozen Hail Marys, three Apollo Creeds, and a handful of How's Your Fathers. But it was useless. On Sunday I hated myself. And so I regressed, albeit briefly, and lay stagnant, unstable, like a veritable sack of couch potatoes, neither use nor ornament, propped up in front of the telly, and the last thing I wanted was to speak to anyone, so when the phone rang, I let it go to answer machine. Which is when I received the following voice message from Keith:

'All right, mate. I've just got this terrible feeling that you're sitting at home moping and feeling sorry for yourself and pissed off that you pigged out yesterday. If I'm wrong and you're right as rain and off out celebrating your joy, then I'm happy to be so wrong. But if I'm right, then ... I dunno. Cheer up, mate! You're allowed to treat yourself once in a while, for God's sake. It might not be good for your diet but it's good for your soul. Your soul! Anyway, take care and speak soon ... Oh, and everybody here loves you.'

At which point, in the background, Patricia and her precocious children, Ben and Dina, all shouted, 'We love you, Stanley!' and laughed. 'You see?' said Keith. 'Seeya later, mate. Give us a bell. Bye!'

At the time, hearing the message made me feel even more pathetic than I already felt. The idea that someone knew me well enough to know that I'd be sitting at home in a nauseating heap, too miserable to even sob, let alone pick up the phone, upset me. Am I so predictable? Is my pathetic personality so widely acknowledged?

But then, listening to the message again a few hours later made me shudder and shake with dirty great tears of something approaching joy. I think I may be slightly emotionally unstable. I think I may have to take that possibility on board.

Then, before those tears had a chance to dry, Ange called and asked me if I fancied a healthy dinner some time. I said that I most certainly did and, immediately, I got back on track with the diet – apples and lettuce and grapes, oh my – and as my weight began once again to crawl in the right direction, I began to cheer up. I started whistling again. By the time dinner at Ange's rolled around, less than a week later, I was positively chipper, not only at the prospect of a healthy meal, but also at the prospect of spending a little more time with Ange.

I felt nervous as I was getting ready to leave the house. I shouldn't have felt nervous. My belly was shifting around. It shouldn't have been doing that. I couldn't, I can't stop thinking about how much I want Ange naked, on a bed, savaging me with her body, her cavities. I feel like I'm fourteen again, like I love her.

Halfway through the meal, the conversation turned, as conversations often do, to sex. Ange couldn't get over the fact that I've only slept with two people. I couldn't get over the fact that she's slept with over fifty, and none of them were me.

'It must be worse to have slept with two than with none at all,' she said sensitively. 'Because you know what you're missing, don't you?'

'Hmm, yes. That's very true,' I replied. 'Thanks for ramming that home.'

'But how do you cope with the frustration?' she wanted to know.

'What makes you think I cope with it?' I replied.

We talked about Ange's sexual partners, her predatory man-eating ways. I asked her what kind of men she liked best. She asked me what I meant. I said, 'For example, short men or tall men?' She told me tall men. 'Small men or large men, cockwise?' Large men. 'Black men or white men?' In response to which Ange informed me that she didn't think she could ever sleep with a black man. Naturally, I called her on this. Specifically, I called her racist. Naturally, she denied it. 'I just don't find them attractive,' she said.

'But that's idiotic,' I replied. 'It's like saying, "I don't find Taureans attractive" or "I don't find lawyers attractive." There are as many different types of black men, as many different black "looks", as there are fish in the sea.'

'I don't fancy fish either,' she said, stupidly.

'Fair enough,' I countered cleverly. 'But to say you don't fancy black men is like saying you don't fancy freshwater fish, or you don't fancy bream, whereas with other fish you have no problems. Or, in other words: you're a racist.'

'I can't believe you're calling me that,' she said at this point, seemingly on the verge of becoming quite upset.

'I can't believe you're being so overtly racist!' I cried. 'OK, let's calm down here,' I suggested, more to myself than to Ange. I poured some more wine. I drank some more wine. 'What would you think,' I said, 'if a black man said that he refused to sleep with white women, that he just didn't fancy white women?'

She paused, as if to suggest – at least as far as I read it – that she was about to lie. Then she lied. 'I'd think it was fine,' she said. 'It's a matter of personal taste.'

'Hmmm,' I said. 'Well, it seems to me it's personal taste informed by personal prejudice. OK, let me try another tack. Tell me – honestly now – don't you fancy Denzel Washington?'

'No, I don't,' she replied, scowling racistly as she did so.

'OK, what about Kanye West?'

'Nope.'

'Right then. What about Thierry Henry?' I was feeling confident. Every woman I've ever met can't help drooling over Thierry Henry.

'Nope. Look, I'm sorry, Stan. I just don't fancy black blokes.'

I sighed. Could I ever love a racist? Probably. Just not a black one. I'm joking. In reality, I couldn't bring myself to believe that what Ange was saying was really true. But I felt that to call her a liar as well as a racist might be verging on the offensive.

'OK,' I said. 'When you go on holiday, do you like to sunbathe?'

'Yes,' she said, 'and I can see where you're going with this.'

'Good,' I said. 'That'll give you time to come up with a decent answer. Have you ever been to bed with a white bloke with a deep tan?'

'Yes,' she said defensively. 'I really fancy white blokes with tans.'

'Well, what's the bleeding difference?!' My exasperation was beginning to flow over.

'OK, OK,' she said. 'I'll tell you what it is.'

'You're racist?' I offered.

'No,' she said. 'And I really wish you'd stop saying that.'

I apologised. Sincerely.

'Have you got a type?' she asked. 'What's your type?'

I started to shrug. 'I really don't think I do have a type,' I replied, avoiding the obvious, because I couldn't see that it would get me anywhere. 'I'm incredibly unfussy.'

'You must have a preference,' she said. 'In your head. An ideal.'

I shook my head. 'Conscious?' I offered. 'But really, I'll take whatever I can get.'

'OK, well you're probably a special case. Most other people – let's call them "normal people" – they have a type. My type is tall, muscular white men, with thin noses and large, square chins. What I don't like, however, are African men. And this is probably going to make me sound more racist than ever, but what I don't like about them are their physical features. I like blue eyes and hair I can run my fingers through. I don't like short, wiry black hair. You know? I like pale ginger blokes. And I know a lot of people don't. Loads of people don't fancy gingers. Are they racist? I don't think so. It's personal preference.' She paused, then added angrily, 'For fuck's sake.'

I laughed. She had worked herself up into quite a little froth. But I was also scheming, and dreaming. 'I'm pale,' I said. 'And certainly ginger-ish.'

'Yeah, but you've got a face like a bag of elbows,' she said. 'And you're too fat.'

I smiled and retaliated quickly with 'Fucking racist,' but I was hurt.

I hid it. I think.

She laughed.

'No, but seriously,' I said. 'This personal-preference thing. It's tantamount to prejudice.'

'Oh, God ...'

'OK, OK.'

We changed the subject. But I maintain that not fancying black people is racist. And maybe the reason it rankles so much is something to do with me, and my popularly perceived level of attractiveness. For if I can label Ange racist for not fancying black fellas, then surely I can label everyone else racist for not fancying me.

Indeed, if I believe that every woman who's ever looked at me with even a hint of disgust is prejudiced – prejudiced against ugly people, prejudiced against fat people, prejudiced against me – then that makes me feel better about myself.

Mulling this over, I felt better about myself.

'What's wrong?' said Ange. 'Are you feeling OK?'

'Hmm? Yeah, yeah, I'm fine.' But I have a face that cannot tell a lie.

'No, come on, what's up?'

'Oh, God, Jesus, no, nothing.'

'Pfffffft,' said Ange. 'Come on! Time is of the essence! We could both be dead tomorrow!'

'All right, all right. Jesus.' I composed myself. 'I was just thinking … I keep thinking about that morning at school when you tried to kiss me.'

'Eh?' cried Ange. 'Are you sure this wasn't something you merely imagined?'

I was sure.

Ange and I were in the same registration class. Our registration teacher, Miss Stirzaker, had a bit of a soft spot for me, which is to say, she liked me, and probably felt sorry for me. So she told me nice things sometimes. She said I was very bright and funny and that I shouldn't allow some of the less intellectually well-endowed children to get me down because they didn't really know any better and probably just called me names in order to take the attention away from their own shortcomings. Also, a couple of times, after assembly, she gave me the keys to our classroom and sent me up ahead of her, so that I could let everyone else into class, and she could stroll up in her own time and not have to rush back.

The first time I did this, all went well. I bumbled through the milling throng of classmates on the stairs and on the landing and in the classroom doorway, I ignored their mundane, quotidian taunts, I opened the door and everyone piled in.

The second time I did this, Ange and a bunch of her friends were in the doorway, hanging around, and when I arrived, Ange thought it would be a killer wheeze to pretend that she found me attractive. Space in the doorway was scant and I had to squeeze past the bodies that were already sardined in there, so it was easy for Ange to get between my hand and the lock, thus preventing me from escaping into the classroom. This she did.

'Oh, Stan Cattermole,' she said. 'Ooh, you sexy thing, you.' And while she said this, she ran her hands over my chest, arms, and back. I was hideously embarrassed. Naturally her friends found all of this hilarious, and their giggles and whoops spurred her on. 'Kiss me,' she said. 'I want your tongue in my mouth.' She put her hands on my cheeks, twisted my head to face her, made me look at her. She licked her lips.

Then, I guess, she saw the terror in my eyes – the terror and the shame and maybe even something of the love I thought I felt for her, and she relented. She stopped humiliating me. She stopped stamping all over my heart. I scrabbled the key into the lock and pushed open the classroom door. I remember there was bright sun shining into the classroom, in contrast to the darkness of the corridor outside, and I remember feeling an overwhelming urge to vomit.

Of course, we were only thirteen or fourteen then, and this was nothing but a bit of meaningless, malicious fun, immediately forgotten by everyone except me. At first Ange didn't remember it at all. I ran through the details and, eventually, the penny dropped.

'Oh, God, yeah,' she said, followed by a tiny, guilty laugh. 'It was just a bit of fun though. I mean, you know that, right?'

'I suppose,' I said. 'But it stayed with me. It destroyed me,' I added, perhaps slightly melodramatically. Perhaps not.

Ange assured me she was sorry she had hurt me. I believed her.

'I had a massive crush on you,' I confess.

'Ah,' said Ange.

'Quite,' I said.

'Sorry,' said Ange.

'Still do if I'm honest,' I went on.

'Oh, come on,' said Ange, with slight pleading in her voice. 'Don't say that.' I looked helpless. We both knew I'd already said it. 'Don't spoil this,' she added.

'Does it have to spoil it?' I asked.

'Stan,' she said, her voice hard, authoritative. Her teacher's voice.

'I just thought, you know, you're quite a loose woman. I'm ...'

'Oy, you cheeky fucker!' she barked. 'I'm not that loose, and besides, look, listen, Stan. I think you're a really excellent bloke, and I think it's great that we're in touch again after so long, but honestly, I don't want anything more than friendship with you. And if you don't think you can handle that ...'

'I can handle it,' I told her. 'Jesus. I'm not in love with you or anything.'

That night I walked home from the tube station in the rain.

'I'm in love with her!' I told myself. 'Again!' I cried. 'After all these years! Still in love with the same bastard woman! Damn it.'

I hate January.

CHAPTER SIX

PICKING UP

Things are picking up. Thank God.

This morning, after a good healthy breakfast of eggs and bananas, I boarded the number 3 bus to Oxford Circus to give blood. I hadn't been on a bus in quite a while, and I have to say, it really took me by surprise. What really amazed me, moved me even, was the intimacy. I guess what I'm really talking about here – really – is the proximity of the other human beings, many of whom – and I feel like a colossal pervert even mentioning this, but if you take the bus yourself sometimes you'll know it to be true – many of whom are *women*.

Good God in heaven. All I wanted to do was give an armful of blood, maybe save the lives of a few desperate children. But things are never that simple. Instead I was forced to bear witness to a cavalcade of sumptuous young ladies, getting on the bus, getting off the bus, ceaselessly brushing past me with their clothes and their flesh and their fresh feisty smells.

I thought of Charlie Kaufman in *Adaptation*, that scene at the Orchid Show, trying and failing to concentrate on the orchids he must write about, distracted by women. 'One looks like a school teacher,' he muses. 'One looks like a gymnast.' Well, that's pretty much exactly how I felt as we sailed through South London, heading north. One looked like a Polish waitress. One looked like a human-rights lawyer. One looked like that girl on *Grange Hill* who had a brief career in pop. One looked like a New Cross intellectual with whom you could go to the Tate Modern and kiss passionately in the Turbine. One had eyes like a cavern under the sea in the deepest darkest dead of night. One had large hoop earrings and a saggy-faced dog in a bag.

You see all sorts on public transport.

One looked like Ange.

I looked away.

I found myself thinking about the Japanese too. People point to the Japanese – with their weird cartoon erotica, their soiled-knicker vending machines, their schoolgirl obsessions, and their pixellated private porn parts – and they snicker and think, 'My oh my, what an inscrutable race of smiling, damned perverts they are,' but I really think that any race insightful enough to have commuter-train simulation rooms in brothels is way ahead of its time. You may find it offensive, but it taps right into a lot of men's fantasies, and in an ideal world, not just men's.

So, I must confess that my journey was filled with thoughts of this nature, and by the time I arrived to give blood, most of it was lodged in my nether regions.

Once inside the blood clinic, I had to fill in a form, just to make sure my blood was good. Do I have HIV? they wanted to know. No, I do not. Do I have hepatitis B? Nope. C? Nope. Have I ever received payment for sex? Oh, come on. Have I had sex in the last twelve months with any of the following: needle-wielders, fudgepackers, Third World backpackers? No, no, no. Have I in fact had sex at all? Oh, leave me in peace, for God's sake. I just came here to save children's lives. Why must I be made to feel inadequate at every single turn?

I heaved a sigh, made for the couch.

But as I lay there, opening and closing my fist, being leeched, I felt positive. Things were picking up. I could feel it in my water.

Outside, on the way back to Oxford Circus, I was approached by a pretty young chugger. 'How would you like to help a deaf child?' she asked.

'Pardon?' I said.

I chuckled. She must get that all day.

Sweet though she was, with her lips and her hair and her eyes full of hope and drama-school training, and sympathetic though I am to deaf children, and indeed deaf people of all ages, on this occasion I had to decline. 'Sorry,' I said. 'I've saved enough children for one day, don't you think?'

She smiled pitifully, thinking, 'London is full of loonies.'

Speaking of things picking up, I've spent the last week reading a book called *The Game*. It is, after all, time to move on.

The Game is the story of how journalist Neil Strauss went from AFC to PUA, then found an LTR with an HB10.

> **AFC** = *Average Frustrated Chump*
>
> **PUA** = *Pick-up Artist*
>
> **LTR** = *Long-term Relationship*
>
> **HB10** = *Hot Babe with a high rating on the physical-appearance scale*

As you can see, there is an awful lot of jargon in pick-up, and as you can see, much of it is excruciatingly embarrassing.

The story goes like this: after years of fearing rejection to the point of not even being able to talk to women without stammering and blushing, Strauss is commissioned to write a piece on America's burgeoning pick-up community. Consequently he becomes immersed in this world; eventually he becomes addicted. In the course of his research, he meets all of the pick-up gurus – including (allegedly) the guy on whom Tom Cruise's character in *Magnolia* is based. He learns all their tricks of the trade – their demonstrations of value, their false time constraints, their peacocking, their NLP tricks and traps – and basically he transforms himself into some kind of RoboStud – a bald, ripped, soulless, pre-progammed seduction machine.

The game in question – also branded by other PUAs as Real Social Dynamics – is basically an attempt to make a science out of seduction. Furthermore, naturally, it is an attempt to make a profit out of that science. The money-making aspect is important. This is not philanthropy, as many of the gurus attempt to imply. It's business.

So I read the whole thing with a very jaded and cynical eye, but there was one paragraph which hooked me despite myself. It described a meeting Strauss had with a PUA called David X. Now David X was apparently one of the best in the business. No shitty stick in the world could protect this guy from a constant deluge of enthusiastic muff. And the bit that caught my eye was Strauss describing X as the ugliest PUA he'd ever met. He was 'immense, balding, and toadlike', with a rash of warts covering his giant face. It was at that point that I thought, 'OK. Maybe I can give this game a go. Maybe it's time I got Game.'

So. Apparently, the first thing I need is a name that is not my own. A seduction name. A pulling name. This is because, essentially, 'the game' is all about manipulation through deception. Strauss is told early on in his journey, 'It's not lying. It's flirting.' It's something he repeats to himself every now and then, usually before he tells some great big horrible lie. 'It's not lying,' he says. 'It's flirting.' No, it's not, Neil. It's lying. And you know it.

Just as I know, of course, that I'm never going to be able to do this. Certainly not to the extent of the various characters in the book. Not to the extent whereby the attempted seduction of a woman becomes instinctive, an habitual reaction to seeing an HB in the street. (Ugh. If it's any consolation, every time I use the abbreviation 'HB', a little bit of sick gets lodged in my windpipe.)

However, although it's very easy to deride Strauss and his cohorts, there is definitely a lot I can learn from *The Game*. Most of it is fairly obvious stuff that only a moron wouldn't already know, of course: look good, feel good, learn a little sleight of hand to impress strippers, shop assistants, and women in the media. But there's some other stuff too, stuff about mastering routines and patterns –

basically all the distinctly dodgy neuro-linguistic-programming stuff used by magicians, shysters, and conmen the world over. In seduction circles, however, we're talking trance words, triangular gazing, the Yes Ladder, and so on. I could, if my conscience allows me, definitely benefit from using some of that.

But first, a name. Ideally, if the masters of 'the game' are anything to go by, it has to be something that makes you cringe every time you hear it. Neil Strauss, for example, became Style. Ugh. The guy who took him under his wing and guided him deep into the seduction community – Eric von Markovik – is Mystery. Ugh. Some of the other names of the main players in the community are: Vision, Papa, Herbal, Rasputin, the Matador of Love ... You get the idea. I would like to say it's one step up from McLovin', but it's really pretty much on a par.

So, a name, a name, let me think. What about Despair? No. Bulk? No. Cyst? No, no, no. Think, man. Positive. Romantic. *Seductive.* OK, what about the Labrador of Love? No? The Toreador of Trim? The Quim Master? Wait. I've got it. The Reverend Poon. OK, OK, I'm being foolish. But wait. I'm trying to establish a presence, both online and offline, so why not – it seems so obvious now – why not *Presence*? Seriously. I reckon I could get away with that. I can see it now ...

HB10: *So what's your name, big fella?*
Presence: *Me? They call me Presence.*
HB10: *Wow. You're making me horny.*
Presence: *Yep. That's what I do.*

OK, now, with the name in place, I need to start working on my game. Of course I'm already doing what I can to improve my physical appearance. The diet is already in full swing and going well, stomach cramps and bad breath aside. Plus, my coccyx is more or less back to normal, and not only have I dispensed with the haemorrhoid cushion, but I've even started running round the park which is just minutes from my flat. It's actually more of a wheezing, lumbering stagger at the moment, but it counts, it's physical exercise, and my muscles are working for the first time in years.

Also, because making the most of what you've got is all important, tomorrow I'm going to have a haircut.

My main concern with *The Game* and the whole science of the pick-up thing is that a) it seems to be – pardon me if I exaggerate – but it seems to be practised – in the main – by total and utter, vile and contemptible morons, b) you'd have to be a sad and desperate, at least slightly misogynistic moron to even seriously consider it, and c) the only way this would work on any woman is if she happens to be a moron.

But what I don't want to do is make any snap decisions. I've been a victim of prejudice too many times not to know that it sucks, so I'm determined not to be prejudiced against 'the game'. I'll try it first, then I'll be prejudiced.

So what I need to do is actually start talking to women – in real life, I mean. No more of this virtual nonsense. The internet is dead. I need to force myself to talk to as many living, breathing, female strangers as possible in order that the pain of rejection no longer holds any fear for me. That's what Style did at the beginning. It's what all PUAs must go through. It is a rite of passage, an initiation, a baptism of fire. I need to get to the point whereby when I approach a woman and open my mouth to speak, my heart isn't beating like bongos.

So I reckon I'll be ready by the spring. I've marked it on my wall chart. In the first week of April, I'll be ready to go 'in-field'. I can't go now because, frankly, I'm a mess. But the fact is, with just a few weeks' concentrated dieting (bar the occasional lapse), and just a week of regular exercise, I've already lost almost a stone in weight. What this means is that if I manage to keep this up, I will no longer be severely obese come the spring. I'll merely be obese. And if I continue at this rate, I will have reached my ideal weight by the end of the summer. At that point, however, I'll have to do something to regulate my diet, otherwise by the time my thirty-second birthday rolls around, I will have completely disappeared.

Joking aside, however, I reckon I'll have lost enough weight to have the confidence to talk to women in April. And not before. I've marked it on my wall chart because if I don't give myself these hideous, terrifying goals, then I'll just stop and turn back into a pork pie.

This gives me somewhere in the region of eight weeks to figure out what to say. Thankfully, this is where *The Game* comes into its own. Ask any PUA – Style, Mystery, Frank 'Master of the Muffin' Mackey – and they'll all tell you, what you need is a stockpile of good 'openers'. An opener is, as its name suggests, a way of starting a conversation when you approach a 'target', or 'woman'. Which, of course, makes sense. It's clearly really useful to have something funny or interesting to open with rather than just saying, 'Hello, what's your name? What do you do?', which, on the handful of occasions I've attempted social congress, is pretty much all I've ever had at my disposal. Unfortunately, the openers recommended by Style et al often smack of either immense cheesiness or downright deception. One example is the very popular 'Fighting Girls Opener', created by Neil Strauss, which goes something like this:

PUA: Hey, did you guys see those chicks rumbling on the sidewalk?
Girls: Wh— [Cut them off before they speak.]
PUA: Yeah, there was a gaggle of girls fighting over this guy. I spoke to him when it was over. Turns out his name was Eros. That's a deal-breaker name right there, Eros. So they were tugging on each other's hair and suddenly one of the girls' boobies pops out. Normally I'm well up for eyeing a ripe one, but this was a strangulated, desperate thing, a real saggy-baggy, National Geographic *booby ...*

At which point, if you allow them to respond, you find you're involved in actual conversation with a woman or women in whom you're interested, the hardest part is over and you can take it from there. That is, unless phrases like 'a ripe one' and 'saggy-baggy booby' don't repulse them utterly and they're just standing there looking at you, open-mouthed, like you've just pooped on their lawn.

I can see, however, how this approach would work, particularly on really dull women, the kind in whom I have absolutely zero interest. So, with that in mind, I've devised a slightly darker, spicier version of the Fighting Girls Opener, something for the more discerning lady, which I intend to use when I'm in-field in April. My plan is to approach a saucy woman in the queue at Pret A Manger and say:

Hey, did you see those two old men in the street just now fighting over a dead cat? [Cut her off before she has the chance to call the police.] Yeah, it was wild, honeycow. They must have been in their eighties, and they both had hold of this cat. One had the head and the other was hanging on to the back legs, pulling at it really hard they were, like it was a Tug of War, until eventually, suddenly – SNAP! – the cat's body just came apart and its guts went flying everywhere. It was like that scene in Trainspotting *when Spud's boozy diarrhoea sprayed all over his girlfriend's parents at the breakfast table … [Glance down at her breadless sandwich suggestively.] Yeah, so think of a number between one and a thousand – make sure it's seven.'*

I don't really see how that can fail, especially considering that by the time I get to use it, I will also be dressed to kill, having taken the advice of PUAs the world over, and peacocked myself to the max. 'Peacocking' is essentially dressing to get noticed. As Mystery says, 'Try wearing at least one item of clothing curious-looking enough to get people's attention.' Mystery himself favours flying goggles. Some would say this makes him look like a gargantuan ass, but it does have the effect that women notice him and will therefore often approach him and make conversation. Even if it's just to say, 'What on earth have you got strapped to your forehead, you gargantuan ass?', at least it's a start, and all you need to do to turn that around is say, 'But don't you see? You're attracted to me. You just came up and started talking to me. You see? By the way, did you see those two midgets in the street fighting over a turnip? ...' And you're away.

Now, to find out a little more, a couple of hours ago I signed up to an online forum. This is basically a place for would-be pick-up artists to get together and compare notes. The forum features, as you might expect, some genuine knuckle-scraping neanderthals, and frankly, some *bona fide* bad eggs to boot. But then that's probably true of most online communities. I decided to give them a chance to show me more than that and I started a thread entitled: 'Any advice for a freaky-looking fat fella?'

This was my opener:

So, the thing is, I'm ugly. Really ugly. Thanks to a combination of a misshapen skull, bad hair, and eczema scars, I'm actually fairly freakish. Plus, I'm obese. I'm so ugly that drunken girls dare each other to kiss me, then run away screaming and laughing like they've just licked an iguana. Even so, simply because I don't want to die alone, I have to put myself out there. So I still go to parties occasionally and suffer the stares, the stifled giggles, and the shifting away as I move close to converse. And once in a while I plunge myself into the icy humiliation of 'the move'. And it never, ever works. So this is how I ended up reading The Game.

Now, even if I say so myself, I do have one thing on my side. That thing is that I am rather witty. I'm sharp, and funny, and bright. But, sadly, fine words butter no parsnips. If you're a cross between the Elephant Man and Jabba the Hutt, you could have the pithiest bon mot *this side of Cyrano de Bergerac cascading from your mouth and women are still going to recoil from you like you're a giant cockroach.*

I've been rejected in some pretty cold ways over the years. Women have laughed in my face openly when I've said hello. One woman told me she only went out with human beings. Another told me she'd be sick if she had to kiss me.

These words stick with you by the way. They become embedded in your heart like poison darts and float around in your system for the rest of your life.

So, seeking guidance, I read The Game. *Then I came here. And what I'd like to know – bearing all of the above in mind – is what kind of advice you would give to a guy like me. And are there any openers you'd recommend for freaky-looking geezers like myself? I look forward to your responses with excitement and glee.*

So, I have to say, while I am very impressed, on the whole, by the level of humanity which is coming across in the answers, I'm astonished at the amount of talk of hats. Fancy hats at that. I never knew the humble hat was such an integral part of seduction. For example, Gigabel suggests, 'Hide your freaky head in a fancy hat'. I'm not entirely sure what he has in mind, but I'm imagining some kind of Panama. 'Clothes are important,' he continues, 'and whatever you do, make sure you drop some weight. Eat healthy, do exercise, maybe even lap-banding ...' I had to look online to find out what lap-banding is. It's not pleasant. In fact, I think I'll stick to peas and bananas for now or, as Muff Daddy helpfully suggests, I'll 'loose' a few pounds and find myself a blind girl ('there are some scorching hot blind chicks out there!').

That makes me laugh. Not just the 'loosing' of the pounds but the seeking of a blind girl. It's almost as if he knew. Meanwhile, Whipcrack tells it like it is. 'Get fit,' he says simply. 'No need to be fat and nasty.'

Then we have The Wizard, who thinks, along the same lines as Gigabel, that I might consider 'bariatric surgery', otherwise known as the gastric bypass. 'You'd be surprised what loosing weight can do for your overall look,' he continues. 'You might also consider a stylish hat and some radical sunglasses ....'

What is this obsession with 'loosing weight'? I'm beginning to think maybe it's not just lazy spelling. Maybe it's something Americans do in the bathroom.

Hat alert! This one from Captain Shaft, for whom the solution is very simple: 'Get some standard peacocking shit. Start with a wicked-awesome hat.' OK, thanks, Captain Shaft.

Of course, not everyone can be a fountain of insight and charm. There is, for example, the inappropriately-named sweetdickwilly, whose response is both hilarious and highly, horribly disturbing.

'When a girl says something like that either punch the bitch in the mouth or put gum in her hair and she will have to cut it like a lesbo and no guy will want her.'

Well, there's always at least one proper psycho in every online community. This one is special though. I have a feeling we'll be seeing this guy on the news one day. They'll call him the Spearmint Killer.

Happily, the rest of the community was quick to pounce on him, making it very clear that Spearmint was on his own.

This next one – again from Muff Daddy – is very interesting, and makes me realise the genuine advantages of belonging to a community:

Everybody here has decided to change their lives and we want to help you succeed. We want you to make other men jealous so they say, 'How the fuck did he get with a woman like that?' We want love to fill the hole in your existence that you're currently stuffing up with food. We don't want you to give up and grow old with your cat, surrounded by porno and video games. We don't want you to fall down dead from a heart attack while jerking yourself off ... We are your real friends. We already care deeply about you, more than anybody you've ever met before in your life. All we ask is that you push yourself, even when it hurts. Especially when it hurts. You're going to have to fight to get what you want, and make no mistake, it's going to be tough. Physical and spiritual ecstasy is within your grasp! You are no longer alone. We are with you.

I think he maybe overdoes it a little suggesting that he cares more about me than anyone else I've ever met – after just an hour of sharing the same virtual space – but still, it's a nice sentiment, and I can't help but feel touched by it. Genuinely. I'm sitting here reading this fellow portly dude's words and I feel moved. I— uh-oh.

Guess who's back: 'If a girl insults me she better believe she's gonna get the gum in the hair. Then I bet the bitch wouldnt do that shit again.'

Jesus. Always with the gum. Seriously, what is it with this guy and gum?

Anyhow, as I say, apart from this one dangerous imbecile, I'm very impressed with the warmth and sincerity of the gaming community. It's not at all what I expected. I feel humbled.

However, having said that, I think on the whole I have to agree with Jack Sharp, who believes: 'There is no easy solution to the difficulties facing you. Rather you must rely on personal strength, willpower, bravery, and learning to like yourself – only these will get you to where you need to be.'

Taking refuge in 'the game', or Real Social Dynamics, or whatever you want to call it, can only get you so far. What you really need to do is learn to love yourself. It may be an enormous cliché – indeed, it may be *the* most enormous cliché there is – but it's true. And that's what I'm doing. That's what all the dieting, the abstention, the exercise, the blogging, and the downright determination is all about. So when, at the end of this year, I'm swimming in HB sauce and getting more ass than my old haemorrhoid cushion, it won't be Neil Strauss I'll have to thank, but myself.

I feel good about myself. Weary certainly, but I also feel better than I have in some time, and I'm excited about the future. I'm excited about the ache in my calves and the dry mud caked to my trainers. And I'm excited about the number of people reading my blog, which is also picking up. It's still really only a steady trickle but, so far, no one has said anything unpleasant, which makes a gorgeous change.

People, it seems, are starting to notice me.

Who knows what will happen next?

CHAPTER SEVEN

SALLY VALENTINE

Traditionally, Valentine's Day is not something that particularly upsets me. Don't get me wrong, I despise it with a passion verging on hysteria, but it's never managed to make me feel any more lonely than I usually feel. Well, not much. This year, however, is my special year, my year for coming out of my shell, so I'm using it as an excuse to make more of an effort. Hence, I've been reading endless crappy articles about how to find True Love at this sickly special time of year. For example, just the other day I was reading the advice of 'gay male-relationship expert' Patrick Perrine, who suggests I 'try a new perspective' and 'think outside the candy box'.

As well as echoing the advice of my PUA buddies and telling me to 'dress for success' – neat clothes, manicured nails, warm hands and fancy hats – Patrick says: 'Pretend you're famous. Work the room like you're Bill Clinton.' Hmmm. In my most humble opinion, this is questionable advice. Work the room like the world's most notorious sex-pest? Let's move on.

'Pretend to be someone you admire,' Patrick continues, 'How would *he* break the ice?' Well, to be honest, I've always been a great fan of Gandhi. So, how would a celibate vegetarian Hindu pacifist break the ice at a potentially sexy gathering? A game of Spin the Bottle maybe? Nah. If I know Gandhi – and I like to think I do – he'd probably just do a bit of low-key mingling, dispensing his wisdom and offering around healthy nibbles: 'Happiness is when what you think, what you say, and what you do,' he'd smile, 'are in perfect harmony. Chick pea?' Actually, that's not a bad opener. I'm going to remember that.

For the moment, however, I have no need of openers. For the moment, and quite suddenly, I'm being opened myself. Like a giant clam. Packed with pearls. I exaggerate slightly, but at the start of this month I was invited out to a concert by a rather attractive cellist. The fact that the cellist in question is Keith's girlfriend, Patricia, does not, I feel, diminish the enormous sense of triumph I momentarily felt. Whether or not it was entirely platonic (it was), this was still a vibrant, sexually alluring woman inviting me out on a date.

'It's not a date,' she said.

'I know,' I said. 'I'm not a doofus.'

'Oh. Good. It's just that you told Keith I'd invited you on a date.'

I laughed, and then I said, all erubescent, 'That was just a joke, Patricia. You know? Funny!'

Damn Keith and his stupid big mouth. Is that what having a girlfriend is all about? Telling her everything your best friend says to you in complete confidence? I don't know. But I pledge to find out.

Our date started particularly well with a trip to the Royal Festival Hall to witness the performance of some 'contemporary music'. The composer was one Luca Francesconi, an Italian chap. I prepared myself for something stirring and romantic.

I was disappointed. No cliché intended, but I like a little melody in my contemporary music. And I like to be moved, damn it! This contemporary music was so senseless and discordant that when a fire alarm went off during the first piece, it took a full minute for anyone to realise it wasn't actually part of the official cacophony.

Eventually, the conductor stopped the contemporary music, out of respect for the contemporary musicians. Then when the fire alarm was silenced, the piece was resumed, with an eccentric-looking man plinking away slowly at his cimbalom, which is something like a cross between a naked piano and a game of table football. Then, at about the same point in the piece that the alarm went off the first time, you'll never guess what happened. That's right, the alarm went off again.

Patricia – who you would think as a professional cellist would know better – was suddenly grabbing on to my arm in an effort to control a violent attack of the giggles.

This time the orchestra played through the ringing, and at the end of the piece, the applause was more of relief than anything else.

The whole thing was excruciating. And hilarious.

Afterwards, we had a little drink, during which I thanked Patricia for having invited me and confided in her that I'm feeling much better about my life than I was even just a few weeks ago at Christmas. I feel more confident, less self-conscious and generally fitter, happier, more productive. Patricia was happy for me. She said I deserved to feel happy. Automatically I thought, 'Do I?' but fuck it, yes I do. Why the hell not?

That night I went to sleep smiling. Four days later, I was running in Brockwell Park on another cold but lovely day, with the air crisp and light like a perfect pancake, and I swear my guardian angel came to me in the form of a fluffy grey squirrel. This squirrel ran ahead of me, for at least a minute, scurrying from one tree to the next, then waiting for me to catch up before running ahead again. This squirrel's behaviour was unusual enough to make me laugh out loud, before it scurried up into a tree and disappeared. A few moments later, I'd completed my circuit of the park and was stretching by a gate, when a young woman walked towards me, slowly. She was wearing a big duffel coat and big jumper and a big dress and big trousers. But she wasn't big herself. She was quite small. Petite. She had long dyed-blonde curly hair that had lots of bits of stuff tied into it. Some of the stuff looked like fishing flies. She had lots of piercings. She looked ever so slightly scary, if I'm perfectly honest. But pretty. Very pretty.

When I realised that she was definitely coming up to me and not just ambling aimlessly in my direction, my heart began to beat a little faster. I felt like a wreck from the run, a phlegm-filled, sweat-stained, sickening mouth-breather of a wreck. I feared she might be about to chastise me for blowing my nose in the park, or else just say something really unpleasant about my appearance; something about the sight of fat men jogging being repellent to her. But she didn't. She just said: 'Hello.'

I blushed and squinted at her, wiped my forehead on the sleeve of my oversized hoodie. She really was very pretty. Bright, grey, piercing eyes. More silver than grey, in fact. And pierced, black eyebrows. I tried to regulate my breathing, which still sounded like it had a slight bark to it. 'Hello,' I replied. It wasn't brilliant, I know, but I figured the ball was still in her court.

'This is a bit embarrassing really,' she said, 'but I think I know who you are. Do you write a blog?'

I nodded vigorously before I could speak. Then I sort of gurgled an affirmative.

'Are you Bête de Jour?' she said.

It sounded really strange. It was a strange sentence to hear. And for a moment I didn't really know the answer. Was I? Not really. That was just an amusing name I invented for a blog I wrote on the internet.

'Yeah,' I said. I was blushing horribly. I felt like I'd been unmasked. I looked left and right to see if anyone else was listening. No one was. I was also embarrassed because the only reason this strange girl could possibly have known that I was Bête de Jour was because – as I'd readily admitted on the blog – I was fat and ugly and went running in Brockwell Park.

'Your blog is really good,' she said. 'You're a really good writer.'

'Thanks,' I said, a tiny bit too blasé perhaps. 'That's really nice of you to say.'

There was a silence. She nodded a couple of times. I knew I was supposed to say something else. Or else she'd just walk away. I nodded. I thought about negging her.

Negging is something practised by pick-up artists. It's basically a lesson from the 'treat 'em mean, keep 'em keen' school of seduction and is designed to make a woman feel just a little bit shit about herself. It'll often come in the form of a back-handed compliment or just a bit of verbal hair-pulling. Apparently women love it. When you treat a woman with playful disrespect by suggesting she's fat, old, or talks too much, you become like a challenge to her, a challenge she cannot resist. A neg is like a red rag to a chubby princess.

A classic neg then, would go something like this: 'You have beautiful teeth. Are they real?' Or you might simply point out a little fault. Tell her she's got an eyelash on her cheek or a crumb of loose skin flapping about on her forehead.

So if I wanted to neg this girl, I could have said, 'I really like your piercings. They're kind of weighing your face down a bit though, like it's sliding off your head. Yeah, like your face is slipping slowly down to the ground, like a cooked breakfast down a toilet wall.'

But I didn't neg her. I just stood there, staring.

'Well, OK,' she said. 'I just wanted to say, you know, keep it up.'

'I just saw a squirrel,' I blurted out. It took a long time coming, but it was well worth waiting for.

She smiled. Nodded again. She liked to nod.

'I'm not usually a great believer in squirrels,' I said, which isn't true, 'but this one was definitely something special. It ran with me for about ten minutes, ahead of me, like it was trying to say something. But then it didn't say anything. It was quite disappointing in the end.'

'I'm not a fan of squirrels,' she said. 'They promise so much, then they just let you down.'

'Yes!' I cried. 'They are evil!' I stopped. Looked into her eyes. 'Cute though,' I said.

Wow. I do believe I was flirting!

'Yeah.' She nodded. 'But appearances can be deceptive.'

Flirting! Good God in heaven! This was the most exciting moment of my entire life! I was a burgeoning internet celebrity and this gorgeous young woman with piercings and anti-squirrel sentiments was actually flirting with me! I shook my head and wiped some more sweat from my giant dartboard of a face.

At which point she introduced herself. And I introduced myself.

Sally was studying photography at Camberwell College of Arts. She was a painter too, but she preferred photography. And she played the guitar. And when I said she was pretty, I was wrong. She was divine. She was absolutely perfect. And [shakes fist at imaginary, malevolent God] I'm certain her boyfriend agreed.

Even if she didn't have a boyfriend, I should probably remember that, so long as the fiery shores of hell remain uncoated with ice, there is no way Sally could possibly have any romantic interest in me. I am ten years older than she is, ten stone heavier than she is, and she is so far out of my league that we are like different species: she an elf, a moon-elf; me some colossal orc or Vogon. Plus, of course, let's not forget, she has a boyfriend. He's like, eighteen or something. She let it slip, not his age, just his existence, just so I'd know that this was not a Romantic Thing. This was about writing. She likes my writing. But we did chat for a full ten minutes before she had to rejoin her friends and carry on drawing trees. And we did make each other laugh. That counts for a lot.

But also nothing. It also counts for nothing.

I spent the rest of that afternoon poring over the work and life of Sally's favourite photographer, Nobuyoshi Araki. I'd never heard of him before, but by the end of the evening – strangely – he was my favourite photographer too.

The next morning I woke up to an email from Sally. My address is on the blog. She found it. She wrote to me. It was lovely to meet me, she said. She felt honoured to know such a great writer in the flesh, she said. If I wanted any photographs taken for my blog, she said, any portraits or head-shots, she would be honoured to take them for me. Erm ... no, I don't think that will be necessary, Sally, but thanks for the offer. I felt the urge to write back to let her know that if she was really keen to help me out, the best thing she could do would be to come to me one morning when I'm at my most needy, wearing only her duffel coat, and then to insinuate herself into my bedclothes, undo the giant buttons on her coat and ... well, you get the picture. I didn't write this of course. Nor did I write it when we moved on to Instant Messenger. But I think it all the time. I'm thinking about it now, this Valentine's morning, buried deep within my bedclothes, as is my wont. I'm thinking about the skin of her taut stomach that I will never see, her face on mine, blood coursing, pulsing, petering out ... poetry. I keep getting distracted by the idea of writing a Valentine's Day poem for my blog.

Sal and I are 'just good friends',
And this is where the story ends.
She loves her boyfriend (of twelve weeks),
Despite the bumfluff on his cheeks.
Apparently, he's 'ace in bed',
A fact now burning in my head ...
(Her truth delights me, makes me glow,
but some things I don't need to know.)
IM is fine but IM not,
To let myself with her besot.
Still, unrequitings are my fate,
And now I fear, it's much too late ...

Far too embarrassed to pleasure myself, I pull on my hoodie and go for a run in the cold.

CHAPTER EIGHT

LOVE IS NATURAL AND REAL

I am human. This much is more or less self-evident. I am human, and I need to be loved. I am also an animal, and I need sex. Ange was right: it is far worse to have fornicated once or twice and lost than never to have fornicated at all. I know what I'm missing and, frankly, I'm obsessed by it. Particularly now. This time of year. All it takes is a couple of sun-blessed days and the early spring starts surging through me, stirring in my bones, feverish, already fermenting. Soon the primeval pulse will flabbergast afresh, breathing unique life into the earth and somehow managing, once again but like never before, to make every single thing on the planet look and feel full of possibility. Before we know it, deciduous bones will slip back into lush summer sleeves; days will lengthen and brighten, slowly pushing back the blanket of night; skirts will shrink, fresh-found flesh will bare and brown, and human beings everywhere will make promises that deep down they know they cannot keep.

Or in other words, I am desperate for a fuck.

It's been such a long time. The last time was over two years ago, and it was hideous. My first foray into the world of flesh was unusual, I accept, but it was tender. There was warmth, and affection, and fun. The second was entirely the opposite.

Sue was a regular in one of the pubs I used to frequent when

I lived in another part of London. She was often there with a group of her friends, being loud, drunken, and shrill. I'd be out with one of a couple of old friends, bemoaning the sickening ills of the world. I'd noticed Sue but I didn't think she had noticed me. Her eyes had passed over me for sure, but I didn't think she'd taken me in. That often happens. If you see someone you find physically repellent, you either stop and stare, sometimes pointing and grimacing, if you're particularly insensitive. Or else you just look through them; they're invisible to you.

I'd noticed Sue partially because she was so annoying and shrill, and partially because, despite myself, I was really attracted to her. She was in her mid-twenties. She was blonde and wore lots of denim. She dressed a little on the loose side, leaving next to nothing to the imagination. Swore a lot. Yet still, somehow, I found her very attractive. Which was why one night, when she rolled over to me, blind drunk at the end of a Friday evening and said, 'Do you wanna come back to my house for sex?', I said, 'Um … yeah, all right.'

Then she kissed me, there in the pub, and her friends cheered, and a flash went off. I should have known something was up. But I didn't. I was blinded by what I foolishly imagined was just brilliant luck, and I assumed that Sue was from the 'he's so ugly, he's kind of fascinating' school, a school I'd hitherto believed to be entirely fictional.

She stopped kissing me. Her hands were still on my face, her cold eyes perusing me. Another flash. 'Let's go,' she said. As she led me out of the pub, one of her friends joined us and introduced herself. 'I'm Cathy,' she said. I told her my name and they both giggled. 'Stan!' cried Sue. 'That's brilliant,' she said. 'Absolutely perfect.'

'Perfect,' repeated Cathy.

Out on the street I asked where we were going. 'Not far,' said Sue. Cathy was coming too, it seemed. My imagination began to kick in. Surely not. Sue grabbed me and snaked an arm through mine, linking me at the elbow. Cathy did the same with the other arm and we walked down a main road in the cold night. 'This is your lucky night,' said Cathy.

Surely not.

As we walked, Sue and Cathy chatted to each other about people I didn't know, shrieking and giggling like inebriated harpies. I really didn't like them at all. Which means I really shouldn't have gone with them. So maybe I kind of deserved what happened next. Maybe. I just wanted so badly to have sex. Before this there had only been Avril. So I'd never had sex with an able-bodied woman. And that had been over two years ago. I was desperate. As I am now. Maybe even more so.

That is my excuse.

We turned off the main road and on to a side street, stopping at a house with a black and red door. Cathy broke away from me and opened the front door. Sue followed her inside and took off her coat. I was very excited and very nervous. I felt a little sick.

I was led through to the living room and offered a drink. I accepted and both women clattered through to the kitchen, leaving me alone. Sue returned, carrying two hefty glasses of some putrid spirit. I don't know what it was, but it was undiluted and tasted of petrol. I took a sip and winced. Sue knocked back half of her glass and made an unpleasant face. I never saw Cathy again.

'Tell you what, I think I might need the bottle, yeah?' said Sue, then she skipped out of the room again. When she returned, she had it under her arm. 'Come on then,' she said, and I followed her upstairs.

Sue's bedroom was very much how I imagined the bedroom of a prostitute might be. A huge bed, with rather tacky tiger-skin blankets, big fluffy pillows and a wrought-iron bedstead with ropes and blindfolds and handcuffs hanging from it. The rest of the room was pretty unpleasant – an overflowing chest of drawers, an overflowing dressing table, dirty wallpaper slipping down damp walls. It was also a bit smelly. Sue lit scented candles in an effort – I presumed – to disguise the smell. Opposite the bed was a PC, switched on, that horrible Pythonesque screensaver filling the window with perpetually extending pipes, and a grotty webcam stuck to the top of the monitor.

Sue then put some soulless soul music on the computer. I believe it was R Kelly. Yet still I didn't flee.

'Do you wanna watch some porn?' she asked.

I shook my head. Not as if to say no, but rather as if trying to understand the question. Did I want to watch porn? Erm ... no? I watched porn all the time. I was here because I wanted to have sex. The opposite of porn. 'I think I'm all right for porn actually,' I said.

I was standing by the side of Sue's bed feeling rather awkward. Sue stood up from her computer and moved to the bottom of the bed. 'Come here,' she said. I did so. 'Sit down here,' she said. I sat at the bottom of the bed. Sue positioned herself behind me. She wrapped her arms around me, leant forward and began to kiss my face. I gasped. I almost couldn't believe it was happening. But it was.

OK, this is where it gets a little graphic. Not massively graphic, just graphic enough to tell the story. I apologise if you find it a little grubby. If it's any consolation, I find it a little grubby too.

So Sue was licking and lapping at my face, moaning, clawing at my chest and unbuttoning my shirt, pushing her tongue in my ear, biting my hair and gasping. All the while she was saying stuff like, 'Oh God, yeah, you're so fucking ugly, I love it. You big dirty ugly bastard.' And so on.

Now I'm quite sensitive about my appearance and I'm easily hurt. Having this woman say this to me – even though she was writhing all over me at the time – upset me, and I couldn't hide it. She saw that I was upset and laughed. 'No, don't be hurt,' she said. 'That's what I like about you. I like ugly men.'

Then she stood on the bed, lifted her skirt and pushed herself into my face. With one hand she pulled aside her knickers and with the other she grabbed my head and pushed it against her. 'See how much I like it,' she said. 'Lick me,' she said. 'Put your fingers in me.'

I did as I was told.

After some more of that, Sue undressed me. All the while she was gasping and moaning, licking her lips at me and going on about wanting me to have rigorous intercourse with her. She didn't use those words, however.

It was a bit much, to be honest. I didn't quite believe it. It was like bad porn. But it was bad porn I was involved in, and although she was a little over the top, she was real; she wasn't merely moving on my PC screen, a bunch of grubby light dancing in my damp eyes. Rather, she was all warm and wet; she was all smells, tastes and noises; she was all over me.

When she pulled off my trousers and reached into my underpants, she got a little bit of a shock. 'Oh. My. God,' she said. Her mouth fell open and she looked at me. 'You never said you had a massive cock,' she said. I shrugged. It's not the sort of thing you just drop into a conversation. Not that we'd ever had a conversation.

Sue's was only the second mouth that had ever conferred oral pleasure upon my penis, and as she slobbered on it, she looked up at me and moaned. She was very spitty was Sue. She spat into her hand and rubbed it all over my penis and balls. She spat on to the head and rubbed it in with her tongue. She looked into my eyes, dribbled down her chin and said, 'I really want your fucking big cock in me.' And then I came. Boof! Just like that. Quite unexpectedly. And rather a lot.

'Sorry about that,' I said. But Sue didn't seem to mind at all. If anything, she was overjoyed. Pushing me back on to the bed, she climbed on top of me, rubbing my sperm into my stomach and chest. 'Move up the bed,' she said. I moved. 'Give me your hands,' she said. I gave.

Then she attached one of the handcuffs and slipped the other round the back of the bars of the bedstead. 'Give me your other hand,' she said. I hesitated. Then I gave her my hand. She cuffed me to the bed. Then she produced a couple of lengths of sex-rope (as I believe it's called) and tied my feet to legs of the bed, tight.

Then she got off me and took off the rest of her clothes. Then she opened a drawer in a bedside table and pulled out some kind of kitchen implement. A long-headed spatula. I recognised it as an IKEA spatula. She used it to slap my stomach. 'Ow,' I said. She slapped me again, harder. 'OW!' I said. It stung. As the stinging sensation subsided, it was replaced by a slightly cold shiver as a wave of panic coursed through me. I suddenly realised I was in an incredibly vulnerable and potentially dangerous situation.

Sue then produced an mp3 player and pushed the headphones into my ears. She turned on the music. It was the *Teaches of Peaches* CD. What on earth was going on? I said, 'What are you doing?' but I couldn't hear my own voice over the loudness of the music. Then Sue lifted my head and popped a blindfold over my eyes. Then she wrapped something that I later discovered to be a bandage around and around my head, holding the blindfold and the earphones in place. My arms above my head began to ache. I wanted to be released.

I was scared.

But then she began to tease me, biting me, licking me, spitting on me, sucking, and occasionally slapping me with the spatula, and I became aroused. The fact of being deaf and blind seemed to both dull and sharpen the sensations simultaneously. Sometimes Sue would get off the bed and I had no idea where she was or what was coming next. Sometimes minutes would pass and nothing happened. Slowly my penis would lose its rigidity and my scrotum would tense and shrivel in the cold calm of the moment. Not knowing what was going to happen next was both terrifying and exciting. It was charged. I felt on the verge of panic. Then suddenly there'd be ice on my testicles, hot candle wax on the shaft of my cock or some kind of greased-up butt plug being shoved violently in and out of my anus.

And scared though I was, I must admit that it was very, very exhilarating. I'd never known anything like it.

Then she'd climb on me, lower her nether regions on to my face and her face on to my nether regions. Then she'd slide down my body and impale herself on me. Then she'd ride me roughly, violently, causing just as much pain as pleasure. I'd never been so much at someone's mercy before, and I can't deny that I liked it, or at least that part of me did. Another part of me wanted to be free again, alone again if necessary, but free.

As soon as it had started happening, by the way, I realised that I was having unsafe sex. I said something, but I didn't hear what I said and Sue made no attempt to answer me. As far as I know. I do know for sure, however, that she didn't stop to put a condom on me. If I'm completely honest, I think the threat of a protracted AIDS death probably turned me on a bit too.

People are weird.

At some stage Sue was licking and sucking on my left nipple and I began to feel something wet and warm on my penis. Sue moved down my body, kissing her way down to my nethers. Then before she got there I felt my penis slipping into a mouth and being sucked and bitten. I cried out. Then another mouth took over. Then I was passed back and forth from mouth to mouth.

Was this Cathy? Someone else?

Not knowing what was going on was disconcerting as hell, but hot. So hot in fact, that with two tongues wriggling over the end of my penis, I came again.

Then I had some of my own sperm spat into my mouth.

People are really weird.

It didn't stop there, however. Slowly, once again, I was teased back to life, more or less – I'd lost a lot of feeling by this stage and was finding it difficult to tell – but things continued for another half-hour or so. Then, quite suddenly, the music was stopped in the middle of a song. Then my head was unbandaged and the blindfold and earphones removed. Sue stood beside the bed, looking at me, not smiling. At the foot of the bed was a tall thin man with white spiky hair and a video camera pointed at me.

I looked at him, shook my head, looked up at Sue.

'What's going on?' I asked.

'You're gonna be fucking famous, mate,' said the guy with the camera, in a thick Scouse accent.

Sue leant over me and unlocked the handcuffs. I sat up, soothed my aching arms and tried to massage some feeling back into them.

'What are you talking about?'

'You've just made your first porn film,' said the guy. 'You're a fucking porn star, mate. A fat fucking ugly fucking porn star.'

Sue untied my feet.

'What?' I said. 'You ... you can't do that.'

'Done it, mate,' said the guy. 'It's done and dusted and there's not a fucking thing you can do about it.'

'Don't be ridiculous,' I said. At which point the guy put down the camera and pulled a Leatherman knife out of a back pocket. He took out the blade, came round the side of the bed and stuck it under my chin. He did all this very quickly. 'What did you say?' he said. 'What did you fucking say?' He was all chains, piercings, and tattoos, by the way. He was – at a guess – something of a psychopath.

'OK,' I managed. 'Take it easy.'

'Just get him the fuck out of here, Tom,' said Sue, and with that she picked up some clothes and left the room.

'You wanna watch your fucking mouth, son,' said Tom. 'How much money have you got?'

When I didn't answer, he headbutted and slapped me.

Eventually, I was allowed to get dressed and leave the house. Tom went through my pockets and found out where I lived. 'Mention this to anyone,' he said, 'and somebody will come round to your house, and they'll kill ya.' Then he took £20 from my pocket and pushed me out the front door.

I walked quickly until I was out of sight of the door, then I stood still, took out my phone and called the police. I explained exactly what had happened, adding that I'd been robbed and threatened with a knife. Part of me was in no doubt whatsoever that this was the right course of action. Part of me wasn't even there. It was like all this was happening to someone else.

The police arrived within ten minutes. I was still there. I met them at the front door. Tom tried to make a run for it through the back garden, but was caught and arrested. Sue was arrested too. I spent most of the next day making statements and looking for somewhere new to live. I stayed with friends for four days, then moved to a different part of London. Three months later I had an AIDS test. I was fine.

I found out from the police that Tom and Sue's house was full of porn they'd shot. They produced ultra-low-quality DVDs and flogged them in pubs and over the internet. They had a site. They were DIY pornographers. As far as I could piece together, they were also trying to put together a speciality series of films featuring ugly men. *Beauty and the Beast* stuff. They'd made one previously. It was for sale online. It was called *Ugly Fuckers*: Part One. I was to be Part Two.

I felt like a donkey in a real bestiality film. Except, of course, I'd consented.

I still fear that some day, somehow, that film is going to turn up on the internet somewhere. Every now and then I search 'ugly' on YouPorn or RedTube, expecting to see myself tied to a bed, bandaged, buggered and loving it. Whenever it's not there, I feel enormous relief. And a tiny, tiny part of me feels disappointed.

People are absolutely fucking mental.

One good thing to come out of it was a visit from a Victim Support lady, which I wasn't expecting. She sat down with me and talked to me about the experience. It was embarrassing. She wanted to know about the damage I'd sustained. The bruise on my face, any other cuts and bruises, the psychological damage. She filled in a form, was very sympathetic and then left, at which point I completely forgot about her. Then, about fifteen months later, completely out of the blue, I received a cheque for over £800.

It felt like royalties.

So that was that, my second sexual encounter. And the truly mind-boggling thing about it was not how much it fucked me up and depressed the hell out of me for the next two years, but how much, at times like this, I'd happily experience the whole thing all over again. In fact, toss in a couple of sweet nothings and a modicum less pain, and I'd probably even pay good money for it.

CHAPTER NINE

SICK

The pain shook me awake like a sociopathic prison guard at first light. It was courtesy of Pip, Philip Pipkin, a friend of Keith's who used to be something in software till he was made redundant about a year ago and is now considering a career in brutal, cold killing. Or at least dabbling.

Pip lives with his mum. Six months ago, at his mum's behest, he insured her pet poodle at a monthly premium of £17. As the months crept by, he began to worry about money. His redundancy package was running out fast. The last thing he wanted was to find another job, so instead he started cutting back. Grimly, he cancelled a couple of direct debits: a postal DVD subscription and a gym subscription, neither of which he ever used, amounting to a saving of £50 a month. £600 a year. He was pleased, grudgingly, but he felt he could do better. His mother tried to help. Did he really need all those sports channels, she wondered?

Pip was livid. Not the sports channels. Anything but the sports channels.

Suddenly he found himself focusing all his impotent, mid-life-crisis rage on his mother's dog. His first thought was to cancel the insurance. He couldn't afford it any more – it was as simple as that. He'd explain to his mum that the dog would have to take its chances like everybody else. But then he thought, 'But what about the money I've already lost on this animal? Isn't there some way I can make a return on my investment?'

It was payback time.

'How hard can it be to break a dog's leg?'

'Depends on the dog,' I said.

'It's not like it's a Great Dane or anything,' he said. 'It's not like it's going to retaliate. It's a scrawny little poodle, a toy dog, and it's old. Weak.'

We were in the pub, drinking. My pain was in the post.

'On Sunday I was round at my mum's,' said Pip. 'And Steve was there, snuffling about.' That's the dog's name. Steve. Steve the fourteen-year-old poodle. 'He's not even very friendly any more,' he said. 'Plus he's started shitting indoors, which is annoying. To say the least. So I'm doing the washing-up after dinner. Stacking the machine. And he's mooching around my feet. So I crouch down and I say, "Sit", and he sits. Then I say, "Give me your paw," and he gives me his paw. And I'm there, with Steve's paw in my hand, thinking, "How much would I get for a paw broken in two, maybe three places?" I apply a tiny bit of pressure and he whimpers and scampers off.' Pip looked at me, beseeching. I shook my head. 'It would have to be a swift, clean break,' he added.

At which point I put it to him that, if he breaks the dog's leg and receives money from the insurance company to fix the dog's leg, then surely – correct me if I'm wrong, and I may very well be – but surely that money would have to be spent on fixing the dog's leg? He nodded, thinking. 'You might be right,' he said. He nodded again. 'You're right. There's only one thing for it then.' He nodded a third time, looking grim. 'Steve must die.'

Pip is a funny old goose. A fairly unremarkable black-haired white man with slightly hooded eyes and a turtle's beak, he is nearly ten years older than me, yet he still speaks and thinks like a child. I don't know what I expect really. I think that, for some reason, I had it in my head that, when they turned forty, boys became men. Silly of me.

'I've got to make it look like an accident though. Help me out here. You've got an imagination. What are your thoughts?'

'Just poison it,' I said, coldly.

'It's traceable,' he said. 'Mum'll probably order an autopsy. I don't want to end up doing time for killing a dog. That would just be embarrassing.'

'Suffocate it,' I said. 'Leave a plastic bag in the kitchen, make sure your mum knows it's there, put the bag on Steve's head and keep him there till he stops breathing.'

'Jesus.' He shook his head, disgusted. 'That's sick,' he said.

I shrugged. 'Murder ain't pretty.'

'Maybe the most humane way is to shit in my mum's bed,' he said.

It took me a moment to understand. 'What, and blame Steve?'

'Well, she would probably just jump to that conclusion.' He shrugged. 'Then I could say, "Well, he is old, Mum. Maybe it's his time."'

I am very glad Pip is not my son.

'Or here's another suggestion,' I said. 'Why not – brace yourself – why not get off your arse and get yourself a job? You're going to have to sooner or later.'

Pip scowled at me. He doesn't want to get a job. He really enjoys not working. His days fly by in a flurry of indoor games and outdoor sports. Not flurry. A barrage. He plays a lot of tennis and serves up a surgical storm. Which is why we were in the pub after my humiliation at Pip's cruel, dog-worrying hands. We were having a restorative drink. In twelve hours' time, with the anaesthetic of the alcohol worn off, I would wake up in agony.

Seven days after that, lying in the same bed, in the same position, I would realise without pleasure that the pain I'd experienced a week ago, compared to what was happening in my crumpled body now, was something akin to a walk in the park. And like a lot of my pain so far this year, it was all Ange's fault.

She'd invited me back to hers to eat. Just a meal. No licentiousness. Just two friends enjoying one another's company like grown-ups. The day of the meal, I phoned to confirm. There was no answer. Fifteen minutes later Ange called me back sounding groggy, like she'd just regained consciousness after a lengthy and painful operation. She said she'd been in the bathroom when I called, being sick from her bottom. She'd been vomiting for most of the day, from both ends. She seemed really dazed. I asked her if I should come up and see her. She said she didn't know, which was really a yes in a shoddy disguise, so I drove to Hackney, stopping off along the way for some bad magazines (*Heat*, *Now*, *Soaplife*), because she likes that sort of thing, and some carrot and coriander soup, because soup is the food of the ill.

Turns out Ange had the norovirus, and was in a terrible way. When repugnant stuff wasn't forcing itself out of at least one of her orifices, she was just lying around in terry towelling, all shivery and delirious. She was actually very sweet and sickly sad and I felt tender as opposed to lascivious towards her, which made me think that maybe it really was love that stirred in my fundaments every time I thought of her.

In lucid moments, Ange would complain that she looked 'a right state', and push some of her lank hair around her forehead, like that made a difference. It's true that with vomit drying on her dressing gown, she was far from her best, but it didn't matter. She still looked good enough to eat.

After forcing a bit of the soup inside her, she fell asleep. I wrote her a little note saying I'd call in the morning and I let myself out quickly, before I submitted to the urge to kipper through her personal belongings and writhe next to her on the bed. Naked.

A day later she was a lot less feverish, and the vomiting had stopped. She was still spending a lot of time on the loo but she was at least well enough to start talking about getting back to work, which was obviously a good sign. Meanwhile, I had begun to ache, which was a very, very bad sign.

The next day I woke up in the powerful grip of the nascent virus. My skin was in pain. All over my body it ached and crawled like something trying to escape from a death camp. My bedroom was colder than a witch's fridge and yet sweat poured out of me like cheap wine. Every few minutes a tiny dwarf in my gut jumped up and down, jabbing at my innards with a sharpened spoon. I couldn't keep my eyes open, but closing them made me nauseous. I felt like I'd taken a handful of mysterious pills from an old lady's handbag – I felt spaced and confused, like I didn't know what was going on. But I did know. I knew exactly what was going on. I knew that, very shortly, I would be stuck to the loo, throwing up between my legs.

And so it goes. The day passed, with my body in revolt and my brain spinning. At the height of its powers, the virus made me delirious, and I slipped in and out of consciousness, with dreams, fantasies, and fears all coming together and getting it on in my addled brain. Ange came to visit. And Sally. I saw Pip crouched at the side of my bed like Annie Wilkes in *Misery*, with thick blocks of wood and a hammer. But eventually it all passed, one day bled into another, and that day, too, eventually passed.

By this morning, I was feeling decidedly better. Still a little flimsy in the stool department, but the running and retching were over with. Then, earlier tonight, Ange came round on care duty. Payback for my kindness. Score. She came round after work, with the ingredients for a first-class leek and sweet potato soup. She looked wonderful in my kitchen, and despite the fact that she's made it perfectly clear she isn't interested in me sexually, part of me couldn't help thinking that with a little manipulation, maybe she might – you know – be interested in me sexually.

Then Keith joined us. We all ate soup, watched a film and Keith and Ange left together.

Oh.

There was nothing fishy about it, per se, but I couldn't help imagining foul misdeeds. Ange, for all her inestimable qualities, is a slut. And I mean no disrespect by that. In fact, her sluttishness may very well be the most inestimable quality of all.

And Keith. Good old Keith. I loved the way he swanned in here tonight with his fisherman's jumper and his stubble, his skunkweed, his pirated DVD and his tales of celebrity shoulder-rubbing. He works as an art director on adverts and pop videos, so he meets the occasional celeb. He doesn't enjoy it, but he does get the opportunity – if he thinks it's going to impress someone – to drop a few names. Tonight he dropped a few names.

And now I'm alone.

I sit for a while, thinking dark thoughts, then I shuffle through to the bathroom for a shower and a shave. It's late but I want to feel good when I wake up tomorrow, and not like a tramp waking up after a fight.

I step on the scales.

Well, will you look at that. Every cloud, as they so rightly say, has a silver lining. In this case it's most probably stomach lining, but it all counts. Chalk it up. Seven pounds in two days. Now *that's* impressive. And although I feel weak now, and still with the occasional twinge, I do feel somewhat purged. Not exactly Born Again, but certainly Wide Awake. In fact, I might go so far as to suggest that the norovirus has actually done me some good. For a while there it was like being eaten alive from the inside out by a double-headed anorexic poltergeist, but at the end of it, I genuinely feel positively lithe.

I hope Keith gets sick now.

That's what he deserves.

Payback.

CHAPTER TEN

PAYBACK

I'm afraid I did something unforgivably insensitive. To Keith. As well as secretly wishing illness upon him, I wrote him a letter. I wrote him a letter because he'd disappeared. Incommunicado. He wasn't answering his phone. He wasn't responding to messages. I even went round and banged on his front door before finally, out of frustration, I resorted to writing a letter. Then – and this is the insensitive part – I published the letter on the internet.

Then, to add self-serving oafishness to unforgivable insensitivity, I attempted, publicly, to justify my actions. 'There are things that need to be said,' I wrote. 'Even if they sting.' What balls. What an egotistical monster I truly am.

Still. We all make mistakes.

It began with a phone call. Patricia called me. She was upset.

'She was crying,' I wrote, pompously, superciliously, in a blog post entitled 'The Long, Dark Soap Opera of the Soul – An Open Letter to a Friend'. What a pompous towering cock I am. 'She said that you'd betrayed her,' I wrote, 'that you'd slept with someone else on Friday night. She didn't know the name of the woman you slept with, but of course I do. You slept with Ange.'

Of course none of this had to do with sexual jealousy.

'I'm amazed,' I wrote, like it really was my business. 'I'm disappointed.' Right. 'I'm shocked and hurt and totally bewildered. I don't know how you could do this. I don't know how you could do this to Patricia. I really can't get my head around the fact that you've gone and jeopardised the very thing you've always yearned for, that which you've described a million times as the best thing that's ever happened to you. And for what?

'Ange is great, don't get me wrong. She's a fabulous woman. She's warm, witty, and wonderful. But she's hardly the most emotionally mature patient on the mental ward, is she? She said to me sometime last month: "I'm not a very good girlfriend. I'm a good fuck, but I'm not a good girlfriend." … I'm guessing that's what swung it for you. The sex. I understand it's a very powerful force. I hope it was worth it.'

Sour grapes ooze like grease through every word. This is ugly.

I have mentioned only briefly on the blog the fact that I may still have a bit of a thing for Ange. But I kept it really lighthearted. None of the twenty or thirty or so regular commenters – some of whom have become quite close virtual friends – have any idea. They don't know that I worshipped Ange at school, that I stroked my pillow and thought of her almost every night for the better part of two long, hard years. They have no idea how upset I am at her coming back into my life and not offering herself to me, for old times' sake, if nothing more. They all think my self-righteous indignation is caused by my upset for Patricia. Even those who feel that washing Keith's dirty laundry in public without his consent was a despicable thing to do – even they think I did it for the right reasons.

Of course, I'm not so twisted and evil that I don't feel terrible for Patricia. I do. I really do. But honestly, and obviously, there is definitely jealousy in there too. I'm not certain my reaction would have been quite so rancorous, nor so ostentatious, were it not for that bitter sting of ghastly self-pity.

'I know I shouldn't,' I wrote, 'because it's ludicrous, but I can't help feeling a little guilty for bringing the two of you together. I keep thinking, if only I hadn't got sick, or if only Ange hadn't got sick before me, or if only I hadn't got back in touch with Ange in December, or if only you weren't such a selfish fucking short-sighted arsehole.'

Ha!

'But this isn't about me.'

Ha! Ha!

'It's about you and Patricia; it's about you and Ben and Dina; it's about you and Ange. And neither you nor Ange are answering your phones tonight. Hopefully you're round at Patricia's and you're going some way to starting to sort this out, one way or the other.'

But wait, what's this? Could this be a moment of self-awareness?

'I'm sorry I'm coming across all self-righteous. Maybe if I had the opportunity, I'd be a treacherous son-of-a-bitch too, and maybe you'd be up here, poncing around on the moral highground, all holier than thou and smug as a Samaritan. Maybe. But I doubt it. You're not as self-righteous as I am. And I'm not as selfish as you are.'

Ha! May Malevolent God strike me down.

Publishing that blog post feels like the worst thing I have ever done. Or at least, I don't think I've ever felt so bad about my behaviour before. Not even after a disastrous date I'd had a few years ago with a woman called Janet, who thought we were soulmates till I crushed her with careless, cowardly cruelty. That was bad, but this, for being carefully calculated, was very much worse.

As soon as I read it for the first time online, I realised what I'd done. But, already, it was too late to take it down. It would be cached somewhere, someone would dig it out and wave it about with glee. Nope. The damage was done and a big ugly ball was suddenly in motion.

I had to live with it. It was the least I could do.

One of the first comments said: 'I'm so sorry his betrayal has touched you. Bravo for having the courage to address it.'

Courage, right. Bravo.

Another referred to an Australian blog, the author of which had also been betrayed by her husband. She blogged about the inevitable dissolution of their relationship, his apology and her eventual forgiveness. It was heartbreaking. But it ended well.

Patricia read it, via my blog, to which she'd been directed by Keith, who was spitting feathers and broken glass. Ange was now aware of the blog too. The whole situation quickly left my hands and spiralled off like a fully blown balloon, fit to pop and suddenly let loose around the room in tight circles, screaming.

I tried for a couple of days to call both Keith and Ange to apologise, but I couldn't get hold of either of them. Naturally I thought the worst.

Then I got an email from Patricia. 'Hello Poppet!' she began. 'It would appear that I'm suffering from a terrible inertia today. I can't seem to do anything to its conclusion.' She had been in something of an emotional flurry, as you might expect. Not flurry. Maelstrom. An emotional maelstrom. But she had come to a decision. She knew what she had to do. She had read the account of the Australian infidelity to its conclusion, from original sin to sweet forgiveness, and all was clear. So she spent a day with Keith, thrashing through the ins and outs. Then she told him. They were through.

I include this extract, as I don't want to besmirch it by rewording it clumsily. This is what Patricia wrote about Keith:

He's never betrayed me with anyone else before, as far as I know, but he has hurt me with his impulsiveness – putting himself before me, always putting himself before me, to such an extent that I don't really matter. Richard never did that. Richard put me first always. He loved me. He truly loved me. And then he died. Nice one, God. Fair play to you.

When it comes to the way they both treated me at least, Keith has nothing on Richard. I do love him, Keith, but as far as I can see it, he doesn't know how to love properly. People who know how to love properly don't sleep around. I think it's that simple. Maybe they can learn how to love. Maybe Keith could learn how to love me. Maybe. But that's too bad because I'm not going to give him the opportunity. He can learn to love someone else. And I can find someone else who doesn't find loving me SUCH A FUCKING CHALLENGE.

She also requested that I publish her email on my blog. I think it was a little piece of payback for her, but she also thought I'd be doing Keith a favour. She quoted the Australian woman she'd encountered online, the one who eventually forgave her husband: 'If he can still face everyone after this, then he is learning to face himself.'

So in a way it was my duty to publish it.

And so it went up.

Keith doesn't really come out of it smelling of roses, I must say. And the fact is, even if he is a smiling damned villain and treacherous, conniving, back-stabbing, adulterous dog, Keith is my friend – my very best friend – and I feel really bad for the public washing and ironing of his dirty, rancid, love-rat laundry.

But I know he'll understand.

'Are you out of your fucking *mind*?' he screams.

He doesn't understand.

'No,' I reply, nodding vigorously. 'You said it was OK!'

'I said it was OK to publish Patricia's letter. What choice did I have? What I'm pissed off about is the whole fucking thing. You had no right, no right at all to write about my fucking personal life on your stupid fucking blog.'

'Oh,' I say.

I'm round at his place in Peckham. We're sorting things out. Keith is not in a good way. He's been smoking junk. No, hold on, not junk. Skunk. He's been smoking skunk all day and, frankly, I think he might be developing a psychosis for it.

'What kind of a friend are you?' he spits, seriously.

'I'm a good friend,' I said. 'You know that, come on, I just ...'

'I don't know anything of the fucking sort!' he shouts, really very angry. 'Not any more. To have people knowing intimate details about me, about my relationships. You *fucking* prick.'

'But it's not even your real name,' I point out. 'What do you care? No one reads the thing, anyway. Ten people maybe. And a couple of cowpokes in Buttcrack, Arkansas.'

He calms down, lights the end of a joint, pushes air into his cheeks and holds it for a few seconds, before swallowing it down again. 'Yeah, fuck it,' he says. 'You're probably right.'

I am relieved, and a little nervous. My heart is beating a little faster than it should, and if I'm perfectly honest, I'm not sure that Keith's right. About me being right. In fact, I have this paranoia that someone somewhere might cut and paste the whole sorry soap on to a forum for disgruntled ladies and Keith might inadvertently become an internet synonym for the emotional brutalities of betrayal, before finally being tracked down, unmasked and horrifically emasculated in a public place. And I will be to blame.

He offers me the joint, but I demur. 'I'll take a pipe if you've got one.'

'You'll fucking what?'

Oh, dear. He seems to have turned again. 'Do you happen to have a pipe?' I repeat, as innocently as I possibly can. 'I thought you had one.'

'Are you out of your fucking *mind*?'

I nod vigorously. 'No,' I insist. 'I just don't want to die of lung cancer. Is that not cool?'

'Cool? *Cool*?' He is screaming again. 'What the fuck has *cool* got to do with this? What do you fucking know about *cool*, you treacherous fucking cow!'

'Look, Keith. If you haven't got a pipe, that's no big deal, man.'

'Oh, is it not? Is it *cool*, is it? Well, I'm sorry to piss on your pipe parade, fatty, but if you want to smoke my drugs, you'll do it like a fucking man.'

'And what's that supposed to mean? How does a *man* smoke drugs exactly?'

'In a joint. A man smokes drugs in a joint. With tobacco. Lots of tobacco. A man doesn't give a damn about cancer. A *real* man gives *cancer* to cigarettes!'

'That's Chuck Norris, and he's not a real man, he's a fictional character.'

Keith is sitting in an armchair, arms folded, shaking his head. I watch as the slow shake segues into a silent weep. Then his shoulders and the nest of his forearms are shuddering rhythmically and his head falls on to his chest.

'Hey,' I say soothingly, moving across the room and crouching beside him, a slightly uncomfortable hand on his upper arm. '... Hey, hey,' I continue. 'What's with all the emotion?'

'I've had a really bad week,' he says.

'I know,' I say.

'I think I might be existentially constipated.'

'I know.' I take the joint from him and relight it.

And this is how he is for the rest of the evening. One minute he is screaming and spitting, the very anus of antagonism. The next he's gibbering and shaking, juddering with grief, tears popping from his eyes like fat from a frying burger.

'I'm really sorry,' I say.

He shakes his head and looks away. 'Worst birthday ever,' he says.

Oh, yeah, it was his birthday a couple of days ago. I forgot to mention. I didn't really get him anything yet, but I'm going to get him something nice. When I think of something.

'Yeah, yeah, when you think of something. Cheers. Happy fucking birthday.'

I feel bad. Not merely because I haven't bought him a gift as yet, but also because I wished him ill, and although it's not one hundred per cent confirmed, it's looking like I might have got my wish.

'Let's just go over what I got for my birthday this year, shall we?

My thirtieth fucking birthday. One,' he says, counting out on his fingers, 'my girlfriend dumps me. Two. My best friend betrays me on the internet. Three. I get fucking MS.'

'I know,' I repeat again. 'It's been a tough week. I'm sorry.'

CHAPTER ELEVEN

EVERYBODY'S FREE (TO WEAR A PAPER BAG)

PatriciaGate is tough on everyone involved, and when it's all over, I make a vow never to wash my friends' soiled smalls in public again. Of course I make this vow in public, with a boastful flourish, and before the month is out, I break it. But really there is nothing I can do. It's all completely out of my hands.

I'm beginning to see how blogging could, potentially, become a problem if a person were clumsy with it. I think I have to decide what it is I'm trying to do with the blog. At first it was a place to log my efforts at self-improvement and help me find a mate. Now it's becoming a place for me to snitch on my friends and gossip about my neighbours.

The thing is, once you've begun to talk to the internet, it does become addictive. Because the internet listens, and thinks about what you've said, and then the internet talks back. And you don't have to be a raving egomaniac to come to thrive on that interaction. (But it does help.) Actually, it's almost the opposite of egomania, because all you really need to get addicted is a passing interest in other people; and the enthralling things they say. Especially if they're talking about you.

I confess. I've become addicted. The internet thrills me; blogging about my life gives me an outlet. I'm slightly concerned, however, that the thrill of writing about my life is actually somewhat sharper than the thrill of actually living it. At the moment, the two seem to be feeding off of one another.

The reason this is a problem is because sharing your life on the internet comes with responsibility, and sometimes disguising names might not be enough.

So I'm trying to do the right thing, but I keep getting it wrong.

So I beat myself up.

It's what I do.

I do not self-harm. Not with blades, at least. I tried it once and it bloody hurt. It hurt a lot more than a few short sharp slaps to the face or paunch, which is the kind of self-abuse I favour at times of emotional hardship. Usually while I'm looking in the mirror. And I fall into a bout of this after the long weekend at Keith's.

But you know, the thing about self-harm of any hue is that it's terribly, terribly destructive. Even on a small scale. If you imagine a young boy slapping himself in the face and crying, your instinct is to reach out and stop him, give him a hug. So it is that I see myself in the mirror, jabbing at myself and cussing my reflection, my face contorted in a failed attempt at crying, and I think: 'Oh. You poor sad thing. Come and let me give you a hug.'

Of course, a man cannot hug his own reflection, so in lieu of the hug, I begin to entertain the notion of 'positive thinking'. I give it a shot, figuring I have nothing to lose.

Then I find out – through a carefully planted link – that Keith – my best friend – has set up his own blog. Apparently it really is payback time.

'Breathe,' I tell myself. 'It'll all come out in the wash.'

I reach for *The Little Book of Calm* that always sits atop the row of books on the middle shelf of the bookcase by my bed, just in case, but I am stymied at the first pass. It isn't there. 'Why isn't it where it always is when I need it?' I cry. Pablo senses my distress and looks up from the bottom of the bed, where he lies snoozing and dreaming of cows. 'What have you done with my *Little Book of Calm*?' I ask him. '*Where is my Little Book of Calm*??'

Pablo pities me, I know.

I love him for it.

I give him a little snuggle by way of apologising for shouting and he snags my sleeve on a claw. Then he rolls on to his back and stretches himself opulently. At his full length, he is a fat fur stole, so I try, subtly I think, to get him around my neck. But he bats me away. He is pretending to be angry, swishing his tail and scowling at me. Luckily, I have something for these moments. What I have is an empty crisp bag, tucked in on itself so that it's now a triangular plastic cushion about the size and weight of a healthy cockroach. It's the best toy any cat ever had. The secret is in the lack of friction when the thing is pawed across the carpet. It flies around the room at the mercy of the cat's clawful instincts, and it's Pablo's favourite toy of all time. Indeed, now that he's getting on in years, it's just about the only thing that can trick him into having a good time when I feel guilty about making him grumpy. I slump to the floor by the bed to look for it and there, beneath a layer of dead skin and cat hair, is *The Little Book of Calm*.

Thanks to Pablo, the necessity for tranquilising epigrams has passed, so I save the book for later and, together, we have a little play. Then Pablo sashays out to the back garden to flex his personality in front of his peers, outwit foxes and do whatever else it is he does when my eyes are not upon him with a loving melange of admiration and envy.

Then it is quiet, and to stop myself drifting back into a dark place, I pick up *The Little Book of Calm* and dip in at random.

'Start Christmas Now,' I am counselled. *Surely not in March*, I think. 'It probably took a lot of trial and error over the centuries,' *The Little Book of Calm* intones, breathily, 'but Christmas cards and lullabies finally have a unique ability to soothe. Use them (silently) all year round.' I close the book and contemplate. I try to focus on the message in this curative nugget of wisdom. *Trial and error*, I ponder. *But now, after centuries, Christmas cards and lullabies finally have a unique ability to soothe.* So therefore I should use them all year round. But – silently. Hmm. So that nobody can actually hear them. And therefore nobody will be successfully soothed.

I ponder some more. Have I read it wrong? Am I just not Zen enough?

I move on, feeling disappointed, ashamed, and ever so slightly less calm than before.

'Wear Donald Duck Underpants.'

I glance at the cover to make sure I really am reading *The Little Book of Calm* and not *The Little Book of Infuriating Non-Sequiturs*.

'Choose a few childlike accoutrements to remind you of the irreverent, uninhibited, joyous side of life.'

I sigh. I'm not Zen enough.

'Pretend You Believe.' 'Recognise the Difference Between Having and Living.' 'Reaffirm Your Friendships.'

I throw *The Little Book of Calm* into my Little Box of Bunkum and decide I can do better myself.

So, I pull up a pen and scribble down a selection of lexical amulets to help me remain upbeat and optimistic. And then I get to thinking, Hey, I can actually help others with this stuff. Because, as the last couple of weeks amply prove, helping others is pretty much what I'm all about. Or at least the new me is. That's the new me to a silver T. So I start writing a kind of a manifesto for ugly people and other members of the Great Unwashed. But I get nowhere.

Then I remember *The Sunscreen Song* and think – Hey! – why not use that?

So I find the song online and stay up all night paying homage.

When I'm done, I have to say, I'm pleased. I feel it is the best thing I've written for the blog by a preposterously long chalk. I am certain that the internet is going to explode when I post this little beauty. By the time autumn comes around, I'll be on the Jonathan Ross show talking about my controversial acceptance speech for the Nobel Peace Prize. 'Was it weally necessawy to be so wilfully iwwevewent?' he'll say. I'll say, 'Pardon?'

So I post it. And I even recommend it, smugly, on various

recommendation sites, waiting for the flurry of up-jutting thumbs. Not flurry. The cacophony of thumbs and cheers and praise.

And I wait.

And I wait.

And nothing.

A few comments from the regulars, yes, which pleasure me deeply, don't get me wrong, as they always do, but where – *where* is the cacophony?

I am upset, and on the verge of petulance .... Stupid internets. What do they know?

But then I reread my manifesto, and I feel better. It works.

It's good, I think. Time will vindicate me.

It's Easter Monday, by the way, when I finish writing it.

I'll leave you to draw your own conclusions.

Everybody's Free (To Wear a Paper Bag)

Ugly ladies and gentlemen of the internet ... wear a paper bag over your head. If I could offer you one tip for overcoming overwhelming feelings of ugliness, that might as well be it.

The long-term benefits of wearing a paper bag are open to question, but in the short term they're great at replacing the shame of a hideous face with the embarrassment of wearing a paper bag. It's a trade-off. Still, this tip, along with the rest of my advice, should probably be taken with a hefty pinch of salt. I will dispense the rest of this advice now.

- *Remember at all times that physical beauty really is only skin deep and that even though Enrique Iglesias has moist women queuing up to fellate him, he is famously, unconscionably dull. If this makes you feel better, hang on to it for all you're worth, and don't give a second thought to George Clooney, who not only is better looking than half a dozen Enriques, but is also a scintillating conversationalist.*

- *Think beautiful thoughts. While you're about it, buy beautiful things, listen to beautiful music, and read beautiful words in the not necessarily entirely vain hope that some of this beauty will rub off on you.*

- *Read. The more you've got going on inside you, the less you need to worry about the car crash that is your physical appearance. Or indeed your life in general.*

- *Practise your comebacks for when the cruel barbs fly. Perfect them in front of a mirror. 'Madam, I may be ugly, but I am also stupid and very bad in bed. Oh.' That sort of thing. Be careful, however, not to self-deprecate to the point of self-loathing.*

- *When the barbs do come, try hard to laugh them off; let them bounce off you without causing damage. Don't be overly sensitive, and don't be too hard on yourself if you are.*

- *Don't be afraid of mirrors. While they may not exactly be your friend, they are a reminder that you're bold enough to face who you are, and to love yourself.*

- *Love yourself. Wear your ugliness like a badge of honour. Remind yourself that any old imbecile can be pretty but it takes real character to carry off a look like yours.*

- *Rejoice in the fact that, when people do like you, they really do like you. They're not just trying to get into your pants because you look good, and they're not with you for the cachet your company brings.*

- *Avoid people who want to make themselves look good by surrounding themselves with freaks.*

- *Surround yourself with freaks. (If this simply is not possible, forget about it. It wasn't the best piece of advice in the world in the first place.)*

- *Accentuate the positive. If there's really nothing in your appearance to be remotely positive about, accentuate the negative.*

- *You're only as ugly as you feel.*

- *Don't be intimidated by superficial fuckwits who cannot offer the world anything more than a camera-ready smile and a pig-ugly soul. You are better than they are. Just not as good-looking.*

- *If you happen to be as ugly on the inside as you are on the outside, you probably need more help than I can give you here.*

- *Floss. Good teeth mask a myriad of sins. If you don't have good teeth, get some.*

- *Work on your body. God may have given you a baboon's behind for a face, but there really is no excuse for being fat. Besides which, your body is your temple. Worship.*

- *If you do believe in God, remember that He loves you. If on the other hand you have sanity on your side, thank God you're only ugly.*

- *Dancercise. If you have nowhere to do it but in your own living room, well, that's probably a good thing.*

- *Remember that there are five senses and being ugly marks you down on just one. So make sure you concentrate on the others: smell good, sound good, practise sensitive tactility and sprinkle a little cinnamon on your genitalia every day, just in case you get lucky.*

- *Wash. Good hygiene counts for so much in this world. If you really need to be told this at your time of life, there may already be no hope for you.*

- *There is ALWAYS hope.*

- *Embrace metrosexuality. Pamper yourself with oils, powders, and unctions. Moisturise daily. If your skin is soft, supple, and touchable, chances are someone somewhere will want to touch it.*

- *Wear good clothes. The expression 'You can't polish a turd' is a vicious, pernicious lie. You most certainly can polish a turd. Indeed, it is your duty as a human turd to polish yourself daily, and a fine wardrobe is some of the best turd-polish money can buy.*

- *Smile. Even if you have a mouth like a block of blue cheese, smile like you really mean it. The whole world may not smile with you, but the best people will.*

- *You are NOT as ugly as you imagine. Are you? Actually, maybe you are. If you are, then really, the dancercising, flossing, and good clothes will help. But if you're genuinely not, you may actually have Body Dysmorphic Disorder. Look into it.*

- *You are NOT as Body Dysmorphic as you imagine. You're just fat. Eat less. Dancercise.*

- *Wear a hat. Hats are the icing on the cake, the fairy on top of the Christmas tree, the fan of glorious feathers that turns the fat ugly peabird into a glorious cock. A good hat can be like sunshine above the clouds; a beautiful day atop the miserable blanket of smog that is your face. A hat can be the ultimate signifier of dignity. Remember, without that hat and those snazzy threads, Humphrey Bogart was just another ugly bugger in ill-fitting dentures, waving a gun about and grimacing like a gargoyle.*

- *Avoid corrective surgery like the plague that it is. Don't go under the knife unless you absolutely have to, or else part of you will always regret the other parts of you that you threw away.*

- *Pleasure yourself intensely. Use pornography if you feel the need, and use it shamelessly, but don't let it get a hold on you.*

- *If possible, sleep with people less attractive than you are. Both sides can only benefit from the union.*

- *If possible, sleep with people more attractive than you are. Both sides can only benefit from the union.*

- *When you mess up, when you embarrass yourself or just stutter or dry up because you're too nervous, don't beat yourself up over it. Other people forget quickly; they have their own stuff to think about. Also, the best way to help them forget your humiliations is to do something magnificent.*

- *In the words of Ian Dury, be magnificent. Dury was crippled with polio but was so magnificently charismatic that many people tended not to notice.*

- *Do not blame other people, even if you feel they might actually be to blame. You really are the master of your own destiny.*

- *Do not hate yourself. I know that's often much easier said than done, but keep it close to you at all times, and always believe it. It's incredibly important.*

- *Kindness lurks in the most unexpected of places. When kindness creeps up on you and takes you by surprise, allow it to reaffirm your faith in humanity.*

- *Have faith in humanity, because faith in humanity is faith in yourself.*

- *Be careful whose advice you buy, and be very suspicious of those who supply it. There are a lot of cynical, heartless people out there whose sole aim in life is to exploit your insecurity.*

- *Oh, and take that paper bag off your head. You look ridiculous.*

CHAPTER TWELVE

EVERYBODY'S BLOGGING NOWADAYS: NO HARD FEELINGS

In the Cattermole residence, Easter was always a baffling and ridiculous time of year. Chocolate-bingeing, egg-painting, bunny-jiving, treasure-truffling, and fresh, fluffy chicks were all pretty much *verboten*. Rather, Easter was a time for recognising what dreadful unworthy sinners we all were – but especially me – and for having my nose rubbed in the blood of Christ until I felt suitably chastened.

My parents were fairly hardcore hyper-hypocritical Catholics. My mum had this weird habit of dabbing water on her eyes at Easter. It was to show how upset she was at the crucifixion of Christ. It used to drive me crazy.

First, I never understood why she was so upset that Christ was crucified when it was my understanding that, when Christ came to earth in the first place, that was his sole intention. Crucifixion was his thing, his *raison d'être*. Christ without the crucifixion is like Noah without the flood. Second, and much more importantly, if she was really upset enough to cry, then why didn't she just *cry*? If I feel upset about something, I don't sprinkle salty water on my cheeks, I just get right on with the weeping. Similarly, if I need to void my bowels, I don't dump a bag of stinking old meat in the loo. I void my bowels.

Since the age of thirteen, when I finally stopped really believing that I actually believed in God – and simultaneously began to feel less guilty about everything all the time – I haven't really bothered with Easter. Ordinarily, I barely notice it. It hobbles down the street like a pantomime Trojan horse, flashing its painted smile, lingering in vain, tragic and ridiculous in equal parts. 'Oh, look, there goes Easter,' people say. 'Eww, looking a bit shabby. Mini-egg?' This year is different. This year I buy masses of chocolate and booze and I celebrate the Regurgitation like a proper heathen, with nought but sexy hedonism and base earthly pleasures in mind. To hell with Jesus, I cry. To hell with Him.

This Easter *I* am Christ. I am a 17-stone, thirty-year-old, adolescent Christ who rises from the dead and comes bouncing out of his cave like a giant priapic ram. I am Christ in a Tarzan loincloth, swinging through veritable Jungles of Knowledge with my best gal by my side. I am Christ Solo at the wheel of the Millennium Falcon, making the Kessel run in less than twelve parsecs with Leia's shiny buns bouncing slowly on my thighs. I am Malachi 'Buck' Mulligan, stately, plump, unflappable, and immense. I am a real slam-bang, honest-to-goodness, three-fisted humdinger.

Or in other words, I get laid.

And dear, sweet Jesus in Heaven, it is good. It just feels *so good*, I can't begin to put into words how good it feels, the naked, primal pleasure it brings. It's like nothing I've ever experienced, and what I have to do now is learn – if I'm ever going to do this kind of thing again, and my God I'm going to make every effort – I have to learn how not to get so damned attached. I have to learn how not to be so emotionally whimsical, grabbing on to every frond of affection and wanting it, needing it so earnestly and so recklessly.

I've also decided it's better not to blog about it, because for one reason or another, I am beginning to think it isn't such a great idea to write about my personal life online so readily, so thoughtlessly.

Then Keith surprises me by beating me to it.

Keith's blog is entitled 'My Name Is Not Keith' and his first post begins: 'I've started this blog because, if I may speak frankly, I'm fucked off about this stupid fucking life of mine.' I read on through gritted eyelids. 'Today I am mostly fucked off about the following things.' Number one: 'It's 95 per cent certain that I've got MS.'

He'd been keeping his dodgy hand pretty much to himself until the weekend we spent together before Easter, when he opened up a little. The first doctor he saw was apparently 'about as much use as a chocolate cock'. Then he saw a specialist, who told him that the regular bouts of numbness and unusability in his hand showed every sign of being MS. He was pretty sure that that's what it was. Currently, Keith's waiting for a series of tests which will confirm that prognosis: a lumbar puncture, some blood tests, and, apparently, a bunch of steroid injections. He's got an appointment in a couple of weeks. In the meantime, the spasming continues. It doesn't hurt, but he did drop a joint the other weekend, which I picked up and smoked. This made him cry, so I rolled him another, but it wasn't really the joint that upset him. It was the whole thing. Keith is really scared. Me too, as it goes. But I'm there for him, and I need to make him see that.

Number two is: 'My ex-girlfriend is fucking my best friend.'

Ah. Yes. I know it sounds bad, put like that, so blunt and bald. It's um … yeah, it's bad. At least, it's not good. Maybe I'm not Christ after all.

All right, I admit it. I'm not Christ. I wonder would it make it any better if I implied that what passed between Patricia and me was revenge for what passed between Keith and Ange? No, I don't believe it would. Perhaps it's just as well then that revenge had nothing to do with it. I may be a disappointing friend, but I'm not petty.

Keith is petty. But I have to take my hat off to him. His blog is very stylish payback, thoroughly in keeping with the nature of my own offensive behaviour. If I absolutely insist on playing it all out in public, then two can play at that game. *Touché*. I write a little post on my blog and link to Keith's blog with a photograph of three ladybirds all fucking one another. It seems like the decent thing to do. And I'm all about the decency.

The first comment I receive pretty much sets the tone for the majority of the feedback I am to receive. It's from 'Thomas' and it says simply: 'You got with your best friend's ex? And he's very possibly about to be diagnosed with MS? Ow. Beast indeed!'

I even receive my first piece of hate mail on the back of it all. Thankfully, it's from someone who can neither spell nor punctuate, so I am able to look down upon it and dismiss its contents as the ravings of a madman.

But it's getting out of hand. Suddenly people who've shown me nothing but kindness, encouragement, and virtual love are now castigating me. They are very disappointed. And they are right to be. I behaved like a monster. I am a monster. I try to tell myself, even now, that I hadn't really been aware of what I was doing, that it just happened, and that's true, it did just happen, but I was well aware of it, and I could have stopped it at any moment. I wasn't raped. I was perfectly in control, or at least I could have taken control, if I'd really wanted to.

Although there can be no doubt that I am guilty of transgressing the unwritten law – Thou Shalt Not Sleep With Thine Best Friend's Ex (Or If Thou Dost, Thou Shalt Wait At Least Six Months, And Be Upfront About It) – I still feel that circumstances were extenuating.

'Go on then,' says Keith. 'Tell me what happened.'

He is still pissed off. Of course he is, but he wants to know the details. We're in a pub, working through it all. I shilly-shally.

'Come on,' he says. 'It's the fucking least you can do.'

Is it though? Surely the least I can do, if I want to do something to engender some positive feeling, is never to mention it again.

'I'm asking you,' he continues, 'as a friend. Tell me what happened. From the beginning.' He crosses his legs and crosses his arms. 'Come on. We're doing this.'

I just sit and fidget, sighing and not meeting his eyes. Like a horrible piece of vermin. 'Do we have to?'

'Absolutely,' he says. 'We absolutely have to. Yes.'

It never occurs to me that I could actually just say no. Probably because I don't really feel like I can. You don't say no to your friends.

So I tell him.

I tell him that Patricia asked me to childmind while she went out with friends to drink and dance and talk bad about boys. He nods. He knows I get on well with Ben and Dina, so I tell him of Patricia's determination not to have them suffer because of the break-up. They miss Keith, obviously, and some of their mum's sadness is bound to rub off on them, but there's no reason for them to miss out on their favourite babysitter. I tell him that I wanted to see them too and that I jumped at the chance.

He bades me continue with a sharp, impatient wave.

I tell him that Patricia left more or less as soon as I arrived and that Ben and Dina and I fell straight into some Wii stuff. I tell him that Dina beat me at bowling using her left hand, with one eye closed.

He asks me what she was wearing.

I tell him she was wearing her Hello Kitty pyjamas because she'd just got out of the bath.

He says, 'Not Dina, you shit. What was Patricia wearing?'

I tell him she was wearing a short satin dress with no arms and no back, long black boots and very sheer stockings.

He says, 'You fucking cunt.'

I tell him, 'I told you! This is a bad idea.'

'Just get the fuck on with it.'

'Jesus,' I say. 'All I said was "stockings". Good thing I didn't mention the pearl necklace I gave her.'

Keith glares at me, like steel. It is fairly convincing, but I can see he wants to laugh.

'*Joke!*' I chirrup. 'Come on, I'm *sorry*. It was a pearl-necklace gag, that's all. I couldn't stop myself. I'm sorry. It was out of my hands.'

He expresses more malevolent disdain and vehemently insists

I resume my report.

I tell him that Patricia returned at fifteen minutes past one. She had the glazed expression and slightly stained teeth of one who has drunk too much red wine. I don't tell him this. I tell him she raced upstairs to use the loo, then tiptoed in to watch the kids sleep for a moment.

I tell him she'd been drinking White Russians and wanted to continue. She offered me one and I accepted. I don't tell him that it did occur to me that if I had a White Russian, on top of the couple of glasses of wine I'd already had, I would probably be over the limit and therefore not able to drive home.

I tell him that Patricia then set to work making the drinks and talking about her evening, what she'd been up to.

He asks me what she'd been up to.

I tell him she went out with some friends, they had dinner then went to some cocktail bar in Soho. I tell him she said she had fun. I don't tell him she said it was the best night she'd had in ages. I don't tell him that when she came back with the drinks and sat down, the first thing she said was, 'It's weird, but all these guys were trying to get into my pants tonight.' I don't tell him that I said that, all things considered, it was not in the slightest bit weird that a lot of men were trying to get into her pants and that she was a very desirable woman. And because I don't tell him that, there is also no need to explain that the only reason I said that was because I was trying to build her confidence, for God's sake. She'd just come through a difficult break-up and she needed someone to value her.

Vermin.

I tell him that I then told her what we'd got up to while she was out – the cake-making, the picture-painting, the play. I don't tell him that we re-enacted *Hellboy* for half an hour and then giggled and romped our way into a version of *Pirates of the Caribbean* with me as Jack Sparrow, and later Jack Ptarmigan, Jack Frigate, and Jack Blue-Footed Boobie. I don't tell him this because I don't want him to start feeling like not only did his best friend jump into bed with his girlfriend but that he also started playing Daddy to her kids. I don't want him picturing himself in that scenario and thinking that he's thrown away the best thing that he'll ever have, the greatest thing he'll never have again.

I tell him that we made a cake which Dina decorated with blue icing sugar and that I showed it to Patricia and that Patricia got a little emotional and talked about Richard for a little while.

I tell him that Patricia then said something about her breasts.

He asks me what she said.

I tell him that she said, 'Do you know that my breasts swell up something rotten if I don't have regular sex?'

He nods and rolls his eyes slightly, then asks me what I said in reply.

I tell him that I was speechless and that a slightly uncomfortable silence followed. I don't tell him that I was also immediately thrilled at the thought of what was just at that moment beginning to look like a possibility. I'd thought of it often, but that's a meaningless fact. I can't think of any woman I've ever met, within a fairly broad age spectrum, whom I haven't mentally entertained, at least briefly, in an erotic context. I don't tell him I finally managed to say, 'I didn't know that, no. Is that a medical condition or, or ...?'

I tell him that Patricia then declared that we were to have one last drink and told me to finish the one in my hand. I tell him that I did as I was told.

I tell him that when she was in the kitchen I had a Vincent Vega moment in the living room, looking in the mirror and telling myself, 'Just one more drink, and then I'll go.' I don't tell him that I had to adjust my erection when I stood up and that I was fully aware that the second drink would put me way over the limit and I was already imagining Patricia asking me to stay and me saying yes and her creeping into my sleeping bag in the night and clips of us kissing passionately were flashing across my internal screen, along with her swollen breasts which so needed my kneading. It would be an intervention. An act of genuine selfless kindness.

I tell him that Patricia returned with more drinks and that we said 'cheers' and drank from our glasses. I don't tell him that we drank to Patricia's toast of 'Here's to being free!' or that she gave me the wrong glass and that the one she gave me had traces of her lipstick around the rim and that I drank it anyway, and deliberately sipped at the lipstick stain.

I tell him that Patricia then started flirting a little.

He asks me how. He asks me what she said.

I squirm a little and tell him that she was talking about the advantages of being single.

He asks me what they were.

I tell him that she spoke of being able to do whatever she wanted and go wherever she wanted and go out whenever she pleased, dancing, drinking, and seeing friends.

He points out that he never stopped her doing any of that stuff and I tell him that nobody is saying that he did. I don't tell him that Patricia also spoke of the immense fun of being able to flirt with anyone she wanted, to let good-looking men buy her drinks and sniff at her hair like slavering dogs. I don't tell him that she also spoke of the freedom to kiss people who are completely inappropriate. Nor that she caught my eye at that point and added, pointedly, 'If that's what I want.'

I tell him that at this stage I was starting to feel, physically and emotionally, very awkward. I don't pretend that I didn't see what was coming, because that would be silly. I have an active imagination, and although it wasn't a situation I'd been in before, it did seem kind of obvious. I watch films. I've been in films! And I've seen *The Graduate*. Besides, the evidence was glaring: she was drunk, she was fetching drinks; she was talking about her breasts and her sex life, about flirting and kissing inappropriate people. It was screamingly, gaspingly, writhingly obvious, and I began to feel seriously nervous. I tried to conceal it by enjoying my drink slightly ostentatiously. I don't tell Keith any of that.

I also don't tell him that I then complimented her on her White

Russian-making skills even though there was far too much Kahlua in mine, or that my voice came out like a quiet, unimposing, frightened little squeak.

I tell him that Patricia then smiled and said, 'Come and sit down with me.' I tell him that I did. I tell him that I took another sip of my drink. I tell him that Patricia took my glass and placed it on the coffee table in front of us. I don't tell him that I stared at the glass and attempted to appear bemused, but merely ended up appearing afraid, or that I actually gulped audibly. I don't tell him that Patricia said, 'I know you find me attractive,' or that at that point I snapped and cried, 'All right, listen! Patricia, stop! Please! I don't know what you're thinking ...'

I don't tell him that Patricia responded with nothing less than a leer and the words, '*You* know what I'm thinking,' or that I responded to that with a stream of bunkum along the lines of, 'I don't think you know what I'm thinking – what you're thinking, I mean. *You* don't know what you're thinking. You've had a lot to think, to drink I mean, and you don't really know what you're saying. You're drunk and you've probably eaten too much too, and you're upset over Keith, and your breasts are swollen and ... and your hand, Patricia, your hand is on my thigh.'

I don't tell him that I then said, 'Patricia,' firmly, as if I were speaking to a dog, and that Patricia looked into my eyes and said the words, 'I know, I know. But I want your cock.'

I don't tell him that in one quite spectacular movement, like I'd been scalded with a plate of prairie oysters, I said, 'Whoa there!' and sprang up from the sofa and back to the fireplace, or that Patricia laughed heartily, then pretended to be hurt, whimpering, 'Do you find me so repulsive?'

I don't tell him that I said, 'Oh, *stop*. Don't. Please. You know I think you're amazing, in every sense, and I'd give my right arm to ... you know, but this is all wrong. You're drunk, for a start, and you're just trying to get back at Keith. And it isn't fair on me, frankly.' I don't tell him that, although I stopped speaking at that point, in my head were the words: 'One kiss is all it'll take and I'll fall madly, deeply, irreversibly in love with you.' But they were there all right. Self-knowledge is important.

I don't tell him that then Patricia stopped smiling, or that when I refused to sit back down next to her, as per her patted-hand instruction and tried instead to sit in the armchair, she snapped at me and said: 'Come and sit over here! Jesus, I've said you're right. I'm not going to rape you, for God's sake.' I don't tell him that she then smiled and re-patted the sofa next to her, and that, primarily because I didn't want to appear petty, I sat down. And I don't tell him that as I sat down, Patricia stood up, moved in front of me, facing me, lifted her right leg and climbed into my lap.

Neither do I tell him that, with her hands on my chest, she said, 'Listen. You're not taking advantage of me, OK?' I don't tell him that when her hands then moved from my shoulders to my neck and to my ears, a shock ran through me and each one of my limbs suddenly became awash with a sea of effervescent goosebumps, like my skin had been instantaneously converted to Braille and that Patricia – who was Helen Keller on MDMA – said, '*I'm* taking advantage of *you*.'

I don't tell him about Patricia's naked thighs on my legs where her dress had ridden up over her stockings, or her hands on the sides of my face and her lips and breath on my neck and ears, and I don't tell him how part of me wanted to grab hold of her wrists and push her away, to get up from the sofa, grab my coat and storm out of the house, drive home over the limit in an almighty huff, calling the police as I go. 'Yes, officer. There's been an attempted rape. A beautiful woman climbed into my lap and tenderly kissed the side of my face. I want to press charges.'

I don't tell him that, at the same time, another part of me thought: 'Hold on a minute. Mate, this is – in many important ways – the best thing that has ever happened to you, bar none. There isn't a court in the land that would convict you if you just allowed what is already happening to reach its natural conclusion.

Even Keith, once he's calmed down, will understand. Patricia likes you. She thinks you're funny and clever and great for her kids, and she just wants someone to ease the swelling in her breasts.'

I don't tell him how Patricia took me to her bed that night and wasn't so drunk that she entirely regretted it in the morning. I don't tell him that, in actual fact, she also did it again in the morning.

Rather I tell him that Patricia was drunk, that she wanted no-strings sex and that in order to make that happen, she started kissing me. I tell him that, after a few seconds, I started kissing her back.

He makes a disgusted face.

I tell him that I stayed over and we had sex. I tell him that we did it again a few times over the space of less than two weeks and that I was a little too sincere in my adoration despite the fact that I tried to hide it.

I tell him that Patricia had to remind me about the no-strings part and that I was so overwhelmed by infantile clinging and adolescent yearning that for a couple of days I felt tragically, tearfully, terrifically sad that it couldn't go on for ever, but that then I snapped out of it and realised how it might all be affecting him. Which is to say, Keith.

Keith asks me whether I snapped out of it because I had a genuine pang of conscience or merely because I'd read his blog.

I tell him it was more a silky-smooth combination of the two.

He asks me if I thought about him at all, throughout the whole thing.

I tell him of course I did but I tried not to.

He asks me if I would ever have told him.

I tell him of course. I'd have had to.

He asks me if I'm aware that she was just using me.

I tell him that she told me as much to my face.

He asks me something else and I get a bit sick of his moral highgrounding if I'm honest, so I remind him, 'You weren't still together, you know. I mean, nobody cheated on anybody. Oh, except you. You cheated, didn't you? Let's not get too carried away with this whole wronged-innocent bullshit, if we can help it.'

He tells me that what I did was worse.

I say, 'You *what*? You're saying it's worse to sleep with a mate's ex than it is to fuck someone else when you're in a relationship?'

He nods earnestly. 'It's much worse,' he says.

'OK, OK.' I accept his lies. 'No hard feelings then,' I say and I lift my glass for clinking.

'Well, let's not go crazy,' says Keith.

I shake my glass like a Blues Brother and insist, '*No hard feelings*, come on.'

Faux reluctantly, he clinks my glass. 'No hard feelings,' he relents. 'Well, not many.'

'To Patricia!' I add, gallantly.

We raise our glasses.

'And all who sail in her,' adds Keith, not so gallantly.

Meanwhile, somewhere in a sweaty orchestra pit on the other side of London, Patricia's breasts begin, imperceptibly, to swell.

I imagine.

I have a little ponder before saying, 'I hope you realise, I'm going to have to finish the story. I'm going to have to write my side of the story online.'

Keith shrugs. 'Whatever,' he says, then with a glint, 'me too.'

I have an urge to ask him to be careful, to ensure that he doesn't inadvertently turn my blog from the pulsing, poignant, pregnant, living masterpiece that it is into something cheap or childish or trivial by embarking on a campaign of schoolyard tittle-tattle or naysaying my version of events. But I do not succumb. I say nothing.

He says, 'No, really, write what you like. Just play fair.'

'When have I ever ...'

He holds up a calming hand and bows his head to wait for my silence.

'Play fair and try not to exaggerate quite so wildly.'

'Wh— '

The hand.

'And whatever you write, try to remember that, whatever happens, whatever heinous sins you commit in the future, you'll always be my friend ...'

I soften and think, *awww*. It's the Mork calling Orson moment.

'... You did a pretty treacherous thing in my opinion – and in the opinion of the great British public – but I forgive you. I'll never quite think of you in the same way again, of course, but I do forgive you. I can't pretend I'm not disappointed either. Neither can I pretend you're the person I thought you were. But I forgive you.'

I decide to accept that. 'No hard feelings then,' I say.

'Not too many,' he says.

'If it's any consolation,' I say. 'I was madly, insanely in love with Ange when you slept with her.'

He raises his eyebrows, laughs and claps his hands once. 'If only that were true,' he says. 'That would be hilarious.'

CHAPTER THIRTEEN

LOST WEEKEND

'I'm going up North this weekend,' says Keith. 'To see the old man. You wanna come?'

'*This* weekend?'

'Yeah, come on,' he insists. 'We need to get away from all this bad feeling. We need a fresh start. Spring. Fecundity. You like all that. Nature. Clean air. We can make it into a road trip. A buddy movie. It'll be excellent. Let's get out of the city for a couple of days.'

'You had me at grass,' I reply.

'I never mentioned grass,' he says. 'Plus, it'd be a good opportunity to stop stalking Katinka. You know, leave her to get on with her own life for a while. Give her some space.'

I make a sarcastic face.

Katinka is the name of a young Bulgarian woman with dark, unevenly cut, medium-length hair and cold, bright eyes like inscrutable almonds. She's been living upstairs from me for about a month and I've developed a healthy fascination with her. We've only had a couple of brief exchanges thus far and, to be honest, they didn't go brilliantly, but I refuse to allow her obvious disdain to interfere with my fantasies.

The first exchange was the night she was moving in. I passed her in the hallway, where her stuff was piled up in boxes and bags. There was also a lot of strange electrical equipment. Silver boxes with rows and ranks of knobs and dials. She had a friend helping her. Rather than just walk past her with a nod, I stopped to say hello and introduce myself. Spread a little warmth, that's one of my mottoes. For who knows what might happen? I might end up accepting an invitation for a housewarming glass of wine. One thing could lead to another and ... bingo! Sadly, it was not to be. No bingo, no wine, no reciprocation of warmth. On the contrary, in the tiny exchange that followed, not a single, solitary smile played upon Katinka's plump, kissable lips. In fact, throughout our entire exchange, she looked at me as if to say [imagine generic Eastern European accent here], 'In my country, you would be in cage.'

Even so, I couldn't help myself: I became utterly enchanted by her. I'm so desperate to be enchanted, I know, but still, could it be? Could Katinka actually be ... The One?

She isn't The One. She isn't even Bulgarian. She's Hungarian, but I figure that pretending I think she's from Bulgaria will play well. Why I think that, I cannot say.

A few days after out first meeting, I passed her in the hallway again, rooting through the communal mail. 'Morning!' I chirruped. 'Anything nice from Bulgaria?'

'I am Hungarian,' she replied, cold like a killer.

'Ah, yes. My mistake. Anything nice from Hungaria?!'

She blanked me. Quite right too. She had a bunch of letters in her hands. 'Who are these people?' she wanted to know. So peremptory her tone, that I couldn't help but find it both irritating and amusing. And ever so slightly arousing. She read out a few names from envelopes like she was reading from a Sex Offenders List, mispronouncing as she went. I explained that some of them are other people in the house, that there are seven different flats, including the basement. I told her also that a lot of the mail that collects around the front door is junk for old residents, and that the landlord comes and picks it up every few weeks.

She scowled at me. 'Every few weeks?' She continued scowling. 'I must to speak with landlord.'

'OK,' I said, squeezing past her to the front door. 'Well, good luck with that.'

And then it happened. She looked up at me, and she smiled. It was ever so faint, her smile, and as soon as it happened, she suppressed it and replaced it with another scowl, like a woman at a sombre church gathering whose breast had inadvertently flumped out of her low-necked top while she was chatting to the priest about Adam and Eve. All she could do was scoop it back inside and stare at the ground, pretending it had never happened. But it had happened all right. She knew it. I knew it. The priest knew it.

'What?' I said, smiling myself, like a sap.

'Nothing,' she replied. 'You are going for run, no?'

And then I realised that her smile was actually a mocking smile, that she was laughing *at* me. Granted, I do look fairly ridiculous when I go running, with my baggy grey tracksuit and the little purple hand towel that I hang round my neck. I need that towel though, I really do. I sweat like a claustrophobe in a suitcase when I'm running. Much more than I used to. The more weight I lose, the more I sweat. I think I have hyperhidrosis.

'Yeah,' I replied, slowly. 'Is that funny?'

This time she laughed openly, then covered her mouth. 'No, no. Sorry. I must to go now.' Then she trotted off upstairs, leaving me feeling ridiculous, and I have to say, ever more enchanted.

A couple of days after that, I was becoming fed up with hanging round my front door, listening for Katinka's footfalls in the hall – it was leaving a nasty, stalkerish taste in my mouth – so I plucked up the courage to go upstairs and talk to her. I cooked up a premise. My opener was, 'Oh hi, Katinka' – all casual like, and even slightly surprised, as if she'd knocked on my door – 'I was just wondering if you were in need of the internet ... I could give you the key for my wireless if you um ... if you ...' I must say I was actually rather relieved when she didn't answer the door. It was quite a creepy thing to say, I realised. I was beginning to worry that I was becoming a genuinely creepy bloke. The episode with Patricia had me yearning ever more obsessively for the company of womankind, and I could feel myself being pulled in strange directions. I stared at women more when I was out in public. I attempted to smile occasionally, but it never came out right. I worried that I was becoming a genuine creep, the kind of man that women notice and instinctively recoil from, not just with disgust – I was used to that – but with a certain amount of fear too.

I confided this in Keith one night, with the consequence that he now brings it up at regular intervals, occasionally calling me Sutcliffe.

I am looking forward to letting go of London for a couple of days. We could both do with washing the cobwebs out of our heads. So we fill my car, whose name is Heathcote, with goodies and we drift North to spend a couple of days with Keith's dad, Gordon, and Keith's dad's relatively new young wife, Sylvia.

I've never really spent any time in The North before. I'd passed through it on my way to Scotland, but I'd never stopped. Not because I thought it was an uncivilised backwater filled with foul-mouthed trolls, short-sleeved Neanderthals, and phlegm-hawking, urine-soaked sex-pests. No. I'd never been and I honestly had no opinion either way.

A few hours in, however, and that quickly changes.

Gordon was always something of a hero to me, if that's not over-egging the pudding a tad. He was the dad I never had. He did things my own dad never did. He showed me affection, kicked balls with me and facilitated fun and happiness. When he split up with Keith's mum a few years ago, I was more upset than when my own mother died.

Last year, Gordon, fifty-five, married Sylvia, eleven years his junior, after less than a year of going out. Keith says his dad just wanted to get a ring on her finger before she tired of his saggy flesh and ran off with someone less close to death. But I don't think he really believes that. Gordon may be close to death in some respects, but in others he's more vital than many a man half his age.

Gordon and Sylvia live in a really funky flat in Newcastle city centre, for which they pay – if you compare similar in London –

nothing. In fact they pay 25 per cent less than I do, between them, for about 75 per cent more space. I can't believe this when we arrive on Friday, but after a couple of days in The North, it makes a lot more sense. There is a trade-off. You get to live at least 25 per cent less expensively, but life in The North is at least 75 per cent less enjoyable, and the people a good 85 per cent less evolved. Or maybe I should spend more time there before I dismiss it so definitively? Nah. Just this once, I think I'm going to go with knee-jerk discrimination. Follow my instincts.

On Saturday night, Sylvia – athletic, assertive, and droll – takes us to Jarrow (henceforth known as *Jarra*) to meet her mum and step-dad, Doreen and Vic, who live in a dark flat which smells suspiciously of leeks. Now, obviously, I've got nothing against old people – aside from the intense fear of slow decay and painful, undignified death they automatically arouse in me – and Doreen and Vic, seventy-six and eighty-five respectively, seem on first inspection thoroughly pleasant examples of the genre.

Doreen is all self-knitted cardigans and dark-toothed smiles, desperate to prepare endless pots of tea and sandwiches containing some kind of pudding apparently made of peas, which I manage to resist.

Vic is much the same, but less smiling and mostly immobile. Wearing an immaculately knotted tie beneath his chunky wife-knitted cardy, he has a neck like a pelican's pouch, thick, super-magnifying glasses and a large crucifix which he wears with considerable pride.

As Doreen makes the first of seven thousand pots of tea, Vic asks us about our first impressions of the North-east. Keith responds, hugely diplomatically, concentrating his answer on Durham, which we visited the night before and which is genuinely eye-catching. Vic seems satisfied with Keith's answer. He knows an awful lot about Durham Cathedral and proceeds to impart all of it, one scintillating nugget at a time, from the history of Saint Cuthbert to the Reformation to the famous Sanctuary Knocker. In fact, he speaks for so long on the subject of sanctuary that everybody else actually begins to yearn for it.

Vic is very proud of the North-east. He loves Jarra. And he loves the church. Doreen, meanwhile, loves knitting, pease pudding, and the North-east folk scene. Together they share a passion for Chinese food, Scrabble, and – thankfully – alcohol.

Within half an hour of being at Doreen and Vic's, something becomes abundantly clear. It is this: Vic knows best. So when it comes to ordering the Chinese for the evening, there is no question of anyone choosing what they actually want, because Vic has his heart set on the set meals. Vic is a set-meal kind of guy. And as no one else really cares that much, Vic gets his way, and just as Gordon is leaving to pick up the order, Vic shouts after him, 'Don't forget the porn crackers.'

Vic actually says 'porn crackers', not because he can't pronounce his R's or anything, just because he genuinely seems to forget there is an R in 'prawn'. Of course, at that age, you do. Yet, simultaneously, he seems unaware of what he's said, because when Gordon repeats it back to him quizzically, he seems to think that Gordon is making a joke. Furthermore, it is a joke much to Vic's liking. He repeats it three times, interspersing the repetitions with his strange, slightly disturbing laugh, like Father Christmas but slowed down to about a quarter of the speed. 'Porn crackers,' he laughs. 'Ohh ohhh ohhhh. The mind boggles.'

After the set meal, Doreen suggests a game of Scrabble. We've been drinking slightly heavily by then, so this seems like a fine idea. But first Keith, Gordon and I nip outside to smoke. There is no smoking in Vic's house ever since a crafty tumour made off with a chunk of his lung a couple of years ago. Which is absolutely fair enough. So we go out into the garden, huddle together and smoke a joint like naughty kids.

Back inside, we split into four teams: Doreen and Vic, Sylvia and Gordon, and me and Keith – the young 'uns – on our own. The first sign that this is not going to be an ordinary game of Scrabble comes when Vic, who has picked an A and thus is first to select his seven tiles, selects only three then passes the bag to Doreen. Keith and I exchange looks, then Keith points out that Scrabble is played with seven tiles. 'Well, we have our own rules here,' Vic explains. 'We pick three each at the beginning, so that nobody gets all the best letters. Then we pick the last four.'

'So what's the point of going first?' asks Keith, genuinely bemused.

Vic shakes his head quickly as if trying to dislodge the pained expression which has settled there.

'And you could just as easily pick four I's and three E's,' I add. 'I mean, there's no saying that you're going to pick good letters just because you pick seven at once.'

'These are our rules,' says Doreen, smiling but slightly uncomfortable. 'If you don't like them—'

'When in Jarra,' Vic interrupts.

'... ruin a perfectly good game,' adds Keith.

Now I happen to be a bit of a pain at Scrabble, in so much as I'm one of those people who memorises lots of those otherwise futile words which only other Scrabble-word freaks ever encounter. That's generally how I win, by throwing in a *DZO* or an *ICTIC* or a *QI* when my opponent least expects it. So I begin to realise the full horror of what is afoot when Keith's first word *LIGER* is disallowed on the grounds that it is 'stupid and made-up'.

'We only allow proper words that everybody's heard of,' says Vic.

My mouth falls open. It's like they've taken the only thing that's really valuable about Scrabble – the possibility of improving your vocabulary – and they've stamped all over it like low-rent Nazis who can't afford to burn books.

The only dictionary in the house is one of those pocket-sized things with about sixty words in, and although there is a computer with internet access, Sylvia says it probably isn't worth the effort, as the dial-up modem is slower than – she glances at her stepfather ...

'If we just use words everybody's heard of, then there's no problem,' Vic says again.

A few turns later and Zyqoxi, the gypsy god of Scrabble, gives Keith the following letters: A, D, E, F, K, U, and Y, with a C in a good space on the board.

That Vic is blessed with a healthy puritanical streak has already been well-established, but when suddenly *FUCKED* is sitting in front of him, in his own home, under his own roof, on his own Scrabble board that he bought from the Salvation Army charity shop, he looks for a moment like he might shit a squirrel.

He starts shaking his head before the words come. 'No, no, no,' he says, breathless, wheezing with exasperation. 'You can't have that. You can't have dirty words.'

'But it's in the dictionary!' cries Keith, appalled. 'And I presume we've all heard of it.' He looks around the table for support. 'Fucked!' he repeats, seemingly astonished by its obviousness. 'From the verb to fuck,' he continues, really quite disrespectfully. 'I fuck, you fuck, he fucks, we all fuck!'

By now Vic is glaring at him like he's taken out his penis, detached it from his groin and pushed it forcibly into his wife's puckered mouth.

'No dirty words!' declares Doreen.

'Not acceptable,' adds Vic, grimly.

'Vic is right,' I say, equally grimly. 'You've gone too far. Nobody wants to hear that kind of language.'

'Not at the dinner table,' adds Gordon with a sly smile.

Keith apologises and play is eventually resumed. A couple of turns later I turn *LOG* into *BLOGS* with the *S* on a triple-word score. Thrillingly, the same *S* makes *SPIES* of an adjacent *PIES*. I am very pleased, and in for a bag-load of points.

Again comes the familiar slow moan that seems to preface each of Vic's sentences. 'Ohhhhh, no, man, come on now. Play the game.'

'What's that supposed to be?' asks Doreen, her face contorted in vexed confusion. Scrabble has clearly never before been such a painful experience.

This time it's Keith's turn to join them. 'Yeah, come on, Stan.

Don't be ridiculous. What the hell is *BLOGS*? It's just rubbish, isn't it? You're just wasting everyone's time. If you can't think of any proper words, why don't you miss a turn and change some of your letters?'

I am particularly dischuffed with this latest outrage, and for a moment I fail to see the funny side. It is a triple-word score. I scowl, viciously.

There is, however, one advantage to playing Jarra Scrabble, in that whenever a word is played which is deemed an illegal move, you don't forfeit a turn. Instead – much more sporting and, of course, *ludicrous* – you just pick up your tiles and try again. So when *BLOGS* is refused, I try with *JABENS*. Then I plump for *BANSH*, followed by *JASHNEB*, *SHABJEN,* and finally, *SHNJA*. Each time I play a new word, I promise that this time, *this time*, I have a real one. *SHNJA* proves to be the straw that breaks the camel's back for Vic, and he tosses down his tiles, refusing to play with people who simply aren't going to try.

So that's that. Having destroyed the game, Keith and I nip outside for another cheeky one and by the time we get back, the Schickel & Lane DVD is on.

Schickel & Lane are apparently a north-eastern folk duo of the most top rank. *Winning the Blaydon Races* features twenty-seven of their favourite tunes, set to some of the most risible music videos ever produced. It seems like a very odd evening to us, but of course it isn't. It's just that this is what they do in the North. Wrecked as we are, it is very funny. We stifle our giggles like twelve-year-olds.

One of the first videos we see is for a version of 'The Lambton Worm' and features Schickel – or Lane, I cannot tell – striding purposefully through a group of wholesome children like a U-certificate sex offender, smiling and singing at them. Drunken grumbles drift round the living room and aspersions are cast upon the honour inherent in Schickel's – or Lane's – intentions towards those innocent children.

Suddenly Keith says, 'Oh, God, now I remember! I read about

these guys in the *News of the World*! They're Satanists. They own a pub in Middlesborough or somewhere, and the cellar was full of all their Satanic regalia, loads of robes and horns and platinum dildos.'

'And children's skulls,' I add.

'This video was banned in Ireland.'

'That audience are all drugged and those children have been trepanned. Schickel & Lane drilled holes in their heads to let the evil out, but then at the last minute, instead of letting evil out, they put more in.'

'With their penises.'

'They worship Baal. That man is only dancing with a brush because he knows that if he doesn't, he'll be sacrificed to Baal.'

And so on. It isn't the most respectful behaviour, obviously, but Sylvia and Gordon are tittering along indulgently, so we feel encouraged. Doreen just ignores us – I think she's turned off her hearing aid – but Vic is fuming. Every comment we make is like a slap across his face. Eventually he just gets up from his chair and goes to bed without saying goodnight. Then we stop. And feel really, sincerely sorry.

It was agreed previously that we would stay the night, although by the end of the evening I think we've probably outstayed our welcome. But we stay anyway, on a couple of foldaway beds in the study room, where there are lots of Reader's Digest books and an old PC with a tortoise modem. I switch on the PC to check my blog for comments, an activity to which I must confess I have become ever so slightly addicted. When the PC is quite ready, I start to type in the address. Which is when the most unsettling search history in search-history history pops up before my eyes.

I get so far as the letters B and E when the first lot of pages drops down. Most of them are pages from either *benaughty.com* or *bestnudists.com*. I call Keith over. We are both very amused by this, but not particularly scandalised. They are saucy, yes, but they seem like fairly innocuous pursuits for a pensioner with a penchant for porn. When he was in his teens, he probably procured a peck of sepia-tinted but decidedly blue postcards and carried them around in his wallet, as I'm certain young lads did in the thirties. Nudist websites are the modern-day equivalent. It's almost sweet. Then we type some other letters into the address bar to see what other skeletons are stacked neatly in Vic's cyber-closet.

Clothesfreeforum.com seems innocent too, charmingly so, as does *spybeachbabes.com* and maybe even *secretvirgin.com*. Well ... maybe. But then there are others, which are clearly a tiny bit darker. *Teenist.com*, for example. *Younglittlegirls.com* for another. And perhaps even more disturbing, *privatebeast.com*, where punters pay top dollar to see women having sex with horses and dogs. We go to a couple of the addresses to see what exactly we're dealing with here. Thankfully, Private Beast is just a couple of preview pages, pre-payment, giving you a glimpse of what to expect if you give your credit-card details. So it could have been fairly innocent surfing on Vic's part. It could have been research or merely strictly legit, wholly ordinary, everyday fascination. Not very Christian certainly – at least not the kind of Christian who moralises and winces at the sound of a sexual swearword, but still, nothing to call the police about.

I ask Keith if he'll mention it to his dad, but he says he won't, because his dad will tell Sylvia, and Sylvia might tell her mum, and that might cause a lot of unnecessary upset and pain and turmoil. 'It's just some old bloke looking at porn,' he says. 'Mostly harmless,' he adds.

'Should I clear the search history?' I ask.

Keith shakes his head. 'Nah, just leave it,' he replies. 'Turn it off and walk away. Maybe wash your hands.'

The next morning at breakfast, Vic is in superior mode, gloriously, gloatingly so, with great dollops of self-righteousness all over his face. He is dressed to the nines and ready for church, his crucifix shining and the finest, most noble headmaster glower you've ever seen stuck fast to his face. Imperious. Unforgiving. Honourable. Implacable.

The atmosphere over the breakfast table is taut, and any

attempt at small talk withers quickly in the indignant air. Eventually Doreen breaks through like a *whip*crack of thunder. 'I think you boys owe my husband an apology for last night,' she says. 'You said some things which ... well, I won't repeat them.'

Keith glances at Sylvia, who rolls her eyes at the ceiling and looks faintly embarrassed. I'm not sure, if I'm honest, for whom.

'Oh, I'm sure they didn't mean anything by it,' says Gordon. 'It was just a bit of fun.' Those words echo within me. I've suffered a lot at the hands of other people's bits of fun. Ange pretending to want me for the malicious glee of her friends; me hanging in front of the school, stripped cock-naked with tears streaming down my face.

I feel bad. We were unnecessarily offensive. Whether we considered Vic a preposterous human being or not was neither here nor there. We were guests in his home and we should certainly have behaved with a great deal more respect.

'Doreen's right,' says Keith, equally shamed. He looks across the table at Vic, and holds his gaze. 'I'm sorry,' he says. 'I'm sorry I accused Schickel & Lane of being paedophiles. That's a very serious and not at all amusing allegation and I am genuinely sorry.'

'I'm sorry too,' I say. And I am. 'We said some terrible things.'

Vic is nodding his head, but still scowling, as if we have a lot more grovelling to do before we will qualify for even partial forgiveness. His self-righteousness is strident. Perhaps overly so. For all his undoubted justification for feeling angry, there is something in his holier-than-thou bullishness that begins to grate.

I shake my head penitently. 'Some of the things we said were barely legal,' I say. Gordon looks at me quizzically.

'I feel bad for what we said,' says Keith.

'Me too. It showed an embarrassing lack of respect,' I add. 'I feel really dreadful.'

'Me too,' says Keith. 'Pardon my French, but I feel like a horse's cock for some of the things we said last night, I don't mind telling you.'

As he stares at Vic, an instinctive wave of anger quickly turns to something darker and breaks slowly over the old man's face, seemingly calming him, washing away his ire. Keith holds out his hand and apologises. Vic shakes it. It's eerie. It's like someone is making a pact with the devil, but it isn't quite clear who. I shake Vic's hand too and say again that I am sorry. Vic looks to Doreen and says, 'We'd better get going, love. We don't want to be late for church.' And after saying their goodbyes to Sylvia and Gordon, off they go to worship.

As soon as the door is closed, Sylvia turns to Keith and says, 'He's still not cleared his history out then?'

Keith smiles, shakes his head and pours more tea.

On the way back to London, Keith and I talk about getting old. We talk about the body breaking down. We say we don't want to imagine Vic sitting at his PC, staring at young nudists and squeezing his 85-year-old manhood. But we imagine it anyway. We talk about the North and how it smacks of death.

We don't talk about betrayal.

We talk about dying. I ask Keith to promise me that if I ever get to the point where I'm leaving smells and noises and little pools of urine all over the house, where I shy away from all things new and I'm too unhip to hide my own porn trails, then please, he has to promise to take responsibility, to take me to one side with a roll of superstrength clingfilm and do the decent thing. Or if suffocation is too hands-on, then disembowel me, behead me, hang me from the nearest lamppost, anything. Just make me stop. Out of mercy.

We don't talk about Keith's MS.

We talk about the future. We talk about fresh starts and a whole universe full of possibilities.

We talk about spring, which finally, outstandingly, magnificently, has definitely sprung ...

CHAPTER FOURTEEN

LIFE & DEATH

In the spring I like to stay up all night, playing and pretending and then, before the first light spreads into my peripheries, I like to go for a drive. I like to drive out of London, if I have time, down through the Kent countryside to the coast. I like to hatch myself from Heathcote, walk along the beach before the day has properly taken hold and breathe, deeply, deeply, in and in and in and in until my lungs hurt, all the tension of the big bad world breathed in and then . . . s l o w l y slowly breathe it out again. I used to do this more when I still lived in Kent. Now I do it less. Right now, fizzing in the very cervix of Spring Fever, I promise myself I will do it more frequently. And I mean it.

My car is called Heathcote, incidentally, because I am pretentious and self-aggrandising. I am also lumbering and slightly depressive, but when I head out with Heathcote into the spring I am free. Heathcote and me, we are both of us free, both of us fashioned from a brand-new mineral compound of helium and mercury; Heathcote all shiny, fresh-serviced, and spry; me weightless, commotionless, careless, and gay. Both of us feeling, together as one, light, bright, and feisty, positively reborn. I open the windows and Heathcote shifts into the sharp light like he's had fifty brick tumours removed from his boot. Off we soar!

I adore the spring.

This is the nearest I get to the great road trips of the past, to Raoul Duke and Oscar Acosta, to Billy and Wyatt, to that semiliterate, diuretic bore Kerouac and his dullard cuckold of a friend. But where was my sidekick? I should have brought Pablo, but Pablo doesn't like to travel. No matter. On this drive, Heathcote is my sidekick and we soar, high as a kite on the passage of time, we feel for once that the Mighty we seek is upon us, within us even, and the weather is on our side and beyond reproach. Too much heat and I puff up in a rash, but this is perfect for me and my sensitive temple. April is the coolest month by far: fecund, sharp, and distinctly moist, the sun bright and brittle like a tiny fist of fire, unfurling from afar the very first beckoning tendrils of summer.

Spring Fever is upon me. I am exhilarated. I see the good that there is to see. I feel it. I'm getting better. I feel alive. I'm learning too. The more mistakes I make, the more I learn. I feel like I'm learning and growing every day. Every week at least. I'm moving very decidedly in the right direction. And now I must consolidate. It is time to lay a sheet of spiritual compost over these tiny mustard seeds of inner strength, and await the first shoots of contentment. Hence, the detox. I need to cleanse myself.

I have fallen back into bad habits. I am weak. Wilfully so. I turn my back for a second and BAM! I become a two-headed piglet with six mouths, a Shetland pony with a tapeworm. Easter provided a damn good excuse for a couple of weeks, and then I found others. I became complacent. Now it is time to get back in the saddle and ride that sturdy ass to the Kingdom of Heaven. It is time to uncork the Tree Syrup.

'The what now?' says Keith.

'The Madal Bal Natural Tree Syrup,' I reply. 'It's a safe and natural detox system with no chemicals and no preservatives,' I add. 'It allows the body to cleanse itself naturally of accumulated toxins, to grow spiritually and to shed pounds and pounds of unwanted flabbullum.'

'It's a liquid fast?' he asks, sounding knowledgeable.

'It's a detox,' I reply, sounding ignorant.

'Well, if it's a detox, you need to make sure you're properly toxed first. Otherwise it's a waste.'

Of course, he is right. So we pass a weekend of THC and MDMA, then I sleep well, wake bright and early and starve myself for five days solid, losing thirteen pounds in the process.

'I don't think that was very wise,' says Keith. 'You could have died.'

Meanwhile Ange calls and tells me she feels terrible. She feels weird and guilty and sad about everything that happened, with Keith, with me, with Patricia, and about not being in touch for a while as a consequence.

She feels sad too because, a few days ago, her mum died.

Ange's mum had been ill for a couple of years, but stable, so when a second stroke segued into a fatal heart attack in the space of a week, Ange fell into a state of shock. Although she was always there for her mum and was even holding on to her when she died, Ange seems to want to convince herself that she was somehow to blame or that she didn't do everything in her power to make her mother's life better than it was. She explains that she'd taken it all quite badly. She tells me she got drunk, had sex with a stranger she picked up in a KFC, cried during the sex, ran home in the middle of the night without any knickers on and took the rest of the week off work. Pangs of jealousy are drowned in waves of sympathy.

She asks me if I'd like to come to the funeral, and I tell her I would be honoured.

I am honoured. The funeral is phenomenal, a thoroughly moving celebration of a life tremendously well lived. And it makes me rethink my opinion of the people of Dartford too. For some reason – blind prejudice, I guess – I have, over the years, come to assume that every last one of them is a soulless cretin, no more capable of genuine human emotion than a bucket full of piss and clams. But that was wrong of me. And her funeral brings that home.

Violet Charlton had two miscarriages and a stillbirth before Ange came along, all healthy and bouncing and bold. Then, even though they wanted more, Violet and her husband Ed stopped trying to have kids of their own. They thought they'd quit while they were ahead, and Ed had a vasectomy. They loved kids so much, however, that – as well as cherishing Ange, obviously – they did everything they possibly could for everybody else's kids. Perhaps they realised more acutely than most how truly sacred young life is and they wanted to do everything within their power to nurture it, and to make it great. And so they became community child-carers in a way which would never be possible today. (I am led to believe that, these days, before you can so much as blow a raspberry at someone else's child, you need a qualification in infant husbandry and certification in triplicate from the local council.) In the 70s and 80s, however, children were not made of sugar glass and you could still throw half a dozen rocks into a crowd of people without necessarily hitting a paedophile.

So, basically, Ange was raised in a community crèche. And although she never had any siblings of her own, other people's kids were always around and she never wanted for company.

Naturally, as she spent a lot of time looking after their kids, Violet spent a lot of time with the young mums of the area. Consequently, she got to know them, and when they had problems – problems of a sensitive nature – they would confide in her, and Violet discovered that she had a knack for sorting the mums out, giving them the right advice and helping them help themselves to get their lives back on track. And so, as well as her role as community child-care consultant, Violet became the first port of call for any young couples in need of any kind of counselling. As far as I could gather, she gained a reputation as a kind of a cross between Drs Ruth and Spock.

Consequently, her funeral, where I learn most of the above for the first time, is a very emotional affair, with a long line of friends and relatives taking turns to pay tribute to Violet, to tell their stories of how she'd helped them better their lives, and to thank her for all that she'd done.

When the tributes are all done, we listen to 'The Green Green Grass of Home' by Tom Jones. I don't think there is a single person in the church who isn't crying.

I never met Violet, but the testimonies I hear at her funeral make me love her, and hope to have someone like her in my life, and vow to cherish the people I do have in my life.

Keith is at the funeral too. It's the first time he's seen Ange since they slept together. Ordinarily, such a meeting might have been slightly fraught, but death has a way of putting things in perspective.

'There's something I need to tell you,' says Keith.

It's the morning after the funeral, and we're on an early train back into London. We're hungover from the brandy and the emotion – mostly the brandy – and Keith looks serious.

I already know the result of the MS tests. The specialist told him there was good news and there was bad news. The bad news was that he does have MS. The good news is that he has a very mild form of MS and apparently there's no reason it should get any worse than the intermittent tremors he experiences now. Although it might. But there's no reason it should.

And that was that.

Now he says, 'There's something I didn't mention.' He looks me in the eye. The right eye. It twitches. 'There's something in my brain,' he says. 'The size of a blueberry.' He smiles. 'And it's not supposed to be there.' He laughs flatly, shrugs and looks out of the window.

The specialist gave him a brain scan and they found some anomaly, a small, dark patch. A shadow. It could be anything. It could be nothing. Well, not nothing. It's definitely something. But it could mean nothing.

He's booked in for more tests in the next couple of weeks.

'I've got a blueberry in my head,' he says softly.

I'm shocked. I feel sick and appalled that this has been allowed to happen. The trembling hand was bad enough, but that that should lead directly to something as terrifying as a blueberry in the brain is just … it doesn't seem right. If I believed in God, I'd be shaking my fist at the sky at this point, questioning everything.

Instead I just shake my head godlessly and tell Keith that I'm sorry.

'That's pretty fucked-up luck,' I say.

He shrugs. 'It could be worse,' he replies.

I agree. It could be worse. But it's still pretty bad and, frankly, it doesn't seem fair. Life doesn't seem fair.

Last night I had Ange crying on my shoulder, sobbing that her mum was her life and she won't know what to do without her. I gave her tissue paper and told her everything would be all right. Would it?

This morning there's Keith, all wet-eyed and worried for his life, looking elsewhere as the grey Kent countryside blurs past him like quotidian hyperspace. I tell him everything will be all right too. Will it?

We hang by a thread.

In other news, I've got a date with Sally!

Yusssssssssssss!

CHAPTER FIFTEEN

LOVE HANDLES

To be perfectly honest, I never expected to see or even hear from Sally again. Our instant messaging had fallen off as quickly as it had begun and I noticed that she didn't comment on my blog any more. So when from nowhere I receive an email asking me if I fancy meeting up for a bite to eat, I am overjoyed. The fact that her invitation coincides with a speed-dating event I have booked myself on to in a fit of self-loathing is doubly satisfying.

So suddenly I have a decision to make. Do I spend the evening with twelve women I've never met before, who probably won't be remotely interested in me, or with one adorable young photographer with bright silver eyes and a ring in her nose, who happens to think I'm brilliant?

With joy in my heart and butterflies in my belly, I give my speed-dating place away to one of the readers of my blog, and wish him all the very best.

I honestly don't know beforehand whether our meal is a date in the conventional sense, or whether we're just brand-new friends meeting and eating together. Nothing happens to suggest it is anything other than friends eating food together, bar the particularly potent erection I'm hiding under the table throughout the meal. Although, having said that, Sally is quite complimentary about how much weight I've lost and how my eyes are apparently 'quite penetrating'. Then there's the fact that, as of only a couple of weeks ago, Sally is single.

If I were anyone else, I would say it were screamingly obvious that something is going on between us. But I am not anyone else. And despite the fact that I feel like a different person to the one who stood in my kitchen six months ago eating cat food, I still find it incredibly difficult to accept that a woman as young and attractive as Sally could possibly be interested in me. I am fat. I am fat and I am ugly. Seriously. Ready wit and an excellent penis aside, what could possibly be in it for her?

But as we eat our pasta and drink our wine, I remember, physical appearance is not the be all and end all for everyone. Maybe Sally's just a bit deeper than your average art student.

At the end of our first date, if that's what it is, we hug goodbye, and Sally gives me a tiny wet peck on each cheek. Furthermore, we agree to go to the cinema some time, maybe at the weekend. A second date! If that's what it is.

The journey home is like a dream. Although I refuse to allow myself to believe that Sally is really into me and that before very long, I will be given carte blanche to slowly move my entire face over every inch of her naked body, I am still very much more exited than any man has ever been. I am walking on air. I leap on to a 37 bus like Gene Kelly. I tap up the stairs like Fred Astaire, and although the bus is packed with drunks and ninnies, it doesn't matter a jot. I am in heaven, and my heart beats so that I can hardly speak. I shimmy to the back of the bus like Tommy Steele and trip over the exposed knee of a drunken teenage girl. She tuts loudly and I laugh, apologise blithely and sit on the back seat with a smile across my face like a giant gash in a watermelon.

When I get home I grab hold of Pablo and dance him round the living room, cheek to cheek, until he tells me to stop, then I dance myself up the stairs to bed, wrap myself in headphones and music and, still feeling rather emotional from the excitement of the evening, I daydream vigorously into an old pair of briefs.

The next day I pop round to Keith's to drop off a few DVDs and inform him that I am in love.

'Good,' he says. 'Great. I'm happy for you.' I sense that he isn't really taking me seriously. Plus, he's still clearly down about his brain and his hand and his creeping anomie. He has been sleeping all day.

'Look at you, man,' I say. 'Sleeping your life away. You're on the edge. You need to take some stock, Keith. You need to take a good long hard look at yourself and you need to pull yourself together. I hate to say it, but you need to be a little more like Frank.'

Keith sits down on the sofa and lights the end of a joint. 'I've been working eighteen hours a day for the past week,' he points out. 'I haven't been sleeping my life away. I've been catching up, rejuvenating. Who's Frank?'

'Who's Frank?' I repeat. '*Who's Frank?!*'

I laugh and shake my head as if Keith had just asked, 'Who's Jesus?' or 'Who's Tim Berners-Lee?'

Frank is Frank Tipper, Bermuda-born owner of a mint condition Lancia Fulvia coupé and a number of very expensive suits, none of which he wears with a tie. Frank gets up every morning at 6 a.m., meditates for twenty minutes and then prepares breakfast for himself, his wife Emily (beautiful) and his little girl, Abbey (precocious), before driving to work, where, before he does anything, he spends an hour pumping his body into a state of masculine flawlessness in the office gym. Frank has run twelve marathons, including the recent London marathon, which he finished in exactly three and a half hours.

Also, importantly, Frank is living testament to the power of the internet. Frank came to me via my blog. He is an occasional reader. He said he liked the cut of my jib but could tell I lacked discipline. I'd been bemoaning the fact that my fitness regime seemed to be falling by the wayside and Frank sent me an email offering his support, saying he'd be happy to take me out running. Obviously, when a grown man writes to you out of the blue offering to get breathless and sweaty with you, you do well to be a little circumspect, so first of all, we met for a drink.

Tall like a tower block and bald like a blade, Frank Tipper is – I quickly came to realise – my guardian angel. Like any guardian angel worth his salt, Frank is ripped to the gills. Seriously. A body like a Greek god's personal trainer. I'm not what you'd call a gay man, but I do know a top-notch piece of masculine ass when I see it, and Frank just happens to have a bod *to die for*. Happily, he didn't get that bod by chance – that would just be annoying. No, Frank works hard to keep himself in shape, playing football and squash, and going to the gym three times a week without fail.

'Join a gym' he said. 'You might not like gyms ...'

'I don't like gyms.'

'Doesn't matter. Join one. Life is full of things you don't want to do. Do them.'

I pass this information on to Keith, as I feel he can benefit from it. 'Frank says fear is what people use to stop themselves living the life they deserve,' I add.

'Frank sounds like a cunt,' says Keith.

'Indeed he is,' I retort, 'and a prime example, but you should see his fucking biceps, man. They are *immense*.'

Keith nods his head slowly, impressed.

'Anyway, all I'm saying, all I'm really saying, is that you could use some of Frank's, you know, *drive*.'

'Oh, really?'

I shrug. 'Just saying,' I say.

He nods slowly again. Maybe he isn't impressed. It's becoming annoying.

'What's with this nodding?!' I yelp. 'No more nodding!'

'I'm going to start doing some art again.'

'Oh, for fuck's sake,' I moan. 'Tell it to the shaky hand, Keith.'

Keith has been promising to start doing some art again ever since he stopped doing art, almost a decade ago.

'I know I've said it before,' he says, 'but I never had MS and a brain tumour before. This time it's different.'

'It's not a tumour,' I say.

'It's not a tumour,' Keith repeats.

This happens a lot these days. Keith refers to his blueberry as a tumour and I reply, in my finest Arnold Schwarzenegger voice that *it's not a tumour*. And then Keith says it back to me. Then it bounces back and forth a while until Keith's Arnie, which is not great in the first place, more closely resembles the distress cry of a screech-owl.

'Look, I've made a start,' he says, and he produces a small notepad he's been sketching in.

I glance at his efforts. They are rough. I pay vague compliments but deep down inside I'm wondering if he has left it too long. I wonder if he can still do it. Is making art like riding a bike? Or is it like playing the ukulele? Because the latter you definitely lose if you don't keep it up.

'I just need to get my eye in,' says Keith. 'It'll come. It'll come.'

My second date with Sally – if that's what it is – can't come fast enough. I am excited, bobbing about like a loon off his meds. It's a long way away, however, and before I can get to it, I have my second date with Frank, running in Brockwell Park.

Now, I have a routine when it comes to running. I run – at a leisurely, some would say dawdling pace – for somewhere between twelve and fourteen minutes, and then I collapse. I have a little circuit around the park worked out and I've been running that same route for around three months, and nothing has changed. It hasn't got any easier and I haven't got any quicker. When I meet him at the park, Frank explains: 'It never gets any easier. But you have to push yourself. It'll still hurt – it'll hurt more, in fact, but the more you do, the further you'll get, the quicker you'll recover and the fitter you'll get.' We're already running at this point. I've started wheezing, which is customary around the three-minute mark. 'Today you push yourself,' he says. And he speeds up.

I'm in quite a bit of pain by the time we finish the circuit, and it takes me a little while to recover. I've definitely run a lot faster with him than I do on my own. I feel well pushed.

'OK, let's go,' says Frank.

'I beg your pardon?' I reply, genuinely curious to know what he might possibly mean.

'One more time around,' he says. 'That was just the warm-up. Now you need to start burning some calories.'

I laugh in his face. 'Very amusing,' I say.

'Come on,' he says, unimpressed, and off he goes. I suppose it's a lot to do with pride, which is apparently not a good thing, often preceding as it does some kind of fall, but I can't just give up. I have to give it a go. So there I am, running again.

Probably around halfway through the second lap, the rain comes, hard and cold. It mingles with my sweat and stings my eyes. As I half run, half stumble along, I find myself grabbing at my sides in an attempt to hold off the stitches which are coming now in gangs, like a girdle of pain. I stop and double over, gasping, 'Stitch. Stitch.'

Frank stops and says, 'Catch your breath. Then we'll carry on.' He says, 'Breathe into the stitch. Deep breaths. As deep as you can, and guide that breath to where the stitch is.'

I don't have the breath to tell him to fuck off.

Then I'm running again. A minute later, desperate to slump to the wet earth and die of exhaustion, I begin to wonder how anyone could possibly run non-stop for three hours. 'They push themselves,' says Frank.

Whoa. That's odd. It appears that Frank has just answered a question I asked only in my mind. I look up at him as we run. He is looking straight ahead. So did that actually just happen? Or did I merely imagine it? 'You merely imagined it,' says Frank. 'Keep going. Sprint the last stretch.'

I do as I'm told, to the best of my ability.

Lying on my back in the mud, I feel a strange sense of achievement. If I survive this, I think, I'll almost certainly end up feeling better for it.

I survive it, and the next day I can barely walk, but it does feel good, like a healthy pain, a pain in which I am able to indulge, even to rejoice. I am still rejoicing two days later when I shock and awe myself into another double circuit of the park. Two days after that I'm rejoicing so vehemently, so fanatically, that I begin to think I might be bipolar. I'm up at the crack of 7 a.m., which for a Sunday is like four dawns rolled into one, and I'm naked but for a pair of giant love handles, down on my knees and scrubbing the kitchen floor. I'm meeting Sally in the afternoon, so I clean the house from webs to wainscoting, just in case. We meet at the British Museum. Is it a date? I assume I'll find out sooner or later.

We hug hello. Just a hug. That's OK. It's just a start. That's fine. I feel rigid, nervous that something is going to go wrong.

We go to the museum café for a coffee. 'You look nervous,' says Sally.

I nod heartily, happily. 'I am nervous,' I admit.

Cockily, but perhaps over-eagerly, I had blogged about our previous date/non-date, making it clear that I didn't know where I stood. And happening to mention that I had an erection for most of the meal. A bunch of readers are now following my would-be romantic exploits quite avidly. They share my triumphs as well as my troughs and they root for me in the comments, openly sharing their opinions of the things that are happening to me, and the people who are filling my life. It's a wonderful thing. I feel like I'm part of a blogging community and that the whole experience of blogging has become a big, beautiful, emboldening dialogue.

'It's a bit like living in *The Truman Show*,' says Sally.

She says that reading other people's interpretations of her life gives her the fleeting desire to start her own blog, so that she too can have her say, put her side of the story. Together we imagine a world in the near future where people no longer speak at all in real life, choosing instead to communicate solely through their blogs. She says something about it being really rather tragic that some people are prepared to say things anonymously online that they don't dare say in real life. I agree. Then I realise she's being rather pointed. 'Ah,' I say. 'So. Yes. Is this a date or what?'

She laughs. 'That's more like it,' she says. 'That's what I'm talking about. A bit of balls. A nice bit of spunk.'

'Balls and spunk,' I repeat. 'Is that what you're talking about?'

Flirting! Rather repulsive flirting, but flirting nonetheless!

She nods enthusiastically, her silver eyes flashing like tiny trophies in the sun. 'Balls and spunk,' she repeats, looking into my eyes. 'Man spunk,' she adds. 'So,' she says, 'have you got an erection right now?'

'Raging,' I reply. 'Do you have any plans to actually answer my question or not?'

She smiles and nods. 'Sorry, yes. Um … I don't know what this is. I like you a lot and I like spending time with you. Which is why we're here, right?'

'Sure,' I say. 'Spending time.'

'I don't fancy you at the moment, if I might be brutally honest.' I wince, thinking that, actually, no, no need for that level of honesty, thanks. 'But maybe that will come in time. I'm a great believer that physical attraction is something that can grow. And it already has grown to some extent. You know? What do you think?'

'I think you're lovely,' I say, emboldened by her openness.

She tells me she thinks I'm lovely too, and ever so gently, she touches the side of my face, elbows and all. At which point, ever so gently, I raise the table we're sitting at with my knees, as if to suggest that I have some kind of bionic penis. Sally laughs and calls me a dirty old man.

After the exhibition, during which Sally proves to be thrillingly knowledgeable and stunningly articulate as well as having the most heart-stoppingly soft hands in existence, we walk into Soho, in the rain, sharing an umbrella, and singing a song about singing a song in the rain. It's nauseating. It's perfect.

From thence to a popular Japanese restaurant where we huddle and snicker like lovers in films, childish and conspiratorial. I feel awesome. At the end of the meal, when our heavily lipstuck and liberally lovebitten waitress pads off to take care of the bill, Sally whispers something offensive about her deep into my ear. I laugh like a seal hitting a fan. Then Sally whispers something else. 'Let's go see a film,' she whispers. I gasp with joy, and I savour the moment, Zenlike: Sally's breath on my ear, her hand on the back of my head, and the smell of her. I lean slowly back in my chair and the table rises entirely of its own accord.

After the film, which is good but predominantly irrelevant, we kiss goodbye by Clapham Common. It is – bar none – the best kiss of my life. No disrespect to anything that's come before, but this is pure and feels so right. There is nothing extra-marital, abusive, or in any manner questionable about this. This is pristine and perfect and pure. I make my way home in a daze.

Over the next week, I try to stay calm. I don't want to scare her off so I don't tell her what I'm thinking, but obviously, what I'm thinking is that I'm in love with her. I think about her constantly, but I don't text her, I don't message her. I play it cool. I wait for her to come to me. Eventually she does. She invites me to an evening of free events at the Tate Britain. It's a thing called 'Drawing on Jarman', a bunch of short films by Derek Jarman. Sounds fine to me. I think I remember enjoying *Caravaggio* many years ago, but frankly, it doesn't matter. I'd happily watch Tracey Emin take an Alaskan pipeline of elephant dung if it meant I could spend time with Sally.

We saunter into a screening room called the Lightbox, where *Imagining October* is being shown. Billed as a 'rarely seen experimental short film' and 'a dreamlike meditation on art and politics in the final years of the Cold War', it becomes clear after a matter of minutes why it is rarely seen. 'Rarely endured' is probably nearer the mark.

The only seat is a spongy banquette against the back wall, which we share with two other people, invisible in the dark. We manage to tolerate about ten minutes of the film, but only because Sally allows me to put my hand on her bare knee, and then slowly move it up over her leg, under her skirt and on to her thigh. I am watching pretentious garbage that has nothing to do with either art or politics, peppered with images of semi-naked Russian boys stroking one another and sledgehammer phallic symbolism and I feel probably as sexually excited as I ever have before in my life. Life is queer.

Then we leave the Lightbox and Sally says, with considerable passion, 'What the *fuck* was that all about?' She says, 'Derek Jarman was far too gay for his own good. There was nothing whatsoever to connect with there. Where was the empathy? Where was the human emotion? What kind of reaction was that supposed to provoke? Am I just being inhuman here? Did I miss it? Do you have to be gay to understand what the point was?'

'Why are you asking me?' I reply. I attempt to accentuate my manliness by pulling back my shoulders but I get a little crick in my neck, which hurts so much that I let out a slightly effeminate whimper.

Then we have a wander through the other galleries, gawping at the good stuff. I love galleries. I don't know if it's the beauty of the art, or the quasi-religious heel-and-whisper silence, or what it is, but there's just something about art galleries that always gets me a little excited. Downstairs, I mean. I seem to get terribly aroused just walking around, no matter what I'm looking at. I share this information with Sally in front of *The Lady of Shalott*, and without so much as a glance in any direction, she pulls my head down to hers and kisses me passionately. Simultaneously, and rather cheekily, all things considered, she fondles me on the johnson.

After the gallery we eat at a Moroccan restaurant in Clapham, and when we're all done with the chicken tajine, Sally says, 'So do you wanna see my darkroom then or what?'

I gasp.

'I do,' I say. 'I really do.'

Sally lives in an old Victorian house, or maybe Georgian. I can't be sure. It's definitely old though, with pointy windows. She shares with three others. Her room is at the top of the house, with white wardrobes and furry white rugs on varnished pine floors.

She leads me up the stairs and then, dear reader ...

We do it.

And if it seems like I'm glossing over the details, that's because I am. It's called discretion.

Sally falls asleep first and at just after 5 a.m. I make my way to the bathroom. Studying myself in the mirror, my face framed by shelves full of potions and powders and a bewildering array of special things I have never, ever seen before and cannot begin to describe, I train my gaze upon itself and stare deep into those really rather penetrating, deceptively lovely eyes. I shake my head and half-smile – actually it is a full smile, but only half a headshake – and I two-fifths-whisper to myself, 'You old dog, you.'

I flex my chest as best I can and give my predominantly hairless bosom a pinch. I roll my shoulders. I look ridiculous. I have no poise. A simple move, a shoulder roll, for God's sake and somehow I manage to look awkward and inflexible. Gym. I have to find a gym. I have to become one of those vain, vacuous vermin that line up like commuters, like civil servants on treadmills. I want biceps like Frank.

I flex my biceps in the mirror. Rubbish. They are rubbish.

I smile at my reflection. Even without biceps, I am happy.

I wipe tardy drops of sticky liquid from the end of my johnson with a couple of pieces of toilet roll, tiptoe back into Sally's bedroom and lower myself into her bed. Sally shifts about a bit, then resettles herself against my naked body. My arm encircles her back automatically and her head burrows into the cushion of my man-bosom. I shake off the shame. I look at Sally. I wish I had a video camera. Not in a creepy way. Just ... it would be nice to remember this just in case it doesn't last for ever.

No, don't be silly.

Of course it will last for ever.

I let my head fall on to the pillow and I smile. It's light outside. *I did this*, I think. *This is real.*

I smile some more.

Phew.

Everything's going to be all right.

CHAPTER SIXTEEN

BAD TO THE BONE

'Everything's going to be all right!' says Keith triumphantly.

'Your blackberry's gone away?' I cry.

'Blueberry,' corrects Keith. 'No, no. It's still there.'

'Oh. I'm sorry.'

'But that's not the point. I can live with that. In fact, I have to live with that.'

'Well, you don't have to,' I interrupt instinctively.

'Shut up!' he barks. 'I'm in a good mood!'

I cheer and squeal and whoop, fail to rapper-snap the fingers of both hands repeatedly, five or six times in a row. Keith looks at me aghast. 'Are you out of your fucking *mind*?' he asks.

I have to say I think maybe I am.

'This is a new side of you,' says Keith. 'I don't believe I've ever seen you actually, genuinely *happy* before. I approve, obviously, but if you could just try and be a *little* less insufferable, that would be awesome. Thanks.'

I laugh uproariously, insufferably uproariously. Things have been going very well with Sally. We've been seeing one another for a couple of months now, and to be honest, sometimes it feels good and sometimes it feels bad. And when it feels good, it feels very, very good, and when it feels bad, it feels awful. The best nights are when it's just the two of us over at her house. She cooks up a storm and then shows me photos she's taken or photos she admires, and we talk and we laugh and she seems genuinely to love my company.

Other times she doesn't seem to like me at all. Is this normal? Is this what happens in a normal relationship?

Keith is here at my house. He's making a joint. I knew he would. So I've been planning my speech, the one suggesting that if we smoke, we smoke outside on the fire-escape steps. I try to deliver the speech. But I'm too embarrassed. I know what it's going to lead to. I wait till he's about to light the joint, and I say, 'Actually, let's just nip outside to smoke that. If you don't mind.' I'm trying so hard to be casual, but my voice gives me away. It's too high. It's tense.

Keith stops before lighting, and thinks for a few seconds. 'You're a fucking loser,' Keith informs me. 'You've gone from thirty-year-old semi-virgin to treacherous love-rat to spineless pussy-whipped eunuch in the space of six months. You don't know how ridiculous you are. And you don't know a fucking thing about women.'

I'm really fed up with people telling me I don't know a thing about women. I explain to Keith that I *know* I don't know a thing about women. I really don't need reminding. Reminding me that I don't know anything about women is a waste of everyone's time. Might as well tell me I don't know a thing about quantum mechanics while you're about it, or remind me that I don't speak Russian. Knock yourself out, make a list. A list of things I cannot do. Jesus, it doesn't mean I'm a bad person.

'It means you're a bad *man*,' says Keith. 'You're like half a man. If that.'

I gasp melodramatically and tell him he's wrong, but really, deep down, I'm not so sure.

'Seriously,' Keith continues. 'I know you're giving the impression of being happy, but ...' He stops. 'I don't know. Are you really?'

'Of course I am!' I snap.

He pulls a face which implies the possibility that maybe, just maybe, I'm protesting too much.

But I am happy. Honest I am. I love having a girlfriend. I love being part of a couple. I love the fancy dinners, the cinema trips, and the carefree walks in the park. I love the intimacy of the hand-holding, the hair-drying, and the foot-rubbing. I love having someone to hug in the morning and to cook for in the evening. I love the way my insides spring to life when I get a text message. I love the way I get this indescribable physical sensation in my throat whenever I think of her face, and I swear, these last few weeks have genuinely been the happiest so far in my entire life.

But obviously, there's a downside. I say 'obviously'. Maybe it's not so obvious. I don't really know: this is all new to me. It's just that sometimes, it's not exactly how I pictured it, and I begin to wonder if things are quite how they should be.

Although I have no doubt that Sally really likes me and enjoys spending time with me, I can't seem to shake this feeling that I'm just not good enough for her. Sadly, this doesn't derive from any deeply entrenched sense of unlovability on my part, but from the fact that she's so critical of me, and so easy to exasperate.

A few days ago, for example, she accused me of supporting terrorism. This came in the middle of an argument about drugs. Sally doesn't like me smoking dope. Until recently she smoked it herself, apparently quite regularly, but now, suddenly, she really hates it. Doesn't like the smell of it on me; doesn't like the taste. She doesn't even like me doing it when she's not around.

The fact is, over a period of just a couple of weeks, the smoking of dope has started to become an issue, and for all her ineffable charm, Sally has quite a few issues. They're like meercats. Just when you think the coast is clear, one will pop its head above the parapet and twitch at you.

Of course, part of me wants to say to Sally, 'Listen, Shagpuss, I am what I am and that's that. Take it or leave it.' But what if she leaves it? Another part of me wants never ever to touch another cannabinoid as long as I live and to say to Sally, 'Look! Look what I did for you! See? I'd do anything for you.'

But that'd be worse than bad. That'd be weak.

Naturally, because this is part of my life and because I am

incapable of learning from the past, I blogged about the drug issue. I was pleased to see that – on the whole – my readers agreed with me. Stupidly, I brought this fact to Sally's attention. 'Listen to this,' I told her, reading from my comments. '"If a guy I had been dating for just a few weeks rolled over and did everything I said, I would be bored witless and ditch him for being a pussy." That's Penelope there, with a bit of homespun wisdom.'

Sally glared at me.

I ignored her and continued. '"She needs to get stoned," says Anonymous.'

'Do you think this is helping?'

I gave her an innocent look, which didn't go over awfully well.

'Well, it's not. It's not helping that you go running off to your readers every time there's something we argue about.'

I nodded my head. She was right, undoubtedly, but it was an interesting idea – a man who uses his blog readership as a kind of couples-therapy substitute. Potentially, it could make for a good post ...

'You're thinking about blogging what I just said, aren't you?'

I couldn't tell a lie. 'Well, kind of, yeah, but I mean, I won't, obviously. It was just a thought experiment really. Like a joke. One thing leading on from another, a little bit ironic ...'

'Have you been smoking?'

Hmm.

When I tell Keith about this, he says she should mind her own fucking business.

Keith doesn't like Sally. Or rather, he doesn't like her trying to change me.

'But I *am* loathsome,' I point out. 'Changing me might not be such a bad thing.'

'Yeah, but it has to be on your own terms. You should be looking to change into something *you* want to be, not fitting in with what some little ballbreaker says you should be.'

'Please don't talk about Sally that way,' I say.

He holds up his hands and sighs heavily. 'OK, fair enough. I'm sorry. She's not a little ballbreaker.'

I thank him for his understanding, but really, I have to admit, she kind of is.

For example, she's still breaking my balls about taking my photo. Actually, not just one, but a series of photos. The first time we went out together, she told me that she wanted to be the next David LaChapelle. 'You can be my breakthrough subject,' she said.

'I don't think so,' I told her, feeling ever so slightly uncomfortable.

I find myself feeling ever so slightly uncomfortable with Sally more often than I feel I should. And this is what gives me cause for concern. Like when she buys me chocolate biscuits and cream cakes when she knows only too well that I'm trying to lose weight. We had a little row about this too. At first it was just a pretend row, but then, when she continued to turn up with sugary treats, it became a bit weird. Under the circumstances, maybe it wasn't the best idea I ever had to blog about the fact that she might be a feeder, but it was meant to be light-hearted. Sadly, it backfired. Sally was pissed off.

'So this is your idea of not writing personal stuff about me online, is it?' She read aloud from the post, which was entitled, light-heartedly, 'Looks Like We've Got Ourselves A Feeder': '"So anyway, usually, feeders are men who want to control their wives or girlfriends by making sure they're at home eating and piling on the pounds, rather than out and about looking slim and sexy and attracting other men. So it's kind of an abusive thing borne of hideous insecurity. But I don't think Sally is like that at all. I think she just gets off on being pinned down and taken roughly from behind by massive sweaty fat blokes." You think that's funny?'

I had to admit that I did.

'And I did not say I was going to buy you some baggy clothes so you could grow into them.'

'Oh, didn't you?'

'You're really fucked up,' she said.

Am I?

I worry that I am. I worry that I'm so fucked up that I'm actually bad. Deep down. Somewhere inside. Like my dad. My dad was unfeasibly bad. He was selfish, short-tempered, and mean-spirited. He took no pleasure from life or from other human beings. He drank to excess, thought nothing of inflicting violence on anyone weaker than him, and was, generally speaking, an odious creature motivated by nothing but negativity. But then I remember that none of that applies to me. And if the worst thing I've ever done is share a few personal details with a bunch of strangers, then I'm absolutely fine.

But really, that's not the worst thing I've ever done. Not by a long chalk. Not, in fact, by a chalk so long that it more closely resembles an ostentatious cane. For example, there was Janet.

Six months or so after Avril and I had stopped going to bed with one another, she decided to try and set me up with one of her friends. Apparently we'd met once already, but I was having trouble remembering. Avril was on the phone, reminding me.

'Tall girl with red hair,' she said. 'Very striking.'

'Did I like her?' I asked, although frankly, if I had to ask, then I probably didn't.

'I don't know,' replied Avril. 'She liked you though. That should be enough, surely. Just go out for a drink with her,' she urged. 'What's the worst that can happen?'

'I dunno,' I replied. 'Murder?'

'Oh, she's not going to murder you, Stan. For fuck's sake. It'll just be a drink. It's no big deal. Go on. I bet you're desperate. I bet you haven't had sex since the last time we did it, have you?'

'You'd be surprised,' I said.

'I'd be amazed,' she replied. She laughed her throaty laugh and wouldn't take no for an answer. 'I'll call you back,' she said. Twenty minutes later she was back on the phone, flushed with the altruistic glee of the matchmaker. 'Eight o'clock tomorrow night,' she gushed.

'You've got yourself a date!'

I arrived early at the designated venue and twiddled my thumbs nervously. Janet arrived ten minutes later, all of a fluster and ever so sorry to have kept me waiting. I told her it didn't matter, and I nipped back to the bar to get her a drink.

Avril had described Janet as tall with red hair. This was a little inaccurate. Actually, it wasn't exactly inaccurate. It was just misleading. She was tall, yes, but – and I realise this might seem dreadfully hypocritical – Janet was really horribly overweight. I attempt to justify this hypocrisy by pointing out that I am and have always been repulsed by my own body fat. Always. When I stand before mirrors, I shout at myself. I clutch at my gut and grab handfuls of buttock, slapping my bosom and swearing and spitting and really, really quite harsh. So if I'm repulsed by my own neglect and indignity, surely I've every right to be repulsed by other people's? Or am I just bad?

She did have red hair too, kind of. It would have been slightly more accurate, however, to describe it as copper-coloured, and insanely frizzy. She was certainly striking though. She reminded me of an enormous mid-op transsexual with a terrifying, bright-ginger afro.

The fact is, from the moment she sat down opposite me, I knew there wasn't a chance in hell of our date working out.

The fact is, I didn't fancy her. At all.

The fact is, I thought she was hideously ugly.

I know, I know, I know. Me. With my reputation.

If she had felt the same about me, everything would have been a piece of cake. But she didn't. It would also have been easier if we hadn't got on at all, if we'd had absolutely nothing in common. But unfortunately this wasn't the case either. On the contrary, we got on well. She was intelligent. She read books. She was doing an MA on something to do with Jane Austen. She liked cats. The one thing that might mitigate my overriding desire to flee from her presence was that she seemed – how best to put this? – psychologically delicate.

Firstly, she was very full on. I swear it's not just my Groucho Marx complex, but I do feel slightly uncomfortable in the face of unremitting compliments. Janet seemed to think I was wonderful, and after thirty minutes of conversation, she was already plotting our life together.

'I want to have kids,' she said.

If I hadn't already finished my first pint, I might very well have showered her in Guinness foam. She was scaring me. I asked her if she'd like another drink.

'No, I'll get these,' she said. 'Same again?' And she made her way to the bar.

I had to get out of there. I decided to tell her when she came back from the bar. It wasn't going to work out. I'd tell her so. It'd be fine.

'What are you doing next Friday?' she said, placing another Guinness in front of me.

'I don't know,' I said, my expression surely betraying me. 'Why do you ask?'

'I'm having a few people for dinner on Saturday.' That's how she phrased it. In such a way that, even if she hadn't been as large as she was, it would automatically have occurred to anyone with a sense of humour to make some kind of joke about cannibalism. I can't remember exactly what I said, but it was something about admiring a woman with a healthy appetite. I thought I was being rather witty, but Janet did not. Her face immediately crumpled.

'Why do you want to hurt me?' she said.

I was mortified. 'I don't!' I cried. 'Honestly, that's the last thing I want.'

She smiled a small smile. 'OK,' she said. 'So you'll come?'

I started shaking my head. 'Look,' I said. 'I don't think I should.' I forced myself to speak the next sentence, sure that it would bring about an end to the evening. 'I'm not sure this is going to work out,' I said. 'I'm really sorry.'

Yeah. That would do it.

'Don't you like me?' she said, all plaintive and furrowed. 'I thought we were getting on.'

'We are!' I protested, slightly too much. 'We're getting on great.'

'Phew!' she said. 'That's a relief. God. I thought for a second you were going to say you didn't want to see me again.'

'Oh ...'

I was incapable of finishing my sentence. She was incapable of hearing me. Instead, she just kept on smiling. 'I really like you,' she said. I smiled back. It was a smile born of terror.

'I've just got to pop to the loo,' she said. 'Don't go anywhere.'

'I won't,' I said.

As soon as she was gone, I took a pen from my pocket and searched around frantically for a piece of paper. Finding none, I picked up a beermat and scribbled on it. 'Sorry. Had to go.' I placed the beermat next to her drink and I walked swiftly and decisively out of the pub. I didn't look back.

Her bag and coat were left untended on her chair and I could only hope that nobody stole them.

All the way home, I imagined her reaction on returning from the toilet. She'd look at the table and see a large hole. She'd look to the bar, around the rest of the pub. She'd sit down and wait. Eventually she'd see the beermat. She'd read the note.

I couldn't believe what I'd done. But I'd definitely done it.

The next morning I got a call from an incredibly pissed-off Avril. Janet had just left her house. 'She was crying her eyes out all night,' she said. 'What the fuck do you think you were playing at?'

I had no excuse. No excuse at all. I hate being judged by the way that I look. I hate it when people dismiss me because of how I look, carelessly overlooking any other qualities I might have. I hate shallow people. I hate rude people. I hate mean people. I hate cowards. And I hate hypocrites.

I was odious. I should have known better. I did know better. I knew much better.

Avril swore a lot, and when I hummed and hawed over whether

I'd do everything in my power to make it up to Janet, she hung up on me. We haven't spoken since. Am I a bad person? It seems I have my moments.

'On a scale of one to ten,' says Keith, 'how happy would you say Sally makes you?'

'Jesus, I don't know,' I reply. 'Ten. Most of the time. But sometimes, you know, I feel like she doesn't really like me.' I shrug, helplessly.

'Well, listen,' he says. 'You know how happy I am that you've found someone, but if she doesn't like you for what you are, then maybe you need to think about finding someone else.'

I am appalled at the idea. 'Don't be ridiculous,' I tell him. 'It'll be all right. She'll come round.'

The last time we argued about me writing about her on my blog, Sally said, perfectly reasonably, 'Just stop writing personal stuff about me. That's all I'm asking.'

I promised I would, before adding, 'Define *personal*.'

'Oh, for fuck's sake, Stan, just stop writing about me altogether then, please. If you don't mind. Thanks.'

'OK,' I agreed, deflated.

'You know, you're really quite weird,' she said, but she said it more or less without malice, so I hung on to it like a particularly earnest pitbull.

'You do like me though, don't you?' I asked, pathetically. 'I mean, I'm weird, but ...'

As Sally stared into my face, her expression softened and something approaching awe seemed to seep into her eyes.

Yes, awe.

And when Sally looked at me this way, I didn't feel ugly. I felt like a work of art. And that felt good. At that moment, on the happiness scale, I was a ten. I just wish she'd kiss me a little more is all. But it's OK. Nothing is wrong.

CHAPTER SEVENTEEN

BRAINS

Something is wrong. I can tell immediately. Keith was particularly spiky on the phone earlier, but that's half normal. What gives the game away is the expression on his face when I answer the front door. There's something disagreeable in his eyes. Apart from the sleep-bogeys. I'm pretty sure he's going to say, 'I don't think we should live together,' so it is – weirdly – almost something of a relief when he says: 'I've got a brain tumour.'

I've known for over a month now that my landlady is planning on selling the house and that I'd have to find somewhere else to live soon. Unfortunately I haven't been doing a great deal about it. Then I thought, I might as well move in with Keith. It's not as if we haven't lived together before. We know we get on, most of the time. I know he has a spare room. It made perfect sense. So I sent him a text. He didn't respond. I realise now that he had slightly more pressing matters on his mind. Literally.

'Come in,' I say.

He stomps through to the living room and sits down. 'I've got a brain tumour,' he repeats.

I just look, waiting for the smirk, waiting for Detective John Kimble to come bounding into Keith's face and make everything all right. There is no Kimble. 'Don't be silly,' I say, desperately. I can't resist. '*It's not a tumour.*' Perfect Arnie. But Keith doesn't crack a smile.

'It is,' he says. 'I understand you don't want to hear it, and

I appreciate that – thank you. But you hiding your head in the sand won't make my tumour go away.'

'Please tell me you're joking now, Keith,' I reply. My heart seems to be moving about in my chest.

He doesn't speak. Just shakes his head.

I start to shake my head too. Vigorously. Until my neck hurts. And tears actually begin to form somewhere behind my eyes before Keith finally forces a supercilious smirk and says, 'Nah, not really.'

I am appalled. Then, as Keith sees my wrecked face twist to anger in a single second, his own face falls. 'I do have a congenital cerebral aneurysm though,' he says, 'if that's any consolation.'

I smile gratefully.

It is.

'I thought for a moment you were going to say you didn't want me moving in with you.' I chortle and nod, half-rolling my eyes.

Keith says nothing. He is sitting in Pablo's chair, staring at my feet.

'So I'm quite relieved,' I continue. 'Phew. It's just an aneurysm.'

He continues to ignore me.

'So. Keith. What about me moving in with you then? You didn't get back to me.'

He shrugs. 'Yeah, whatever.'

'Hmm,' I say. 'Well, I appreciate your enthusiasm, I must say.'

'Hundred quid a week rent,' says Keith.

'That seems very reasonable,' I say.

'You're damn right it's reasonable.'

'Well, all right then.' I reach into my pocket and count out eight £50 notes. 'There's June,' I say.

'Have you started dealing drugs again?'

'What do you mean, *again*? I've never dealt drugs,' I point out.

'Have you started dealing drugs for the first time then?'

I tell him no, I haven't. Rather, I came to an understanding with my landlady, whom for the duration of my stay in her humble home has kept herself pretty much to herself, but who decided a few days ago to transform herself into a rapacious hard-nosed harridan. She then decided not to hand over any of my £1,150 deposit on the grounds that Pablo has 'destroyed' her flat. This translates as one patch of carpet and the back of one armchair, both of which have been slightly scratched up. And a table. And a cracked kitchen window. And although Pablo didn't actually crack the kitchen window directly, it was kind of his fault. He'd been in the back garden torturing a half-dead blackbird, so I rapped on the pane in reprimand, not knowing my own strength. Bad cat.

So I had to assert myself with the landlady. I said to her: 'You've got over a grand of my money. You can't possibly be suggesting that it's going to cost over a grand to replace a couple of pieces of – let's face it – fairly crappy furniture, and a roll of cheap, paper-thin carpet.'

She didn't like that.

'You're being ridiculous,' I added.

She liked that even less.

'You're just greedy.'

She glared at me. And she wouldn't budge. Our conversation ended poorly. I said I had work to do and suggested she have a little think about what she was playing at. She mumbled that she didn't need to think about anything and made vague threats about sending round her brother.

I was furious. I turned to my virtual brethren and asked for advice. Apart from seeking legal counsel and requesting receipts for all work carried out, a packet of prawns behind the radiator, and a couple of crates of haddock under the floorboards were among my favourite suggestions. Could I do that? Would that be bad, or just …? No. She'd still sell the flat, and the fish pong would only make the lives of my successors miserable.

All of this I pondered yesterday, surrounded by half-packed boxes and more of a mess than I could really handle, and I thought about the money, my money, which was in effect being stolen from me, and which I could really use rather desperately, and I'm afraid

I had something of a tantrum. I threw lots of things on the floor. Piles of papers. Piles of books. A cup full of pens and pencils and joss sticks and candles.

Pablo, startled, darted from the room. I shouted after him, 'Yeah, go on, run! This is all your fault! You little shit!'

It was then, as I found myself abusing my beloved cat, that I stopped, shook my head, and calmed myself down. 'You're just stressed out,' I told myself. 'The thought of moving. Money. Sally and me, the issues we're developing.'

As I was picking up all the mess I'd made, huffily and puffily, Pablo waltzed back into the room. I called him over, told him I wanted to apologise. He sat down slowly on the opposite side of the room, apparently prepared to listen.

'OK,' I said. 'Fair enough.' I sat down myself, on the carpet. 'I'm sorry I shouted at you,' I said. 'I'm sorry I called you a shit. And I know it's not your fault that I'm out over a thousand pounds.'

He lifted his head slightly, as if he were giving me half a nod. Then he stood up and sashayed across the carpet. He climbed into my lap, and in response to my touch, began to pad and purr.

It's difficult to put into words the validation a cat can give you. Every time Pablo gets in my lap and purrs, I honestly think, *I can't be that bad*. I trust Pablo's judgement, probably more than I trust my own, and the fact that he's willing to spend his precious time with me, the fact that he's able to take pleasure from my touch, these things mean an awful lot. It feels like such a healthy thing, to have cats around.

Pablo will be good for Keith, and good for that ballooning blood vessel up there in his brain. A medical man told him that the blueberry is inoperable. Which I guess means that if they try to remove it, he might wake up and never walk again, never speak again, never move or even think again; or he might wake up and imagine he's Jewish or Jamaican, or like Preston Sturges's father, he might start laughing when he's sad or crying when he's happy. Or of course he might not wake up at all. The brain is a funny old stick.

And terrifyingly fragile. All of which reminds me of my father's brain, which in the end got so confused by the world that it had to have Lord only knows how many volts of electricity shot right into the heart of it.

The medical man also said that, if the aneurysm ruptures, as it could potentially at any moment, then Keith could be dead within seconds. But he also said it might just as easily never happen.

So, in reality, having no clue how long he's got left, he's really no different from the rest of us. Just happens that he has one more tick box to worry about in the Book of Grisly Demises. But then who's to say that I don't have a blueberry timebomb in my brain too?

'Do you think you should be smoking weed with that blueberry?' I ask helpfully.

He grabs the joint off me like a man half his age.

'I'm just saying,' I say. 'The last thing you want is a psychotic aneurysm.'

'No,' Keith replies, his brain full of smoke, 'the last thing I want is to start living my life like a terrified weakling, not doing the things I would ordinarily do just because something that will probably never happen is hanging vaguely over my head.'

'Like the Blueberry of Damocles.'

'It's actually more like a raspberry,' he says. 'Which could of course one day be horribly appropriate.'

I tut and shake my head. 'Oh, come on, man! Where's your positive mental attitude?'

'Don't you dare!' spits Keith. 'You've changed,' he says accusingly.

'Damn right,' I reply. I have changed. I think Elsie noticed it too. Elsie is my landlady, and yesterday she came back to the flat for the final showdown. She was still insisting that returning the flat to the same condition it was prior to my arrival would cost her the full £1,150 of my deposit. I laughed. 'How is that possible?' I asked. 'Explain to me where the money will go, please.'

She ran through the obvious, which would amount to a couple

of hundred quid maximum, then she cited nicotine-stained fixtures and fittings. 'The whole house will have to be redecorated and all of the furniture replaced,' she said. How she kept a straight face I do not know.

But I am not the wilting wreck of a quivering cockstand I was when I moved into her flat. I am changed utterly, unconcerned with what this woman thinks of me, unafraid of standing up for myself. Finally, after all these years, I feel able to assert myself.

So I said to her: 'Look, I'll be honest with you. I actually think you're trying to rip me off and I intend to do everything in my power not to let you get away with it.' At which point she gasped quite melodramatically, but I held up my hand and said, 'Please let me finish' – just like they do on *Question Time*! Then I said, lying adroitly: 'I've already taken legal advice and I'd like you to provide receipts for every item of furniture which you buy and every piece of cleaning or refurbishment you pay for. If you refuse to do any of this, I will have no hesitation in taking you to the small-claims court. I'm sick and tired of being walked all over by people like you.'

Her expression, which had moved from impotent rage to shocked bewilderment, suddenly switched to righteous indignation. 'What is that supposed to mean?' she cried. 'What is this "people like you"?'

Uh-oh, I thought. She's going to play the race card. Or is that a racist assumption on my part? Gah! Minefield. I stood my ground and told her what I meant. 'Grasping ...' I began. I so wanted to use the word 'fucks', but I stopped myself. I was determined to retain the moral highground. 'Liars,' I said. 'If I'm wrong, I apologise. Prove me wrong. If not, you owe me money, and I want it back.'

At which point she started screaming at me. 'Are you calling me a liar? Are you calling me a liar?'

'No, I'm not,' I said, although I quite clearly had. 'But I'm definitely suggesting it. I think it's a distinct possibility.'

But she wasn't really listening. As she turned and left the flat, she carried on screaming, and waving her fists and pointing her fingers. 'You go to hell!' she shouted. And as she slammed the front door, a little bit of plaster fell from the surrounding wall. I shook my head. That was another hundred quid right there.

Half an hour later, her brother was hammering on the front door with his large fists.

Five minutes after that, he left. I closed the door, breathed in the glorious money-stench of the £900 he'd begrudgingly counted into my palm, and did a gloriously self-satisfied little dance.

I repeat the dance in front of Keith, and excited at the prospect of living with someone again, I leap forward and punch him on the shoulder like Fonzie.

He recoils in surprise. 'Please don't,' he says. 'My brain could pop at any moment. One more shock like that, and ...'

'And what, Keith? Eh? And what?' It seems it's time for some tough, stoned love. 'So it goes pop. What happens then? You die, do you? Is that what happens?'

'Probably, yeah. No one knows. It wouldn't be pretty though. We know that much.'

'Do we? Do we really' – I wiggle my apostrophe fingers – '"know that much". Or – and I'm just throwing this out here – maybe we should start looking on the bright side here, eh? Eh? What do you think of that? Let's give that a go, shall we? So – with that in mind – as well as you dying a horrible death, what else might just as equally happen?'

Keith nods his head, slowly, as if coming round to my way of thinking. He hands me the end of the first joint of the evening. 'Well, I suppose,' he says, 'best-case scenario, there's just as much chance that I might actually be immortal.'

I sigh, nod my head. 'Thank you,' I say, pleased that he is back on my wavelength. 'Exactly. And at least,' I add. 'At least it's not a tumour.'

'It's not a tumour,' repeats Keith, in his best screech-owl.

'Come on,' I say, getting to my feet. 'Group hug.'

'It's really not necessary,' he protests.

'Of course it is,' I insist. 'Let's hug it out.'

Keith relents and rises, we put our arms around one another and squeeze, then Keith pulls away suddenly and clasps at his forehead. 'Shit,' he gasps.

'What's wrong?' I say.

He looks me in the eyes.

'I felt it move,' he says. 'Will you fetch me a beer, please?'

Bastard.

If tonight is anything to go by, Keith is going to be dining out on this stinking aneurysm for the rest of his life.

I fetch him a beer.

I wish I had an aneurysm.

CHAPTER EIGHTEEN

WELCOME TO PECKHAM

Despite Keith's refusal to lift more than one paltry box at a time, citing potential aneurysm-related mayhem, and despite downpours so heavy that they had a distinctly biblical flavour, the move from Herne Hill to Peckham went off fairly smoothly. I hired a small van and staggered the shifts over a long bank-holiday weekend. I also squeezed in a couple of trips to IKEA to stock up on still more beautifully designed but absolutely one hundred per cent completely unnecessary stuff. This was in part to compensate for all the rotten old stuff I'd chucked away.

The most exciting part of the spring clean was giving away lots of clothes that didn't fit me any more. As I dumped them in a supermarket recycling bin, I felt an overpowering sense of achievement. I felt like finally my life was going in the right direction.

By Monday evening, it was all done. Not my life, but the move. I closed the front door, opened the kitchen window for Pablo to slink on to the stairwell and tentatively begin exploring his new home, and I slumped down in the living room, like a great big lump of pungent, sweaty lard. At which point Keith informed me that he had killed the internet. Frothing angry with the incompetence of his internet provider, he'd terminated his account.

I pointed out that I had very important proofreading work I had to get on with all week, work that would eventually enable me to pay Keith July's rent money.

Keith pointed out that I didn't really need the internet for that. Surely all I needed was my laptop and my brain? After all, God had given me a decent, non-malfunctioning brain. The least I could do was use it once in a while. I scowled.

I then pointed out that I needed to blog urgently, and to check my comments.

Keith pointed out that I had become addicted to the internet and that I should make an effort to participate more fully in the real world.

I pointed out that smoking grass and playing video games was not necessarily what a lot of people might consider 'participating more fully in the real world'.

Keith pointed out that a lot of people needed to get with the programme.

I pointed out that using terms like 'get with the programme' was probably going to cause the two of us to fall out.

Keith pointed out that I should probably wake up and smell the coffee.

At which point we fell out.

To make matters worse, Pablo didn't come home that evening. Then, to make them worse still, he didn't come home the following morning. And Pablo hates the rain. Something was wrong. He must have got lost, confused, looking for the old house. I should never have let him out so soon. I cursed myself. I cursed Pablo. I thought he had more sense than that. I scoured the streets between the two locations all Tuesday morning and most of the afternoon. To no avail.

On Wednesday I had to meet the landlord, Dudley, because Keith is a blithering, slack-jawed fuckwit who happened to mention that he was going to have a friend staying for a few months. Dudley is an East End type, slightly ferrety, boastful, and annoying. Particularly annoying – aside from worryingly unnecessary, regular mentions of 'Pakistanis' and the 'half-caste girl' upstairs – was that Dudley made a point of saying, 'I don't allow pets either.'

'Fair enough,' I said. 'I don't have any pets.' I hoped I was lying, but there was still no sign of Pablo. I was beginning to panic. Feelings of helplessness were welling up inside me. If Pablo was human, I'd have called the police by now. Every few hours I went back out on to the street. I knocked on local doors and walked all the way back to Herne Hill, unable to stop myself imagining all the horrible things that might have happened to him.

On Thursday afternoon, I typed the words 'PABLO – BELOVED BLACK CAT – CASH REWARD OFFERED FOR HIS SAFE RETURN' into a blank Word document. I added my phone number and a photograph of Pablo and printed off twenty copies. As I picked up the first sheet to examine it, my mobile phone began to squeal.

Timing.

It was Ron, next-door neighbour in Herne Hill, owner of three discoloured teeth and one fabulously untended garden, which was until recently Pablo's favourite stomping ground and miniature-jungle kingdom. I'd already talked to him about Pablo going missing post-move. He had kindly checked his garden and promised to keep his eyes peeled. So when I heard his voice, I was optimistic.

Ron explained that he was with a young man called Tony. Tony had been going door to door in the area asking if anyone owned a black cat. He'd eventually been pointed towards Ron's building. When Ron said yes, his ex-neighbour was missing a black cat, Tony burst into tears.

'I've got some bad news,' Ron said. My heart sank and my stomach turned. He passed me over to Tony.

'He just ran straight out in front of my car,' Tony explained. 'There was nothing I could do.'

Tony was a cat person. He felt terrible. I felt bad for him. But I felt sick for Pablo. I drove back to my old house in a state of shock, not quite believing what was happening. When I got there, I shook Tony's hand. There was nothing he could do.

'It's OK,' I told him. 'It wasn't your fault.'

'I've got four cats,' he said. 'I know how it is. I'm so, so sorry.'

Tony showed me to his car. He'd placed Pablo in the boot. His car was a Skoda. A fucking Skoda. Pablo deserved better than that.

As I lifted him out of the boot, it hit me properly for the first time that Pablo was dead. Never again would he wake me up in the morning, purring and padding and rubbing the top of his head against my sleepy face. My heart ached.

I was surprised by how light he seemed. At first I thought maybe he was lighter because the life had leaked out of his body; because the weight of his soul had departed. Then I realised he'd probably lost a bit of weight in the days he was missing, roaming around Herne Hill wondering where his life had gone. A shock ran through me. Pity and anger and shame. I tried not to blame myself. I'm still trying not to blame myself. But I do blame myself. At least partially.

I'd never held a dead body before. I touched my mother's face before they put her in the ground, but I didn't feel much.

I loved Pablo much more than I loved my mother. Probably because Pablo showed me much more love than my mother ever did. It was easy to love Pablo. It was impossible to love my mother. She made it impossible.

His body was still warm. It had been a clean hit, thank God. He ran into the front wheel with a thud. None of his insides were outside – I don't think I would've been able to face that – but there was blood on his face, already dried. I couldn't tell where it had come from exactly. I closed his eyes, the way they do in films, with soldiers.

I wrapped him in his favourite blanket and placed him on the passenger seat of my car.

Stalled at the traffic lights near Dulwich Park, I looked down at the blanket and let out a low groan.

Back home I laid him down on his favourite chair and I smoothed his fur and cleaned his wound and brushed him. As I stroked the top of his head too hard, I pulled back his eyes and allowed myself to imagine, just for a second, that he was coming back to life. But he wasn't.

Pablo was gone. I thought of Sally. I wanted to be with her. I wanted to hide my face in her lap and weep away the pain while she stroked my hair and comforted me as best she could. I needed her. But Sally was gone too.

CHAPTER NINETEEN

SNAPSHOTS

A fortnight ago, Sally's obsession with taking my picture came to a head.

'I really thought you'd be into it,' she said.

'Well, I'm not,' I replied. 'I'm really not.'

'Well, why not?' she wanted to know, and it pissed me off that she seemed to feel some sense of entitlement. Like I was some art project she had paid for with her body.

'Because you make me feel like a freak show,' I said.

'But I think you're beautiful,' she said. 'In your own way,' she added.

I made a face. My face said, 'Thanks for that. You certainly know how to make a person feel like shit.' Then my mouth said it.

'But I mean it!' she cried.

'I know you mean it!' I cried back. 'That really doesn't help matters.'

'But you don't understand,' she said, still digging a dirty great hole for our relationship. 'For me you have a kind of anti-beauty that's very attractive.'

'Jesus, Sally. There's no difference between that and morbid fascination. I am not an art project! I am a human being!' I smiled but I was pissed off. 'Seriously. You really do make me feel like a freak show.'

'Well, you are a bit of a freak show,' she said. 'And that's part of the attraction.'

I didn't know how to react to this. I just shook my head.

After which, things became rather strained between us, and as if by mutual, albeit tacit agreement, we began to see a little less of each other. Then on Tuesday – the day after the move – she called to see how I was and I told her about Pablo going AWOL. She was shocked and saddened and suggested we meet up for a late dinner on Wednesday night. I readily accepted, and at the restaurant, everything seemed great. We laughed a lot and touched a lot and things seemed easy again. So afterwards we came back to my new home in Peckham, and we made love. That night I went to sleep feeling good, thinking we were back on track and that everything was going to be OK.

At 4 a.m. I opened my eyes and Sally was sitting cross-legged, wide awake in the middle of my bed, her body twisted away from me. She had a little white vest on. She looked like a dream. My bedside lamp was on, blinding me. I squinted, shaded my eyes. 'Are you OK?' I asked. She turned off the light, lay down and pulled the sheet over her body. She said she was fine. Told me to go back to sleep.

I didn't believe her. 'What's up?' I said.

'I had a bad dream,' she said.

'Poor baby,' I said, snuggling up to her and experiencing a wave of tenderness. There's a song by Counting Crows with the line, 'And every time she sneezes, I believe it's love.' It was that kind of moment. Like she'd sneezed all over me. She turned her body away from mine and I positioned myself behind her. 'What was it about?' I asked. And just as I did, something fell from the bed to the floor with a clatter. I jumped. Sally didn't move, but her not moving was so precise, so deliberate, that it had more impact than if she'd jumped to her feet. 'What was that?' I said. I reached across Sally, turned on the light, angled it away from my face and sat up.

Sally continued not to move. 'Nothing,' she said. 'Just my camera.'

I looked at her. She continued to face away from me, but I sensed her eyes were open, waiting.

'Were you taking pictures of me?' I asked.

She turned to face me, looking furtive, guilty. Or not. I don't know.

'Don't be ridiculous,' she said. 'God, you're paranoid.'

'Sally. Why were you sitting up in the middle of the night with your camera and a light shining on to my face?'

'I told you, I had a bad dream. I couldn't sleep.'

I shook my head.

'Oh, what?' she snapped. 'I was awake and I was looking through photos on my camera.' I stared at her. She stared back. 'You're being weird,' she said.

My mouth fell open. 'Me?!' I was aghast. 'Let me see the camera then.'

'You're joking, right?'

'You've showed me photos on your camera before. Show me again.'

'So you don't trust me?'

'Sally. You look guilty. You look like you're lying to me. And you must admit, it looks pretty suspicious.'

'I'm not lying and I don't care how it looks.'

'So show me. What have you got to hide?'

'This is ridiculous.'

'I agree entirely,' I said. 'This is utterly ridiculous. You're behaving like a child.'

'Oh, fuck off.'

And with that, she got out of bed, pulled on her clothes, picked up her camera and left.

To my shame, I did a little pleading. 'Please don't go, Sally,' I said, and I sounded pathetic. I followed her downstairs, wanting to stop her. I tugged at her elbow, and she reacted like I'd stabbed at her with a cattle prod, She turned and froze and glowered at me. I felt guilty. I looked away.

She said she wasn't going to stay where she wasn't trusted. I said I did trust her. Honest.

She left.

When the front door closed, I went back to my bedroom and picked up my watch from the bedside table. It was a quarter past four. How was she going to get home? I got back into bed.

I picked up my phone. I put it down.

Then I picked it up again and started texting.

Then I shook my head, cancelled the message and threw my phone across the room.

I turned off the light.

I thought about how she often flicked through the images on her camera and realised that her explanation was entirely plausible. Why the fuck would she want to take photographs of me anyway? She was right. I was entirely paranoid.

I thought about how her eyes had flashed hatred when I grabbed at her arm, like she expected me to hit her, like she was daring me.

I thought about the fact that tonight we'd spoken about going to Prague for a weekend in August.

I thought about how we didn't really know each other.

And now she was gone. With or without stolen snapshots. It didn't matter. I felt stupid, like I'd fucked everything up.

I placed the palms of my hands over my ears and pushed my fingernails into the scalp at the back of my head until it really, really hurt.

I missed Pablo. And I missed Sally. And as I lay in bed, breathing loudly, staring blankly through the darkness, I realised that, for the first time in a very long time, probably since I was an ignorant, hopeless teenager, I was really, truly alone.

CHAPTER TWENTY

PABLO, PABLO, BURNING BRIGHT

Actually, I'm not alone. Keith is here, and although he neither purrs nor nibbles my earlobes, his company is not to be sneezed at, nor its healing power underestimated. Together we're going to give Pablo the send-off he deserves. Tonight. This feels right. Indeed, this is the first thing that has felt right since moving to Peckham.

Conversely, the last two days have been horrendous. Losing Sally and Pablo within twenty-four hours of one another seems needlessly cruel, and although the loss of Pablo runs much deeper within me, it is the loss of Sally that has me shouting out. Not in grief but in embarrassment. When I think of Sally, I remember, and when I remember, I despair, and when I despair, I pity, rage and writhe in hideous, abject embarrassment. The extent of my embarrassment is profound. It's physical. I cry out.

I really showed my arse to Sally. In the figurative sense. I told her things I should never have told her. Things that nobody else knows, nor ever should. And I did so because I was certain she loved me. Actually, that wasn't it. I told her because I was certain I loved her. And maybe I did, but why did I have to declare it, so readily and so hungrily?

I cry out again, another *aaargh* of frustrated indignity. Jesus. Somewhere serious inside me, something is not right.

I also cry out when I remember the way she looked at me. That look that I interpreted as love, but it wasn't. It was the look of a journalist in the epicentre of a race riot. Outrage and horror masked by professional exhilaration.

But what's really frustrating is not knowing. Was Sally really taking photographs of me, or am I literally insane? Or even figuratively so? Is that really all she ever wanted? Oh God. Oh, the humiliation.

Thoughts of Pablo cut me no slack. I leap, snarl and grunt from guilt to anger to great blankets of sadness. Why the hell did he have to go all the way back to Herne Hill? He was a very bright cat, I was sure of that ... Maybe I've forgotten something. I haven't even missed it yet because I'm too dumb, but Pablo realised and went back for it.

I shake my head.

It's done.

The anger now is futile, counter-productive.

All I can really do now is honour him.

Pablo was always a fan of poetry. Or at least he rarely rose up and flounced away when I read poems to him as he lay sleeping in my lap. Therefore I can only presume that he was a big fan of E. E. Cummings and T. S. Eliot. Furthermore, I also presume that he would probably have rather enjoyed William Blake.

Which is nice to know, for when William Blake was only eight or ten years old – details, apparently, are sketchy – he was out for a walk across a field with his family, when suddenly he became transfixed by what appeared to everyone else an ordinary tree. Indeed, to everyone else, this *was* an ordinary tree. But to little William Blake it was something different. For William Blake saw angels ... 'a tree filled with angels, bright angelic wings bespangling every bough like stars'. This sounds like a suitable resting place for a perfect poem of a cat such as Pablo. So it must be written in the stars that this very tree is situated in Peckham Rye, just a couple of minutes from Keith's house.

So before it gets dark, I set out with Keith to find Blake's Tree of Juvenile Delusions. Within a matter of minutes, guided surely by divine providence, we find it. Or at least one very similar. All it seems to lack is a bespanglement of angels, but we can arrange for those to come later.

We return home to wait for nightfall, and with Pablo still on his blanket on the living-room floor, we become intoxicated. We find choice cat quotes online, and we drink to them. 'Dogs are dogs,' says Keith, 'but cats are people.'

Then we get slightly ritualistic. We sit in a two-man circle around Pablo's body, smoke a chillum and read a bit of William Blake. Then we reminisce with wonderful stories, made sad only by his lousy, miserable death.

There was the time he enraged an elderly neighbour by killing one of her rosette-winning doves. I tried to explain to this furious woman that Pablo would never do such a thing, but when I found him later, there were still giveaway white feathers all over his face. I tried to chastise him for that, but he seemed so proud, and really, it was hilarious.

Then there was the time he brought home a beautiful grey squirrel he'd caught and heartlessly murdered for his own pleasure. I rate squirrels highly and was really quite angry with him. But again, you know, what can you do? He was a killer. He loved to kill. And deep down I simply had to admire him for it.

When he was a kitten he grew very attached to a straw shopping bag a friend brought round to the house. So attached did he become that the friend brought the bag back the very next day, empty, as a gift for Pablo. We then developed this game, Pablo and I, wherein Pablo would climb into the bag and I would swing him backwards and forwards, causing him to grizzle with pleasure. That low, slightly spooky cat-growl that he'd do when I gave him cat-nip. The higher I swung him, the more he would grizzle, until eventually I was swinging the bag around the room in full circles. Then when I'd stop he would stagger out of the bag, still deep-purring but unable to walk in a straight line. This hilarious pastime came to an end one day in the back garden when the bottom of the bag came loose. Pablo flew out and away, high into the air in the direction of the house. He landed just above the kitchen window, where he remained, clinging to the brickwork like a terrified drunken bat.

Then there was the time before he was house-trained, when he was very tiny and didn't really know any better, just a few weeks into our relationship, and he was still shitting everywhere; I caught him shitting under my chair and I lost my rag, picked him up, shouted in his face and threw him down to the ground like a bow-tie I couldn't fasten, hurting him quite badly in the process. He squeaked in pain, and when he righted himself he walked with a limp. Immediately disgusted by what I'd done I went to comfort him, to apologise, and he hissed at me.

Even though he recovered quickly, I never forgave myself for that. It made me question everything I thought I knew about myself. It made me wonder who I was and what I was capable of. It made me question whether I was fit to have children. It made me go into counselling for a while and talk and talk and talk, because that's really all there is to do.

I have still never forgiven myself for that horrible flash of temper that's like my father deep inside me, and I think it's important that I never do. But Pablo forgave me. And that made me love him more than I think I have ever loved anyone.

'Let's buy a house,' says Keith. 'Then we can get another cat.'

'That seems a bit extreme,' I say. 'But maybe, yeah.'

When it gets properly dark and properly late, and only cats and foxes and drunks are out roaming the streets, two drunks armed with a dead cat, a garden fork, and a spade sashay suspiciously over to Peckham Rye, heading for Blake's Tree of Angels.

Now, I haven't dug a hole since I attempted – as I imagine all children do – to tunnel my way to The Bowels of Hell aged five or ten. Turns out it's bloody hard work, and despite Keith's manly arms – and taking into account his diseased hands – it takes us over an hour to get the hole deep enough to ward off our fear of Pablo being dug up by dogs or other vile scavengers.

We begin, or rather, Keith – who sings the outdoors electric, frankly, and makes Ray Mears look like Margot Leadbetter – begins by slicing up and removing a few squares of turf a few inches thick and putting them to one side. Then, our grave template in place, Keith unfurls a large sheet of tarpaulin and we get to digging in earnest by the light of the moon and distant street lights. As I dig, I hear Pablo, already perched above me in the branches of Blake's tree, licking his chops greedily, one fat cherubim feather stuck in his teeth.

When the hole is deep and good and ready and the tarpaulin piled high, I pick up Pablo's body, blanket and all, give him one final hug and kiss and place him deep down inside the soft, wet earth. Then I recite the poem I have penned in his honour:

Pablo, Pablo, burning bright,
Bespangling all with perfect light.
Sleeping now where angels played,
Your life has left me less afraid.
And though your days of play are gone,
The love you made lives on and on.
Bespangling still my heart with light,
For ever Pablo, burning bright.

Believe me, by the time I'm done, there isn't a dry eye in the house.

Then we steel ourselves and cover him over with earth and earth and more earth and more, and stamp down hard on top of him, which feels a bit wrong but Keith insists it is necessary to make Pablo safe, to seal him in there, in the heart of the planet. Then we replace the grassy bits and stamp them down too. For minutes on end we stamp and stomp and sweat and chant like weird warriors. 'His name is Pablo Cattermole,' we chant. 'His name is Pablo Cattermole.' The leftover earth we toss around and kick about the place like tribesmen in the midst of a magick ritual.

'His name is Pablo Cattermole,' we chant.

'His name is Pablo Cattermole.'

That night in bed the loneliness returns tenfold and, feeling helpless, hopeless and overwhelmed with grief, I sob myself slowly to sleep.

CHAPTER TWENTY-ONE

A FRESH START: AUDREY TAUTOU

Allô, Stanley! Please stop your sobbing now, for it is I, the very lovely Audrey Tautou, French film starlet and all-round sex profiterole. 'Ow are you today?

I'm on the Old Kent Road. Whenever I'm on the Old Kent Road, I understand afresh why it's the cheapest property on the Monopoly board. It's like the part of London that evolution forgot, and the perfect location for an existential crisis.

I'm having my existential crisis on the top deck of a bus. If I'm honest, I don't even know what an existential crisis is, but my hypochondria rather pretentiously informs me that that's exactly what's going on.

Something's gone wrong. I've stopped running. I've stopped swimming. I've stopped eating well. I've stopped eating less. My weight is already ouncing back, pounding back up in the wrong direction. I've broken promises to myself – and to the blog readers – about marathon training and gym membership, and as I sit here, stuck at this bus stop seemingly for the rest of my life, there are pizza crusts on the kitchen floor and most of my possessions are still packed away in boxes from the move, which was weeks ago. I need a shave. And a haircut. In the last five days alone I have literally grown trotters and a snout. *Literally*. Imagine that.

I'm on my way to Shoreditch to have a spot of elevenses with Frank. I'm meeting him in a bar – don't be late, time is money, life is short – and I'm stuck on a bus, writing a bunch of Never Asked Questions for the blog. I don't really know what else to write at the moment. Never Asked Questions seem a safe bet. I've got Audrey Tautou never asking the questions.

You look so sexy today, Stanley. You know, I really fancy ugly men. I was wondering if you wouldn't mind coming to my villa in the Seychelles tonight and showing me a good time?

I'm stuck at a bus stop across the street from an enormous Tesco. A pub called the Lord Nelson has what appears to be two fresh bullet holes in one of its windows, each giving way to separate spiderwebs of shattered glass. Across the street a large clump of disparate, desperate-looking people are waiting for a bus. One of them – a man in his forties with lank grey hair and an old suit – suddenly steps out into the road and throws what appears to be a stone at a passing bus. It comes out of nowhere, this act of aggression, and is all the more remarkable for this guy's seeming respectability. Witnesses shake their heads vaguely and look away. The guy steps back on to the pavement, like butter wouldn't melt, like nothing out of the ordinary had happened.

I sigh and grab roughly at my gut. Frank will sort me out.

A quick burst of sunlight is shooed away by angry clouds, and I smile. I'm not in the mood for happy hot weather today.

Oh, but you make me so 'appy! I thought we could fly there in my private jet, which in reality is actually more like a time machine. We'll be there in literally no time at all. Actually, I know this is a bit forward, but are you free right now? ... Ooh, that was fun. Time travel always makes me feel – 'ow you say? – up for it. So – do you like my villa in the Seychelles overlooking the Indian Ocean and miles of private beach?

On the Old Kent Road, an old man on a bench, looking not quite all there, struggles to light a cigarette he's just painstakingly constructed. He's in his fifties, grey skin, short spiky silver hair and beard, a can of superstrength lager in a brown paper bag between his knees. When he finally manages to get his cigarette going, he folds his arms and stares straight ahead, fag hanging from his gob, smoke dancing into his face, and I think that thing I think a lot, that thing that everybody who thinks about other people thinks a lot. I think, 'I wonder what he's thinking.'

I wonder how old this man is. Probably much less than twice my age. I shudder. I need to get out there. Go for a run. I really don't know how it all slipped away from me again. Last thing I remember, I was running three times a week, swimming once in a while, losing loads of weight.

Enough. I turn to a new page in my notebook and begin a list. In times of trouble, never be afraid to start a new list. There is comfort in a well-compiled list. I write the words 'A Fresh Start' at the top of the page. Below the heading I write the word 'problem' on the left of the page, and the word 'solution' on the right.

I suddenly lose patience with the bus. Other passengers are getting off. Why am I here?

I look back out of the window at the old man drinking his lager. I shake my head with despair, then notice a well-dressed young Indian woman staring at me from behind the bus stop. She has exactly the same expression on her face that I imagine I have on mine. A mixture of polite enquiry, patronising pity, and outright disgust. She looks away. I look away. I look back at the old man. He is looking at me. He looks away. I look away.

May I kiss you slowly at first, tentatively, my lips as light upon your face as my breath, until we're both burning up with exquisite anticipation? Then, when you're really aching for me, may I gradually introduce my tongue, teasing you, sucking on your swollen lips and groaning as I taste the sweet nectar of your 'ighly erotic man-spittle? Then, when I'm ready to give myself to you fully, may I go wild on your mouth and face and kiss you with all the savage intensity and barbaric abandon of a woman who 'as been denied any physical affection for 12,000 years?

In my notebook, in an effort to put my life in order, I write the following:

- **Problem:** *massive belly.* **Solution:** *cut out the junk food again.* Piece of cake.
- **Problem:** *bad back.* **Solution:** *medical attention.*
The back problem crept up on me two weeks ago and has really dug in its heels. Now it's constant, nagging, whinging, stabbing agony and the perfect excuse not to join a gym. It must go. I'm looking for an osteopath as I speak.
- **Problem:** *atrophy.* **Solution:** *swimming.*
No excuse not to. Swimming is good for everything that ails you.
- **Problem:** *lovelessness.* **Solution:** *speed dating.*
And fantasy. Never underestimate fantasy. Fantasy is essential.

Ooh-la-la! You are such a generous lover. And may I say that I 'ave never been kissed so perfectly, so passionately before?

'Oh, Audrey. Don't be silly.'

But Stanley, it's true! You are a very sensual man. Gentle yet assertive. Almost feminine in your emotional sincerity, yet at the same time ruggedly masculine. I wonder, would you like to do me in the bum?

'Audrey! I'm shocked. And also a little embarrassed. I've never done that before.'

Then would you do me the honour of allowing me to be your first?

'OK, Audrey. OK. I'll do you in the bum.'

I get off the bus in Shoreditch and make my meeting with Frank with ten minutes to spare.

As I'm waiting, I think about Frank's astonishing, enviable self-assurance, and I wonder where it comes from. Probably from the fact that he is one of those self-made swine who worked his way up from abject poverty to uncommon wealth. This gives him an air of invulnerability, like nothing can be worse than where he came from, so he has no fear.

In his twenties, Frank was in banking, working his way up to management before he got bored and moved on. 'When I first started out in banks,' he told me during our first meeting, 'it was different. Banks *were* banks in those days, and customers were terrified of them. Then it all went soft and people realised they had rights and dignity.' He spat the last word out like a fishbone that had been trying to choke him.

For Frank, technology is the new finance, and therefore the new religion, still fresh enough, and powerful enough, to be feared by the ignorant. So now he's a partner in a new-media company, where he describes himself as a digital guru, only when he says 'guru', he says it like Marc Bolan, so that it chimes not with 'voodoo', but with 'kazoo'.

The man has balls of reinforced concrete. Also, surprisingly, he's late.

In the end I wait for forty minutes, leave a couple of messages, then give up on Frank and go home.

I feel good. Especially good that apparently I didn't need him after all. It occurs to me briefly that he planned the whole thing. The traffic jam, the drunk, the loon with the stone. I see him snapping orders into a walkie-talkie. 'OK, let the traffic flow, boys. Free up the streets. Good job.'

Good old Frank.

Now. What's next?

Ah, yes, of course.

More love, please.

CHAPTER TWENTY-TWO

SPEED DATING: OUR TIME IS RUNNING OUT

I am on heat. I have become transformed. I am a giant pulsating testicle. Sixteen stone of stagnant sticky manwash enclosed in a diaphanous sheath of sweat, hair, and cellulite. One wrong rub and I could snap, crackle, and pop, splashing my spicy clam right in your eye.

Action then, required.

Persuading Keith is actually much easier than I thought it would be. At first he's like, 'What am I, desperate?' and I'm like, 'Duh.' But then I use psychology on him. I say, 'Although you might not be desperate, Keith, at least one or two of the young ladies there will be, and if you play your cards right, and pretend that you can give them what they need, you'll most likely be able to trick your way inside them and damage them for ever, you vile misogynist.'

He gives this some thought. 'OK,' he says.

I tut loudly. Men are monsters.

But women. Aaaaah. There's the rub.

So I still haven't figured out whether speed dating is a wonderful, ingenious idea with the power to transform lives and create wonderful relationships, or something profoundly inhumane, pretty much on a par with deep-frying kittens. In the end, I guess it depends on the person sitting opposite. But even if you luck out and meet someone you can actually get along with, it's still basically costly torture, with an outside chance of something life-altering developing amidst the pain and humiliation. Or do I exaggerate?

I'm still not sure.

The speed-dating event I attend is on the other side of London and isn't, strictly speaking, 'speed dating'. Old-school speed dating, you were in and out, bish, bash, bo— next! Three minutes max to make your mark and work your magic. Tonight we have ten to fifteen minutes. Fifteen if it's going well. Ten if it's a bit ... next!

As we stand at the bar waiting for the first round of dates to begin, I must admit I am very, very grateful that Keith is here with me. If I were here on my own, I'd be bilious with nerves. As it is, I'm just slightly gassy. So as I stand here, trying to surreptitiously swallow another mouth fart, the woman running the evening – perma-tanned and barely able to speak for smiles – explains to everyone how it's going to work.

There are ten women and ten men, which means ten dates each in two and a half hours, with the women assigned their own table and the men moving from date to date like giant, knicker-sniffing wasps. It sounds like quite an ordeal, really, and basically a production line, with the males slowly paraded in front of the females like incomplete consumer durables, holding up their shoddy personalities to the light of quality control, trotting out their stories and their questions and their jokes like tramps emptying their pockets looking for pound coins they know they've already spent. It is a seduction line.

I pop a mint in my mouth, fix my name tag to my lapel and promptly faint.

I don't really faint. Sorry. I've never fainted. Instead I do what I am told, follow the organiser's pointing finger and sit myself down opposite date number one, Gloria.

Gloria doesn't look like a Gloria. Gloria looks more like a Mildred. But appearances can be deceptive, I know, I know.

Gloria has small features: narrow eyes and a tiny pinched mouth which, in my presence at least, refuses to unpinch itself. She has short brown hair and a thin, skeletal face. She looks like she hates me, frankly. But she can't. Surely. Not yet.

Even though I have rehearsed most of what I end up saying to Gloria – or I have at least imagined myself saying it – I am still rather surprised, in all honesty, to hear it coming out of my mouth.

'So, Gloria, tell me, have you ever seen thousands of tiny turtles scampering across a mighty beach on a moonlit night?' This is my opener.

Her expression doesn't falter. The cat's rectum of her mouth opens slightly, however, to release the words, 'I'm sorry?'

'You know, like when thousands of turtles all lay their eggs in the sand. In South America maybe. Then one night, when the moon is bright and high, all the eggs, millions of them, all hatch at once and all these baby turtles start scampering towards the sea. You must have seen it on *The Living Earth* or something. Have you never seen that?'

'What are you talking about?' Gloria is shaking her head as she speaks. 'Why are you asking me about that?'

Wow.

So this is speed dating. I cringe. My cheeks turn cold. I feel sad. 'I dunno, I ...' I shrug. 'I guess I like turtles. No reason other than that. Are you not a fan?'

She shrugs right back at me and curls a single nostril. 'Not really, no.'

'Oh.'

'So what do you do?' she asks, out of nought but contemptuous obligation.

'I'm a pole-vaulter,' I say. I can't help myself. I'm actually quite upset that my turtle opener has fallen on such wilfully deaf ears.

Gloria stares at me with an expression that says, 'So, not only are you ugly, but you're also an absolute fucking idiot.'

'And you?' I say.

'I work in investment banking,' she says. 'I'm a trust-fund manager.'

I laugh. 'Wicked,' I say. 'That's really brilliant. So tell me, Gloria, do you like bats?'

Her face contracts, reminding me, ironically enough, of a startled turtle disappearing into its shell. 'What are you saying? Are you trying to be funny?'

'No!' I cry. I'm not. 'We're here to meet people, to get to know them. I'm trying to get to know you, Gloria. Trying to find out what you like. Trying to find out, specifically, if you like bats. It's not that odd, surely.'

'Yes,' she cries, exasperated. 'It is. What have bats got to do with anything?'

'OK, OK, I'm sorry.' I hold out my hands, palms open and facing out, somewhere between us. 'We've not got off to the best of starts, I think that's safe to say. Probably that's down to the sexual tension between us ...'

I smile, amusing myself enormously. Gloria's mouth falls open like a broken trap. 'I can assure you there is no such thing between us.'

I swear, this woman has absolutely no sense of humour.

'Denial,' I say. 'The second of the first five stages of attraction. It goes like this ...' I count them out on my fingers. 'Fascination, denial, arousal, intercourse, repulsion.'

And that, seemingly, is that. We are only about five minutes into our date and Gloria has had enough. She pushes back her chair noisily, stands up and marches out of the room. I assume at first she's just gone to the loo or some such and will be back in time for her next date, but I realise later – when she doesn't return – that she's gone for good.

I am flabbergasted. And frozen with embarrassment.

I wonder if I've set some kind of record.

I wonder if Gloria has been speed dating before. I imagine not. I wonder if she'll ever go again. I can't see it. I imagine her telling her friends about the freakish mentalist whose idea of seduction was to ramble on and on and on about bats and turtles and pole-vaulting till she had no other option but to storm from the room in an almighty strop. I wonder if one of the other men in the room is her ideal partner, and because of my refusal to have a proper conversation, they will never, ever meet.

I think about this as I sit there, at an empty table, with every other woman in the room trying not to think about the fact that very soon they too will have to spend at least ten minutes with the big ugly freak who – within minutes – has women running screaming from the building. (She wasn't actually screaming.) (And for what it's worth, I am convinced there was more going on beyond Gloria's seeming irritation with my conversational skills. More likely that I was the unfortunate straw on the sagging back of a very tired camel. Surely.)

At which point I briefly consider getting up and leaving myself, but then, with something of a shock, I realise that I have no intention of leaving because, against all expectations, I am actually enjoying myself, and very much looking forward to my next date.

Cindy is actually Lucinda, a posh girl with high, cherry tomato cheeks and bright blue eyes which are sweetly beady. Cindy is so far out of my league that she is actually playing a different sport. Happily, that doesn't matter, because for the time being we are both playing on the same field. Sadly – if I may extend the metaphor till it splinters like a butterscotch hymen in a flux capacitor – I have a set of darts and a catcher's mitt; Cindy has a speedboat and a light sabre.

She also has a spicy blond bob and tiny white teeth which she covers with her right hand whenever she laughs.

'Hi,' says Lucinda, pumping my hand like a lumberjack. 'How are you?'

'Well if you want to know the truth,' I reply, 'I'm a tad hacked off. I don't know if you noticed, but my first date turned a little sour.'

Lucinda doesn't know whether to admit that she noticed or pretend that she hadn't, so instead, she opens her eyes wide and draws her bottom lip into her mouth. It is quite an effect, and I take it as a sign for me to continue. So I continue. 'I don't know what it was,' I say, 'but I think it was because she was a little intimidated by my looks.'

At this stage I should probably mention that, before we left the house, Keith and I shared a bottle and a half of excellent red wine. Kind of pathetic, I know, inasmuch as it was rather cowardly of us, but it's really, really helping.

'You're not bad-looking yourself,' I continue. 'You must have had the same thing once in a while. People get jealous, and they lash out. I guess they don't like to be made to seem inferior.' Cindy is still sucking on her bottom lip, seemingly unsure as to whether to laugh or to run screaming from the room herself. Which I realise would be rather amusing. I tell her so. 'It would be very funny if you left too now,' I say. 'Just got up and walked out like the first one. Go on, I dare you. It would be hilarious.'

'No, I'm all right,' she says. 'I think I can handle your good looks.' I give her a look which is meant to suggest that *many* a woman has made that fatal assumption, but it's probably just more of a leer. 'So what do you do?' she says.

'I'm a pole-vaulter,' I say. If it ain't broke ...

She has a lovely laugh, Lucinda, like cow bells in a wind tunnel, and when she finally lets rip with it, it is a great relief.

'You cover your mouth when you laugh,' I say, rather unnecessarily. Then I realise ... was that a *neg*? Was I gaming this woman? Good Lord, I'm smooth. 'I'm a copywriter really,' I say, 'although not in an interesting way. I've written the copy for websites for both trade unions *and* chartered accountants. My life is that exciting. What about you?'

'I'm a tree surgeon,' says Cindy.

Then it is my turn to laugh. I also cover my mouth, just to make her feel at home. 'But you had to give it up 'cause you couldn't stand the sight of sap, right? Is that what happened?'

The hand comes up again, like clockwork. 'No, honest, I really am. I work for the Tree Council.'

'Get out of it,' I say. 'What Tree Council?' I really think she's making it up, but apparently not. 'That's pretty cool,' I guess. 'What do you think about bats then? You must like bats?'

'I love bats!' she says. 'I even went on a bat walk a couple of months ago.'

'You never did!'

'I did!'

And so Cindy and I talk about bats for a while. And then we talk about speed dating. She asks me if I've done it before. Then she asks me why I'm doing it. 'Well,' I say, 'believe it or not, I don't meet people well.' That's a line from *Adaptation*, which I've always wanted to use.

'What do you mean?' she asks.

'Oh. I guess I mean that I'm a big ugly bugger with a fairly unpleasant physical presence and women are generally discouraged by this.'

'Oh, come on,' says Cindy.

'Oh, come on yourself,' I say. 'You know it's true. Anyway, the reason I'm here is not necessarily to find a girlfriend, although that would be ideal, but more just to force myself into these situations. You know? Because I refuse to hide away any more.'

'Well, good for you,' she says. 'I think that's really admirable.'

'Me too,' I say. 'Here's to me.' And we drink to me. Then – a sign that I am actually quite tipsy – I tell her about the blog.

'Oooh, will I be in it?' she wants to know.

'Maybe,' I say. 'If you play your cards right.'

Then she asks me what it's called and I say that, if I tell her, I will then have to torture and kill her, which I think kind of frightens her a tiny bit. So I give her a winning smile. And suddenly it's time to move on.

Meena is a slightly stuck-up PR girl who tells me that if she doesn't find a bloke tonight, she's going to become a lesbian; Kath works with Meena. She has ratlike features, prominent gums, and an unhealthy obsession with the football player Kaká – how I chortle; Clare likes George Clooney (yawn) and vodka and Red Bull. She also works with Kath and Meena and seems a little upset when I suggest that she might end up spending the night in a lesbian threesome; Meg looks like the actress Emily Lloyd and insists that I should be on television but can't quite put her finger on why, or in what capacity; Jane likes short men with 'really shit-hot bodies' and wants to know all about my eczema. She has a face like a tapir.

Then there's Tilly.

Tilly is very tall and very bottle-blonde. She has a certain superciliousness around the eyes; a certain disdain. I guess that a lot of people who go speed dating feel very strongly that they shouldn't be there and therefore feel superior to all those other *losers*. I further suspect that most of the people who feel this way have the good sense and even the decency to try and hide it. Not so Tilly.

Tilly reminds me of Patsy from *Absolutely Fabulous*, and not just physically. She also has the sneer off to a T and is absolutely overflowing with hideous, hateful self-absorption. It doesn't surprise me one iota to discover that Tilly works in television. She is a presenter on a certain type of – to my mind – fairly odious TV programme. Let's call it 'fact porn', which doesn't actually give too much away. And let's leave it at that.

Tilly is the kind of person – in my most humble opinion – who has a very fixed idea of what she wants from a person, what she requires, and if it's clear to her that you don't fit any of those criteria, then not only will she have no time for you, but also, she'll have no problem making that abundantly clear.

Awkward silence descends for the first time in the evening. I interrupt with the words, 'Well, this is going well, isn't it?', to which Tilly replies, 'Not really, no.' Which I think is a little unnecessary, frankly. Then, having no idea how to respond to that outside of something equally unpleasant, I laugh. It is a high-pitched, staccato, cartoon-character laugh, and completely inappropriate. Tilly looks at me like giant toads have just started pouring from my open mouth, then with the words, 'Actually, I have to make a call,' she gets up and meanders over to the bar. Splendid. That's Speed-dating Desertion Number Two.

The cow.

Next up is Atiya, who is kind of exotic looking. Half Mauritian, half Danish, she is dark and sultry, with an amazing complexion and a wonderful chest, but also, there is something around the eyes that makes her look ever so slightly like a gigantic simpleton. Actually, maybe if I hadn't spoken to her, I would have interpreted this as a beatific openness, a delightful childlike fascination. But I am speaking to her. And she is a simpleton.

Atiya believes in fairies. And as far as I can make out, in Jiminy Cricket. At first I imagine she is joking. But she isn't. She's insane.

Atiya cites her heroes as Aleister Crowley, Kenneth Anger, Walt Disney, and Louise Brooks. Running, rather elegantly, up the vein of her left forearm are tattooed the words, 'Love is the law'. Meanwhile, her right forearm reads, 'Love under will'. Apparently, running down her spine rather like – one imagines – an army of Satanic ants, are the words, 'Do what thou wilt shall be the whole of the Law'. These are apparently slogans coined by Aleister Crowley, the erstwhile Wickedest Man in the World.

Unfortunately, the dark arts are not the only arts in which Atiya is interested. She also makes films and jewellery, both of which – in her search for a soulmate, which is what the speed dating is all about – she enjoys talking about a great deal.

She shows me a film she's made. It's on her mobile phone, which she roots around for and eventually extracts from the huge Mary Poppins-like bag she keeps on her lap. It is slightly difficult to make out exactly what's going on in the film, but Atiya seems to be dressed as Alice, moving slowly through a room which is decorated with hundreds of pairs of latex gloves hanging from the ceiling. She moves through this ridiculous environment the way one might move through an enchanted cave, regularly holding up her hands in exaggerated, horribly acted awe. What makes it even sillier is the fact that attached to each of her fingers is a foot-long fake fingernail.

'You see my nails?' she asks excitedly.

'Oh, is that what they are? I wasn't really ...'

'They are twelve inches long,' she explains.

'Are they *really*?' I say. 'Well I never.' And when the film is done – I watch about thirty seconds of it – I ask her, 'So what does it mean?'

This seems to puzzle her. 'It's whatever you want it to be,' she says. 'It's just life. It's everything!'

'OK,' I say. 'I see.' Then her head disappears briefly back inside her bag.

'Look at my earrings,' she says, resurfacing. 'I'll show you.'

I laugh. 'OK,' I say. 'Come on, own up. You're having a laugh, right? You're doing some kind of social experiment maybe. Or you have a column somewhere. Come on, you can tell me.'

She gives me her delighted simpleton face. 'Life is a social experiment!' she cries.

'Oh, don't give me that,' I say. 'You can't possibly be real.'

Then she laughs and claps her hands together like a homosexual man. 'I'm not!' she trills. 'Nothing is real!'

'Oh, God,' I say. 'OK.' I nod.

The earrings she's holding up are extremely realistic representations of used condoms. I have no idea how she made them, but as I say, they are very realistic. Right down to the teaspoonful of white liquid in the ends of each one.

'What is that?' I ask. 'The white stuff.'

'What do you think?' she replies, beaming at me, so proud.

I just shake my head. 'No, come on,' I say. 'You're scaring me now.'

She laughs. 'It is!' she cries. 'It's real sperm!'

She holds the condoms up to her ears. 'Wow,' I say. 'You're like the porno version of *The Girl With A Pearl Earring*. You're The Girl With The Pearl-Necklace Earrings.'

I look around the room again. A couple of the other couples are looking on, smirking and enjoying themselves. Atiya is the perfect conversation piece. I even think that maybe she's been laid on by the organisers. Maybe she's there every week, just to keep things lively.

Just as our date is coming to an end, Atiya takes a red transparent sweet-wrapper from her bag and holds it up to the lamplight at the side of the room. She then proceeds to look through it like a child gazing into a kaleidoscope, turning it slowly to the left and to the right. 'This is really amazing,' she says. 'Here.' She hands me the wrapper. I stare at her for a while, waiting for her to laugh. In fact, I stare at her as if giant toads had just started pouring from her open mouth. 'Try it,' she insists. 'The world looks so different this way.'

I try it. I hold the sweet wrapper to my face and look through it. I remind myself that Jeremy Beadle is dead, so it's unlikely I'm being filmed for bad television. But where did Tilly get to? Maybe, in Beadle's absence, Tilly's got a hand in it ...

'Wow,' I say. 'Do you think this is how fairies see the world?' I ask.

'Yes!!!' she cries, clapping her hands together three times, as if to summon one.

And that, more or less, is that.

Odd. Really, really odd.

And I could be wrong here – I could be very very very wrong – but there is something in the way she looks at me at the end of our date ... I reckon – as I say, I could be wrong – but I reckon she'd definitely do me. But the fact is, desperate though I may be to bury my face in the nether regions of a beautiful woman, or indeed any woman, it would feel too much like taking advantage of a mental patient. And, besides that, I probably am wrong.

Finally, we move to Melanie.

Melanie is what my somewhat racist landlord would term 'a half-caste'. She is what Keith, particularly when stoned, would call 'a caramel honey'. Apart from a voluptuousness which makes my fingers twitch with desire, Melanie is fairly nondescript in that way that beautiful people can be. You know, perfect eyes, perfect mouth, perfect everything. Adorable. Breathtaking. Like a tropical sunset. With slightly chubby trees waving in the foreground.

Melanie is my final date, and – as I've been glancing over at her every once in a while during the changeovers all evening – she is the one I've been most looking forward to. I sit opposite her at 10.45 p.m.

The first thing she does is to read my name aloud from my badge. Then she shakes my hand and says, 'I don't know about you but if I have to explain what I do one more time tonight, I think I might have to scream.'

'I know what you mean,' I say. 'I tell you what then, how about, instead of the usual chit-chat paddywhack, I just tell you a story?'

And I swear, her eyes light up.

'That sounds great,' she says. 'That sounds perfect. I love stories.'

So, after first ascertaining that she is sitting comfortably, I begin.

'Once upon a time there was a little boy called Edgar Godsick. Edgar was born in a time of great sadness in the middle of a long, dark winter in the north of England. What made matters even worse was that Edgar was born with two heads.'

Melanie laughs. Then she says, 'Awww, poor Edgar.'

'I know,' I agree. 'Imagine that …

'At first, his parents were shocked and afraid, and they made Edgar sleep in a drawer. Then after a couple of weeks, when Edgar's second head didn't look like going anywhere, they grew angry. They seemed to blame Edgar for his congenital singularity. "Why can't you have one head like everyone else, you little monster?" they screamed at him. But Edgar didn't understand. He just looked up at his parents with his little brows furrowed, one set of eyes pointing at his mother, one at his father.

'Edgar's parents took their son to the doctor and said, "Our son is a two-headed freak. What are you going to do about it?" The doctor just smiled, although he wasn't happy, and he said, "Well, what would you like me to do about it?" Exasperated, Edgar's parents replied, "Why, cut off one of his heads, of course!" The doctor looked at Edgar's parents quizzically. "But if we cut off one of his heads, your son will die. And you don't want that, do you?" Edgar's parents looked at one another but said nothing. "Look," said the doctor. "Edgar seems perfectly happy with his two heads. And he's perfectly healthy, so why not try just accepting his extra head and learn to love him anyway? Maybe you could even love him that little bit extra because of his extra head? After all, he's practically twins." The doctor smiled. "What do you think?" he said. "I know your son's second head is a tad unusual, but it's not the end of the world. And they do say that two heads are better than one. Don't they? Eh?" He smiled again. Edgar's parents did not smile back. In fact, they scowled, affronted by this imbecile's levity. "Fine," they said. "Well, if you won't help us, we'll just have to help ourselves." And off they went.

'That night at home, Edgar couldn't sleep. He was hungry. Like most babies, when he was hungry and couldn't sleep, Edgar cried. Unlike most babies, of course, Edgar had two mouths, so when he cried, he was twice as loud. Before very long, Edgar's mother stormed into his room, shouting at her husband to get out of bed and help.

'The thought of Edgar's freakish heads clamped to her breasts made Edgar's mother feel physically ill. So she stopped his noise with plastic bottles stuffed roughly in his bawling gobs. Ten minutes later and Edgar was sound asleep.

'As he lay there, sleeping, his parents stood over him, shaking their heads and fists. "Why did it happen to us?" asked his mother. "What did we do to deserve such an aberration, such a crime against nature?"

'"We mustn't blame ourselves," said Edgar's father. "It's just bad luck."

'Edgar's mother closed her eyes. "Well, I can't live like this," she said. "I can't." And so saying, she marched out of her son's bedroom and into the kitchen, returning seconds later with a large breadknife.

'Her husband's mouth fell open. "You can't," he gasped. "He's just a baby."

'"No, he's not," Edgar's mother snapped. "Babies don't have two heads. He's a freak. He's an animal. The world will be a better place without him." And with that she moved closer to Edgar and raised the breadknife above his heads.

'"No," said Edgar's father. "I've got a better idea."

'Edgar's father then snatched up his son and wrapped him in a scratchy blanket. Placing the scratchy blanket on the back seat of his car, he then drove for four hours to an old church in the small, dark village where he had grown up. He knew the priest there was a good man and would take care of Edgar and give him the life that he deserved. Or else he would assume that Edgar had been sent by the Devil and he would kill him. Either way, Edgar's parents would be shot of him and they'd be free to return to their nice, normal lives.'

I stop.

Melanie wipes a little tear away from her eye, but I assume it is only a pretend tear. 'Poor little Edgar,' she says. 'It wasn't his fault he was born with two heads.'

'I know!' I cry, slightly over-excitedly. 'Life can be so cruel.'

'Did you make that up?' she asks.

I nod and blink.

'Not just there and then though?' she asks.

'No,' I have to admit. I tell her that I wrote the first chapter of the Edgar story some time ago, but that I've never told it to anyone before. She says she is honoured. I agree that she is.

'What happens next?' she wants to know. 'Do you know?'

'Not really,' I say. 'Well, I know that the priest is not very nice to him. You know what priests are like.'

Melanie scrunches up her face. 'Don't even go there,' she says.

'No,' I agree. 'Best not. Then I think he's rescued from the priest and taken round the country as part of a modern-day freak show. I see it as kind of a children's version of *The Elephant Man*.'

'Cool,' says Melanie. 'I like it. I really do.'

'I believe you,' I say, perhaps slightly smugly.

'Is it possible to be born with two heads though?'

'Yeah,' I say. 'Doesn't really matter though. It's just a story. But yeah, it happens now and then. But then there are all kinds of freaks in this world, aren't there? Take me, for example. I'm something of a freak myself.'

'Oh, come on,' she says. 'You're different, I'll give you that. But you've hardly got two heads.'

'No,' I concede. 'I suppose not.'

'Are you a writer then? Is that what you do?'

I tell her not really. But that I'd like to be. I tell her I'd love to write a children's book about a little boy with two heads. I tell her that it is my curse that, instead of writing children's books about boys with two heads, I have instead to write a bunch of corporate guff that no one ever really reads. And why would they?

'So are you trying to write other stuff?' she asks.

'I am,' I reply. 'I'm trying.'

'Good,' she says. And she nods. 'I like a man with ambition.'

Then we talk about books for a while, and simply because Melanie likes many of the same books that I do, I fall just a little bit in love with her. There and then. A short while later, I say: 'So what's your ambition, Melanie?'

'I want to save the world,' says Melanie. And a second later, Satan rings the bell that signifies that the last date of the evening is over.

I ignore it. 'And how do you plan to save the world, Melanie?' I find that I really enjoy using her name. It occurs to me that I might want to use it for ever. I am drunk. But sincere. Then I notice that her glass is empty, so I ask her if I can get her another drink, somehow realising as I do that our date really is over. I guess it's in her eyes.

'I'd like to,' she says, 'but I've really got to get going.'

'Oh, surely you can't leave it there,' I say, ever so slightly petulantly. 'The world needs to be saved, Melanie, and I need to know how it's going to happen. Please.'

Oh dear. I am begging. How unbecoming.

'I'm really sorry,' she says, and to her credit, she does look it. 'I promised one of the other guys I'd go on somewhere with him.'

I turn my head to follow Melanie's gaze to the bar. Please, God, I think instinctively, don't let it be Keith.

It isn't. Oh. Then I feel sorry that it isn't Keith. At least if it had been Keith, and he and Melanie started going out, I'd definitely see her again, and there'd always be the chance that when Keith fucked up, I could get involved on the rebound again.

Actually, I don't think any of that till much later.

'Aaaah,' I say, checking out the other bloke. 'He's quite a catch. Well done.' I sound bitter, and I hate myself for it. So I smile to try and counteract the bitterness, but it's a bitter smile, so it rather backfires.

'It's just a drink,' says Melanie. 'I honestly don't think it'll go anywhere, but he works for Amnesty, and I've got a soft spot for compassionate men.'

'Well, look,' I say, 'I hope it all goes really well and it was magnificent talking to you, it really was.' She reciprocates, which is nice. 'I think you're rather lovely as it goes,' I continue suavely, 'and if you ever want to continue the conversation, you should definitely give me a call.'

'Well, I'd need your number for that,' says Melanie.

'Well, you'd better take it,' I reply, and she takes out her mobile phone and keys in my details.

'Are you going to give me yours?' I ask.

'Nah,' she says. 'This way I get to retain all the power. Which is exactly how I like it.'

And with that, she stands up, gives me a peck on the elbow of my right temple and walks out of my life on the arm of another man.

CHAPTER TWENTY-THREE

BESTIAL OBLIVION

I'm standing in front of the Peruvian Semen Monkeys at London Zoo, and Melanie still hasn't called. Ange, meanwhile, calls me an arse biscuit. 'Do you honestly think that if you had sex with lots of people, you'd be happy?'

I raise an eyebrow, turn the corners of my mouth down and waggle my head from side to side. 'Maybe a bit,' I say.

'You're an idiot,' she says.

It's always an education, coming to the zoo. Today I'm learning a lot about Ange. I learn, for example, that she was only thirteen when she swallowed her first mouthful of male ejaculate. I make encouraging noises when I hear this, then, feeling noncey, I stop. 'That does seem a little on the young side,' I say. Ange points out that she didn't have sex till a month or so after that. 'Even so,' I say. 'Don't you wish you'd waited a little longer?'

'Yes and no,' says Ange.

'You were the Littlest Ho,' I say.

'Better that than wait till you're thirty,' she retorts, killing the conversation dead.

She asks me how Keith's getting on. 'Don't talk to me about that ... arse biscuit,' I say. Keith and I have fallen out over the speed dating. He said some mean things about Melanie. Namely that she was boring, and full of herself. I told him that a real friend would never talk that way about the woman I intended to marry.

'Hypocrite,' he spat.

I had said some mean things about Tilly, whom Keith has started dating.

'He's got a new girlfriend,' I tell Ange. I describe her as a six-foot oven chip in a blonde wig. 'I think he's going to fall in love with her, just to spite me.' Then I'll have to lie awake at night listening to them humping, while I weep and pine for Melanie, torturing myself with images of her hungrily lapping at Amnesty Man's philanthropic cock as he reads out a list of political prisoners he's helped emancipate. Jesus, what chance did I have against that? Next time I go speed dating, I go armed with stories of handicapped children and the sweaters I knit for Ukrainian orphans. No more dumb-ass two-headed-baby bullshit.

'I've got chlamydia,' says Ange, round by the giraffes. Instinctively I call her a bad, bad girl. I don't know why. It just comes out of me. I waggle my finger in her pretty, cum-hungry face and say: 'As ye reap, so shall ye sow, my girl.'

Ange, to her credit, tells me to go fuck myself, before adding, 'And it's the other way around, you dickhead.'

In reality, I don't think Ange is a bad girl at all. A little careless perhaps, but not bad, and she's certainly done nothing to be ash—

'I'm not fucking ashamed!' she spits. 'I'm pissed off.'

A silence descends. I feel bad. I think Ange is great. I wish I had chlamydia.

'Those giraffes are eavesdropping on us,' I tell her. There are two of them. They are eating leaves lugubriously, very close by.

'They're too far away,' she says.

'Well, this is where you're wrong,' I tell her, a sudden spring in my step. 'This is the fantastic thing about giraffes! Everyone focuses on the necks, but they actually have the most powerful ears in the whole of the animal kingdom.'

'You know a lot about giraffes, do you?'

'I know a lot about all the animals!' I declare. 'I used to work here at the Zoo of London many years ago. Did I never tell you that?'

'You didn't mention it, no,' says Ange, playing along with what she knows – or *thinks* she knows – is a lie. (It is a lie.)

'Well, there you go, we're both learning a lot today. I'll tell you another interesting thing about giraffes. Giraffes regularly indulge in all-male sex orgies.' I nod knowledgeably. 'Giraffes,' I repeat, 'are *so* gay.'

'Yeah, tell me something I don't know,' says Ange.

'The female iguana has retractile spines on the inner wall of her vagina, with which she is able to pierce her partner's member and hold him in place long after he has ejaculated. Why she has evolved this ability is not known, although zoologists suspect that it is an attempt to instil in the male a sense of paternal responsibility.'

I ask Ange how her dad's getting on without his wife.

'Not great,' she says. 'He doesn't really know how to do anything. Mum did everything for him.' She shrugs. 'But I guess he'll have to learn, right? Otherwise he'll die too.'

'Of course,' I agree. 'He just needs time to adapt, that's all. I'm sure he'll be fine.'

We're on our way to check out the monkeys. 'How's your dad?' asks Ange.

'I don't really know,' I tell her. 'I haven't seen him since his breakdown.' Ange pulls a face like she doesn't approve but she's trying not to show it. I tell her I've been thinking about him a lot recently though. This is probably due as much to Ange's mum dying as it is to Keith's health scares. I've been thinking I should make an effort to see him, and reconcile with him, before I wake up one morning to a letter coldly informing me that he's dead.

I last saw him when he lost his mind and repeatedly tried to kill himself. I went to see him in hospital and he didn't know who I was. However, I haven't seen him since they zapped his brain with electricity on the off chance that it would start working properly again. And I know that, if he dies now, without me giving him and his new brain one final chance, I'll just feel guilty for ever. And that will *suck*. Whereas if I go to see him, and he's wretched to me, then I'll know: a leopard never changes its spots.

Keith's dad went to see him, soon after he'd had the shock treatment, more or less on my behalf, and he told me that he'd asked after me. I didn't believe him at first, but he insisted that my father had asked how I was. I was surprised, but I decided that I didn't want to know. I decided I didn't care.

I don't care, but maybe it's about time. It is. It's about time.

Ange approves. 'I saw my mum all the time, but when she died,' she says, 'I still regret not spending more time with her.'

'Yeah, but you liked your mum.'

We are outside the gorilla enclosure. I hate gorillas. They've got this big thing about being 'almost human', like that's something to be proud of. Like there's something intrinsically noble about humanity. Don't strive for humanity, you ignorant monkey, strive for bestiality. Nobody questions the humble beast. He does what his instinct decrees, oblivious, doing whatever he chooses with savage dignity and perfect immunity from all judgement.

'It's just Nature's Way,' they'll say, no matter what he does.

I say to Ange, 'Although gorillas are mostly monogamous, they only actually mate once every seventy years. The rest of the time they just sit around spitting poison into one another's eyes and being horribly unpleasant to their offspring.'

Ange has had two abortions. When I ask her for details she just dismisses them as mistakes with men in whom she had no interest, but she also is at pains to point out that she does not want children, 'under any circumstances'.

She says she thinks she is too selfish for motherhood. She doesn't think she has it in her.

'I'm not a very good girlfriend,' she told me months ago. 'I'm a good fuck.' I nodded hopefully. 'I really don't get off on being in a relationship,' she went on. 'I like my independence. And I like my friends. And I don't want kids. I just happen to have a very high sex drive.'

By the time Ange left school, she'd worked her way through five boyfriends. I was at home experimenting with gloves and kittens, she was in her boyfriends' cars, all fingers and thumbs.

We are different people, Ange and me. Different animals. And I remain enormously envious of her. She possesses abilities I do not possess. Sex abilities. And I wish she would teach them to me. I'm tempted to ask her, but I'm afraid she'll just assume I'm trying to trick her into having sex with me. I ask her anyway. 'Would you teach me about sex?' I ask her. 'How to do it, how to *be* it, how to be *sexy*. Teach me what you know,' I say. 'Show me how everything works, what works best, all the little tricks. Whatever.' But she just assumes I'm trying to trick her into having sex with me. 'What do you mean, *tell* you or *show* you?' she asks suspiciously. '*Show* me,' I reply. 'Get naked and show me. Sally showed me some but I need *more*, Ange. Teach me, Ange! Teach me your sex secrets, Ange! Show me love!'

Ange is a really, really wonderful creature. I'm still rather a lot in love with her, if the truth be told, and I think I always will be. I'm certain it's healthy though, so that's good.

'I'm not so sure our relationship is healthy,' she tells me.

'Oh, what do *you* know,' I snap.

'The Peruvian Semen Monkey is so-called because of the male's astonishing capacity for producing and disseminating three times its own body weight in sperm in a single day.'

I look at cum-hungry Ange, the Littlest Ho-Bag. She is salivating.

We laugh. We'd make such a lovely couple.

The next day I read the following comment on my blog: 'Stop wanking and get yourself a woman.'

Touché.

CHAPTER TWENTY-FOUR

FUCK BUDDIES

This was Morag's opener:

I've read your blog from start to finish and I think you should probably come to Brighton and bugger me.

It came in an email. She continued:

I think we have a lot in common. You're bright and funny and can write well; I'm bright and funny (and modest) and can write well. You've got a very large penis, or so you claim; I've got a very large vagina, or so my ex who shall remain nameless claims. You have a weight problem and physical appearance issues; I – according to my ex who shall remain nameless – would also benefit from dropping a few pounds and having a couple of moles removed. You're looking for someone to love, or at least have bumsex with; I'm looking for someone to love, or at least have bumsex with. You see? It's almost like it's in the stars.

I had to agree. It was eerie. It was like Derren Brown was sharing our virtual space, squatting on our fat pipe with both of our names written on a playing card in his back pocket. But I had my reservations. It wasn't just the fact that a complete stranger was approaching me and asking me to do her up the bum. It was also the fact that she kept mentioning her ex. Nameless or not, it sounded ominous. Like there were still feelings.

But, of course, I emailed back. And before long we were chatting on instant messenger.

This was about three weeks ago now.

At the beginning of last week, she suggested that we meet. 'What about Wednesday?' she asked. 'Is there a tiny window in your busy programme of self-abuse?' I admitted that I was a bit nervous at the thought. Morag called me 'a big Jessie' and said, 'Where's your sense of adventure?' She reminded me that life is short.

She was right of course. We had been talking late into the night every night for over a week. We got on really well. It was time to meet up. The fact that we still hadn't seen each other's face was, as Morag put it, 'all part of the adventure'. Even when I offered to swap photos, she refused. She said that if either of us was repulsed, then we could just have a drink or two and call it a night. Or we could become friends. 'You can never have too many friends,' she said.

Morag is Scottish. She was born in Glasgow. She's twenty-six years old and works part time in a cinema. *Bad Lieutenant* is her favourite movie of all time, and her parents are separated. Her father lives in Edinburgh with a new wife and three new sons, and Morag gets on with them all fine, but they don't really have that much in common. Her mother lives in London and writes historical novels, apparently with a fair degree of success. She doesn't get on so well with her. Morag is allergic to cats, but not to the point whereby she can resist touching them. She loves Gabriel García Márquez and has a thing about Magic Realism.

I knew all that. And I loved it. And I was eager to ask more. We were on instant messenger a lot. It's the modern way. 'You ask a lot of questions,' she typed.

'That's because I read somewhere that that's what women want.'

'So it's not because you're necessarily interested in the answers then?'

'No, I am, I am. Honest I am.'

'How fortuitous.'

'Isn't it?'

'Go on, then. Ask me some more.'

And so I did ...

Scat: Did you have any pets as a child?

Morag: Yes. I had four guinea pigs and a dog.

Scat: What were their names, please?

Morag: The guinea pigs were called Edmund, Baldrick, Percy, and Lord Melchett. The dog was called The Dark Lord Tiberius.

Scat: Nice names.

Morag: Thanks.

Scat: When you were shouting for the dog to stop chasing squirrels or stop humping the vicar's leg or whatever, did you say, 'The Dark Lord Tiberius! Stop that at once!'

Morag: He didn't chase squirrels. Squirrels were beneath him. He did hump the vicar's leg though. But we never tried to stop him. To answer your question, however, no. We called him 'Tibs'.

Scat: Awww ... Do you have any recurring dreams?

Morag: Um ... apart from the usual stuff about going to school with my muff out ...

Scat: Your capacious muff.

Morag: Hush now. I dream a lot about my ex-boyfriend, who shall remain nameless. He fucked me over in lots and lots of ways, and sadly, horribly, he has burrowed his way into my subconscious, where he will probably forever bubble to the surface in all of my worst nightmares.

Scat: I'm sorry to hear that. What's your favourite flavour of ice cream?

Morag: Rum and raisin.

Scat: What do you think of bats?

Morag: You've asked me that already. Don't you listen? They're all right. Nothing to write home about. I like vampires though.

Vampires are sexy.

Scat: *What's the most valuable thing you've ever stolen?*

Morag: *Um ... honestly, probably a car. I went through a troublesome phase in my teens. I didn't keep it though. I just drove it around for a bit then left it in a park. Actually, I stole a bus too. That's probably more expensive than a car.*

Scat: *You stole a bus?*

Morag: *Just a single-decker.*

Scat: *Ah, OK. What's the most unusual object you've ever had inside of you?*

Morag: *That is a freaky, borderline-scary question.*

Scat: *I've got to press you for an answer.*

Morag: *Um ... let me think. It depends on your definition of 'unusual' really.*

Scat: *I'm happy to go with your definition.*

Morag: *OK. Probably a bible.*

Scat: *What?*

Morag: *No, just kidding. I did once and for the briefest of periods have an action-man doll pretty much all the way inside of me, so that just his boots were peeping out.*

Scat: *Wow.*

Morag: *Impressive, huh?*

Scat: *Capacious.*

Morag: *Fuck off.*

Scat: *So. Do you believe in God?*

Morag: *Yes.*

Scat: *Oh.*

Morag: *God is Harvey Keitel.*

Scat: *Oh, OK. Thank God for that.*

Morag: *Thank Harvey.*

Scat: *Thanks, Harvey. Have you ever had a threesome?*

Morag: *Hmm.*

Scat: *Hmm is not an answer.*

Morag: *All right then, no.*

Scat: *You see, that wasn't so hard, was it?*

Morag: *But I have had a couple of foursomes.*

Scat: *Oh my.*

Morag: *Exactly.*

Scat: *Oh me, oh my.*

Morag: *I know, I know.*

Scat: *I'm simultaneously aroused and frightened.*

Morag: *That seems like a reasonable response. Ya big Jessie.*

Scat: *Thank you. We will talk about this in more detail at a future date. In the meantime, and finally, what's the most important thing in the world?*

Morag: *The most important thing in the world is Love.*

Scat: *Aaaaaaah. Thank you, Morag.*

Morag: *No, thank you. And I hope I've passed the audition.*

Then, last Wednesday, we met.

And for a short while, it was everything.

Disappointment is a terrible thing. I dread disappointment. It's bleak. It's dead hope.

So when I met Morag in Brighton, at the train station, and she curtseyed, shook my hand and kissed my cheek, I was happy. I was not disappointed.

And when a couple of drinks into our evening, I asked her if I could kiss her and she said yes, and then we kissed, I was happy. I was not disappointed.

And then when we proceeded to get a little bit drunk and to fumble our way into Morag's bed together, and then when we made love as best we could with our lack of knowledge about each other's bodies and the things which give us pleasure, I was happy. I was not disappointed.

But then, some time around 1 a.m., when Morag told me that she really liked me but didn't think that what we had on our hands was a long-term relationship, I was disappointed. So disappointed, in fact, that I had a little cry. Like a *bona fide* big Jessie.

The next morning we went for a walk on the beach and we talked about things. We kept it light. I came back to London that afternoon feeling elated and deflated in equal measure. I was still disappointed, but I regretted nothing.

The next night we spoke on IM and Morag said to me, 'What do you think of the concept of fuck buddies, as a concept?'

I had to say that, as a concept, I thought it was potentially a predominantly good one. I said so.

'Good,' said Morag. 'What are you doing tomorrow night?'

So I guess that the main difference between 'being in a long-term relationship' and 'being fuck buddies' concerns the level of emotional investment to which one is allowed to confess.

I have to say, there is something in me – something slightly old-fashioned perhaps – that baulks at the idea and feels that it's a kind of failure, a kind of settling for second best. And I don't like that. I don't think it shows either of us in a particularly complimentary light. But there is something else in me – something slightly desperate perhaps – that craves consensual physical contact under any circumstances, and that part of me shrugs, says 'Fuck it!' and dives in. Like an action man. Till just my boots are peeping out.

So there we have it.

I was looking for a love buddy. I found a fuck buddy. It's not ideal, but my God, it'll fucking do.

CHAPTER TWENTY-FIVE

ACT OF GOD

It's 7.25 a.m., and there is a loud noise at the front door. There are two men. One of them shouts something and raps sharply at the glass in the door.

Briefly wondering where I am, I jump up off the sofa, panic along the corridor and open the front door in my sleep-clothes: a pair of sweaty underpants and an oversized grey hoodie – one that was way too big for me even at Christmas, when I was four stone heavier. I open the front door to Keith's first-floor flat and see three men gathered below me by the open garden gate. One ratty-looking man with a beard and – for reasons I've still yet to work out – two policemen.

After the customary, and to my mind slightly offensive, double-take, the ratty one says: 'There he is. Bag in your drain, mate.'

I shake my head, bewildered. Am I perhaps still dreaming?

My first lucid thought, on seeing the police, is that there's been a stabbing. Or else one of the shops downstairs has been broken into. But then why would a strange, wiry man with a snout be telling me to *bag in my drain*? And what on earth can that possibly mean? Is he insulting me?

'Wake up, mate!' he yells, smiling, and both policemen chortle into their attack-proof vests. 'A plastic bag got caught in your drain. Out the back. Flooded the shop downstairs.' I'm still not quite getting it. He shakes his head in mock exasperation, playing up for the police. I must still be dreaming. 'Go check your back room, mate.'

Leaving the front door open, I wander to my bedroom feeling slightly shell-shocked.

I push open the door and my face collapses. My mouth falls open in the ruins.

Apparently, it's been raining. Heavily.

I walk slowly towards my computer, as if approaching the charred body of what may or may not be an elderly relative. Halfway across the room, my feet begin to squelch and hiss on the sodden carpet.

I remember that Keith is not at home. He is at Tilly's house, on the fashionable side of town. Hence my sleeping in the living room. When I'm home alone, that's where I lay my hat. That's my home. I set up camp on a pile of cushions on the sofa and I watch DVDs till I drift off at dawn.

Sleeping in the living room reminds me of Pablo.

Life is sad.

Usually, if I'm in the living room, I'd have my laptop in there with me, but because my useless spine was playing up, and on the back of a recent conversation about deskplace posture, I've been trying to restrict computer use to my desk.

My poor desk. Look at it. It looks like a desk on the *Titanic*.

My desk sits against the back wall of my bedroom, along with the head of my bed. Above the desk and the bed is a large sash window, which looks out directly on to the flat roof of the shop below. Although the shop is below the flat, the roof of the shop is actually about fifty centimetres higher than the bottom of my bedroom window. There's a slope. So if you want to climb on to the roof, you have to climb from the window frame, over the culvert – if that's what it is – and up a short concrete slope to the flat roof proper.

In order to avoid flooding, the culvert – if that's what it is – has a small drain for every room.

Unfortunately, at some stage during the night, the drain outside Keith's bedroom became blocked with rotting leaves and other ghastly *ichbar*, while the drain outside my bedroom became completely covered over with a rogue carrier bag.

My window is also open a few inches, which obviously didn't help stem the tide.

My laptop is also open, sitting there on the desk like a raped clam. It is drenched. I cry out. My new keyboard – two days old – is also ruined. I unplug everything – two lots of four-socket extension leads are sitting in inches of water – and I return to the front door.

The police are now next door talking to the little old lady, whose flat has also suffered a soaking. Meanwhile, the ratty guy – who is annoyingly chipper, I must say – is on his way out of the front gate. He smiles at me as he leaves and says, if I remember correctly, 'Don't let any more plastic bags on the roof.' I bristle at this, angry at the implication that I could have in some way averted this catastrophe. 'Nothing to do with me, mate,' I respond, but he's already gone.

I close the front door and return to the scene of the crime. (It certainly feels like a crime.)

When I unplug the various leads from my laptop, pick it up and hold it on its side, a pint of water pours out on to the floor. I don't know what to do. It's like it's bleeding.

I shake it gently till it's more or less stopped dripping. Then I dry it as best I can with a towel and take it into the living room, placing it open and upside down – like an open book, spine up – in a brief patch of mocking sunlight. Then I do the same with the keyboard, my old PC, a pile of books and magazines, DVDs and CDs, a bunch of various lovely bits of stationery, and all of my bedding and mattress.

Then I wipe down the walls and cover the floor with more towels. I then stamp on the towels like I'm pressing grapes, and as soon as they became soaked, I chuck them in the empty bath and replace them with more.

Leaving the bathroom, I catch sight of myself in the mirror. The first thing I notice, apart from the look of defeat smeared across my face, is that, hanging out of the flap of my boxer shorts is the fat end of a crispy piece of kitchen roll.

Ah. My face collapses. I suppose that may well have had something to do with the sniggering and double-taking.

I pull the kitchen roll out of my pants, wander back into my bedroom and throw it into the bin. Then I realise that there's a length of toilet paper in there too. Ah yes. I remember a lot of tossing and turning last night. I was very restive.

When I try to pull the toilet paper out of my pants, I realise that some of it is stuck to my johnson. So I pull off my pants and throw them in the wash basket. Then I stand there, picking at the scraps of bog roll that are clinging fast to the end of my old chap. It's only then that I notice a shadow has fallen across the room. I look up and see the ratty guy again, this time on the roof outside my window. He's crouching down, scraping up all the rubbish and old leaves into the offending plastic bag. He's looking directly at me. I just stare, till eventually he gives me a thumbs-up and moves on down the roof, chortling as he goes.

I continue staring long after he's gone.

My humiliation is complete.

Not only have I just been observed at my embarrassing worst, but also, and worse still, I have just realised that the plastic bag which was without doubt the motivating factor and major cause of the flooding, which had resulted in God knows how much damage to Keith's flat, the little old lady next door's flat, and the shop downstairs, did in fact belong to me. In fact, it was the Curry's bag in which I'd brought home the new keyboard at the weekend.

I am mortified.

I figure out what must have happened, all the while trying to convince myself that none of it was really my fault.

When my window is closed, it rattles something awful. Every time a car passes by outside, every time someone sighs upstairs, rattle rattle rattle. It is incredibly irritating. Thankfully, silencing it is merely a matter of wedging something between the two panes.

Usually I wedge a tissue in there, as there's always plenty of them lying around. On Saturday, however, I used a folded-up carrier bag. On Sunday I was sweaty so I opened the window. The bag, I now realise, must at that point have fallen out on to the roof and floated about pretentiously, as if it were in a film, just biding its sweet time. Then, some time in the very dead of Monday night, it struck, causing absolute maximum havoc.

So, I suppose, it could be argued – at a push – that the flooding, and the damage, was actually somehow, indirectly, my fault.

I wonder what kind of a state Keith's room is in. So I stop staring out at the empty roof and I pull on a clean pair of undies. (I make it a rule never to go into another man's bedroom with my balls bared.) Then, tentatively, I turn the handle on Keith's bedroom door, and I peep inside.

I breathe out.

It's fine.

I walk over to his window and peer through. The roof on his side of the flat is higher than mine, because the entire street is on a slope. All is well in Keith's room. I am very relieved. As I creep out of his room – I have no idea why I'm creeping; I guess I feel guilty – I notice a pair of handcuffs attached to his bedstead. I giggle like a four-year-old and run back to the mess of my life.

When I explain to Keith what has happened, and later when he sees it with his own eyes and smells it with his own nose, he is fairly sanguine about the whole thing. When I remark upon his sanguinity, he replies. 'It's not my flat. If it was, I'd break both your arms.'

He wouldn't do that though. He's not the violent kind.

Someone who knows about such things is looking at my laptop, but their prognosis is not good. The first thing they tell me is that I have to let it dry out for ten days. At least. After that, they reckon there's every chance it will still never work again and everything on it will be lost. The very fact that it's so totally and utterly saturated apparently bodes horribly unwell.

My laptop is three and a half years old and it has so much totally irreplaceable stuff on it that I still feel physically ill at the thought. As well as the photographs, some of which I will one day miss, there is writing. Lots of writing. This is what upsets me. There's a lot of stuff that could one day have been useful. Loads of notes I've made, blog posts I've half written, stuff about my parents, stuff about my childhood ... Loads of stuff. Nearly four years of stuff. Even longer, actually, as I'd written up a few older notebooks which I then tore up and tossed away.

And no, I haven't been backing up.

And no, I'm not insured.

I'm gutted is what I am.

I actually feel literally gutted. But obviously I'm not. I'm merely metaphorically gutted.

I mean, I know no one's actually died or anything, and I should probably just be thinking about something else already and getting on with my life, rewriting what I've lost if it was that important, and in time I'm sure I'll do that, but for now I'm utterly devastated and I really need to go and stand in a corner and think about what I've done.

I blog about what happened and I mention that I'll be offline for a couple of weeks, till September, by which time hopefully I'll have sorted out my old laptop or got hold of a new one.

In the meantime, the entire flat reeks of stagnant rainwater and smells like blue cheese.

Ugh.

My life stinks.

CHAPTER TWENTY-SIX

BOX OF FROGS

Life is like a box of frogs. You never know what you're going to get, but you can be pretty sure it's going to be another motherfucking frog. No, that is not what I meant at all. What I meant was that it's up and down, up and down always, exponential randomness all the way, and there's no predicting it, ever. Not subtle little changes of mood either, but quite violent jags of emotion and circumstance, like one long but distinctly finite concatenation of rhapsodies and doldrums, booms and slumps, woes, whoops, and weary fresh starts rising phoenix-like from every funk.

All of which is to say, I feel good. I feel like things are going in the right direction again.

I had a couple of sessions with an osteopath to address a sudden attack of really quite vicious lower-back pain. As well as cracking my spine like a thumb knuckle and sticking ridiculously long acupuncture needles in my back, he also advised me to do some exercise. So I joined a local gym and am happy to report that I'm thoroughly enjoying it. I don't think I'll ever be a fully fledged ab rat, with wires monitoring my heart rate and isotonic implants, but I do enjoy the ache in my muscles a day after I've pushed myself. I enjoy the feeling that my body is alive and is feeling something close to how it is meant to feel. My muscles were soggy before, practically coming apart, like wet bread. Now, after just a few visits to the gym, they are beginning to feel less soggy. I've still got heaps of fat all over me of course, but these things take time. Hopefully, half an hour on a bike three times a week and lots of swimming will chip away at that. It's good. It's going well. I feel better. Even better than I did when I was getting into the running, as now my whole body is beginning to thrum. There are other changes too. My weight is dropping again, my biceps are firming up nicely, and there is a tiny bit of definition appearing in my chest. You have to really squint to see it, but it's definitely there.

Frank says he can even see it through my shirt, but he is lying. He apologises for standing me up last time we had arranged to meet, but something had come up. An emergency at home coupled with a dead phone. Although it makes me feel ever so slightly guilty, I have to say I don't entirely believe him. I think Frank may be just a little bit irregular, mentally. 'I'm pleased for you,' he says. 'And I expect great things.' I just nod and smile like a simpleton.

Ange and Karen are also pleased for me. 'Let me feel your muscles,' says Karen. I hold up a doughy arm and attempt to flex it. She wraps her hands around my bingo wing and nods faux enthusiastically. 'It'll be great when it's done,' she says. I laugh, take the joke, try not to feel bad.

Ange feels bad. She says she doesn't know what she's doing with her life. 'You're teaching,' I remind her. 'Teaching kids how to … live. You love teaching.'

'So is that all I am? Just another fucking teacher?'

'Well, what do you want to be?' asks Karen.

Ange shrugs miserably and sighs. 'I just want to be less pre*dictable*,' she says.

'I knew you were going to say that,' I say, unhelpfully.

Keith is pleased too, although he's behaving so bizarrely recently that it's actually quite difficult to tell. Keith is up. This year's mortality shocks are probably the best things to have ever happened to him. His aneurysm, which shows no sign of erupting any time soon, and his MS, which aside from the occasional twitch and the odd thirty seconds of digital uselessness here and there, has drifted away as suddenly as it arrived, have left him lustful for life.

Consequently, he has thrown himself into this relationship with Tilly with a reckless passion which I personally feel she doesn't deserve. More importantly, he is also throwing himself into his art. He has turned his revenge blog over to drawing and painting, and within a couple of months, a San Diego literary magazine called *Grass Limb* has paid him a small bunch of US dollars to reprint some of his stuff. I am made up for him.

'So things are going well with Tilly then?' I ask. It's always a little tricky when we talk about Tilly.

'Very well,' he says. He's like me, Keith – probably a little like most other people too – in that he's extremely keen to fall in love. Whether his motivation is the same as mine and he desires to lose himself entirely in the process, I cannot say. But like me, he yearns, and like me, he probably tries a little too hard.

'I've been getting a bit lonely recently,' I confess. 'And jealous. And bitter. You know? I mean, the first sign of a girlfriend with a nice flat and you vanish, never to be seen again. What's that all about? Eh?'

'I know,' he says. 'I'm sorry. I've got no excuse.' He did an elaborate Gallic shrug. 'I'm a bit selfish, I guess. Let's do something when I get back from the Lakes,' he says. He's going to the Lakes. With Tilly. 'You'd be the same though,' he adds. 'If you ever got a proper girlfriend.'

'Maybe,' I say.

He asks me how things are with Morag. I tell him things are fine. But they're not really. The first rule of fuck buddying is apparently: Do Not Get Emotionally Involved, and frankly, I feel incapable of following that rule. My only hope is that Morag feels it too. Keith asks me if I think she does. I don't know. I tell him so. Morag and I have been seeing quite a bit of one another recently, and because we live in separate cities, the fuck tends to slide into more date-like, relationship-like territory, and because this is not supposed to happen, I like it all the more.

Morag too, is pleased about my muscles-to-be. We've just made love. Or rather, we've just fucked. We're fuck buddies. Fuck buddies fuck. Must remember that.

I know that this arrangement should be making me happier than it is, but the fact is I want more. I said so at the beginning, but Morag made it clear that this was never going to be more than no-strings sex for her. 'If you can't handle it,' she said, 'maybe we should just call it a day now.' I told her I could handle it. I can handle it. I am handling it. Of course I am. I'm a grown man. I own my emotions. I tell myself what to think. I tell myself not to fall in love, not to care too deeply for this woman. Instead I am learning how to fuck. And when she looks into my eyes and my whole body heats up and my heart expands and my skin contracts and my poor befuddled brain cries out 'I LOVE YOU!' ... I close my eyes or look away and just keep on fucking.

As we lie there in her gloriously big bed with its acres of duvet and wrought-iron stead, she says: 'I like the way you fuck me, Stan Cattermole.'

I glow. I feel complete. 'Do you really?'

'I really do,' she says. 'And I like your new arms,' she says, squeezing a negligible nascent bulge.

'You wait,' I tell her. 'Give me a couple of months, I'll be like Popeye.'

'Eww,' she says. 'Don't go too far, will you? You don't want to turn into one of those freaks with bodies like giant bubble-wrap.'

'No,' I tell her. 'I don't want that.'

I know what I do want though. What I want is Love, and when I mention this to Morag, the frogs come tumbling out of the box.

CHAPTER TWENTY-SEVEN

LOVE 2.0

Most of our not falling in love took place on Instant Messenger. I'm sure this would seem odd to the point of alien to our parents, but for we who live in a technological age, it's quite normal. Love is different these days. Hundreds of years ago, it must've been so very much harder. There was no broadband then. So unless you lived in the same town, you were at the mercy of painstaking penmanship, perfumed envelopes, and a positively heroic postal service. Now love is different. Whether there is distance involved or not, these days the making of non-physical love is instantaneous, and comes with plug-ins and emoticons and far too many exclamation marks, and the laughter that accompanies it, although allegedly loud, is seen but not heard. Even more shocking for the lexical Luddites among us, these days, very often, love lacks vowels. Call me old-fashioned if you will, but I think that love that lacks vowels will not last.

Happily, when Morag and I message, we are sticklers for good grammar. Sadly, we are not always sticklers for unambiguous communication ...

> **Morag:** *Have you ever been in love?*
> **Scat:** *I'm not really sure.*
> **Morag:** *If you're not sure, then you probably haven't.*
> *I know it's a bit of a cliché, but when it happens, you know.*
> *You know?*
> **Scat:** *Oh, I didn't realise it was that simple. In that case, yes.*

Yes, I have.

Morag: *Really?*

Scat: *Yes.*

Morag: *Who with?*

Scat: *Just some chick.*

Morag: *Stan.*

Scat: *Yes, babe?*

Morag: *Don't be a jerk.*

Scat: *I'm not really, I just ... OK, what do you want to know?*

Morag: *Well, what was her name?*

Scat: *Her name was Zuhal.*

Morag: *Zuhal?*

Scat: *Zuhal.*

Morag: *That's an unusual name.*

Scat: *She was an unusual girl.*

Morag: *Where did you meet her?*

Scat: *I met her at the candy store.*

No, just kidding.

I met her at Glastonbury a few summers ago. She was selling toffee apples to help disadvantaged kittens or somesuch.

I bought all of them.

Fifty toffee apples.

Then we went round the kiddies' area together giving them away to little children.

Morag: *Awww. That's lovely, Stan.*

Scat: *Oh God, I'm sorry. Please say you didn't believe me.*

Morag: *Oh you shit. Of course I believed you. Who would make up such a thing?*

Scat: *Oh come on, disadvantaged kittens?*

Morag: *I didn't necessarily believe that bit, but the rest seemed plausible.*

Scat: *Sorry.*

I actually met Zuhal on a film set. We were both extras on The Passion of the Christ.

Morag: *Oh COCK OFF!!!*

I'm never going to believe another word you say.

Scat: *Our first date was entirely in Latin.*

Morag: *Does she even exist at all in fact?*

Scat: *No.*

Sorry.

And I've never been to Glastonbury.

Morag: *Unbelievable.*

Scat: *Sorry.*

Morag: *So you haven't been in love then?*

Scat: *I think I have. I mean, I've suffered all the symptoms. I've vomited and wept and gone to sleep feeling completely obsessed with someone and woken up feeling completely obsessed with someone, but it's never necessarily been reciprocated.*

Basically if there's more to love than vomiting and pain, then no, I probably haven't.

Morag: *Aww.*

Scat: *What about you?*

Have you ever been in love?

Morag: *Yeah, twice I think.*

Scat: *When you've been in love, you don't think. You KNOW.*

Morag: *Oh yeah. Twice then.*

Scat: *Once with Ollie. And ...?*

Morag: *A guy called Duke.*

Scat: *Duke? Like Mussolini? Il Duce?*

Morag: *I guess.*

Scat: *Was he like Mussolini in other ways?*

Morag: *I don't know much about Mussolini, to be honest.*

Did Mussolini drive a Nissan Micra?

Scat: *Yes.*

Morag: *Did he have Celtic tattoos all over his arms and neck?*

Scat: *I believe he did, yes.*

Morag: *Then yes. He was very like Mussolini.*

Scat: *What was it you loved about Mussolini then?*

Morag: *I think it was more what he represented. He was much older than me and – potentially at least – much wiser. I was only seventeen when we started seeing each other, and we were together for, like, five years.*

Scat: *God, that's a long time.*

Morag: *Then I found out he was seeing not one other person, but about half a dozen other people most of the time we were together. He didn't treat me very well. But he was like an outlaw, you know?*

Scat: *In a Nissan Micra?*

Morag: *Yeah, he used to do graffiti. He wasn't very good actually, but he was brave. You would see his name in some very hard-to-get-to places.*

Scat: *Duke?*

Morag: *Yeah.*

Scat: *He sounds like a dick.*

Morag: *He was a dick. But for a while there, I loved him. I was consumed by him.*

Love is blind.

Scat: *I've always taken solace from that.*

Morag: *I love your back.*

Scat: *I'm sorry?*

Morag: *Your back. I want to bite it.*

Scat: *Oh come on, my back is vile. It's all flaccid skin and stretchmarks.*

Morag: *I like it.*

Scat: *You loved it a second ago. Had you forgotten about the stretchmarks?*

Morag: *No. I do love it. And I love your hands.*

Scat: *My hands are nice. I'll give you that.*

Morag: *Thank you.*

Scat: *I've always thought that if Jesus was real, He'd have hands pretty much like mine.*

Morag: *Um …*

Scat: *Shall I tell you what I like about you?*

Morag: *OK then.*

Scat: *I like the way the skin on the inner walls of your thighs is like the smoothest, softest thing in the universe. Like warm mercury wrapped in the skin from angels' wings.*

Morag: *Um ...*

Scat: *Like the skin on the rice pudding of the gods.*

No?

OK, I like the dark curls on the nape of your neck, I like how your skin tingles when I kiss you there.

I love the small of your back and the swell of your hips and the rise and fall of your belly when you sleep.

I love your breasts, and I love your hair, and I love your eyes and your lips and your sharp ways.

Morag: *You've been watching me sleep?*

What sharp ways?

Scat: *A bit.*

You know.

Morag: *You mean my tongue?*

Scat: *Yes. I love the sharpness of your tongue.*

Even if it hurts.

Maybe even because it hurts. I'm weird like that.

Morag: *You're using the L-word a lot.*

Scat: *No biggie. I love cats and baked potatoes and Chai Steamers too.*

Morag: *You didn't know what a Chai Steamer was till last week.*

Scat: *I know! I've so much to thank you for.*

Morag: *You're funny.*

You make me laugh.

Scat: *What am I, a clown? I'm here to amuse you?*

Morag: *No, you know, the way you tell the story and everything.*

Scat: *Awww.*

Are you sure we should be chatting so much, what with us just being fuck buddies and all?

Morag: *I don't think there are any rules, are there?*

Scat: I guess not.

Or at least if there are I don't know them.

Morag: Me neither.

Are you coming down this weekend then?

Scat: Try and stop me.

Morag: I don't want to stop you.

I want your hands in my muff.

Scat: ...

There is no emoticon for what I'm feeling right now.

I can't believe my luck.

Morag: Believe it.

Scat: OK.

[Believes.]

So yeah, that was right back at the beginning. Although I refuse – for now at least – to say anything, my answer today would be different.

But today things are already different.

'I want to ask you something,' types Morag.

Scat: Ask away.

Morag: I just want to know how this is working out for you.

In your opinion.

Scat: What are we talking about?

Morag: Me. You. Us. Our 'relationship'.

Are you happy with it?

Scat: How's it working out for me? I'm happy, yeah. Thanks for asking.

What about you?

[Time passes.]

Your silence is speaking volumes. Are you not happy?

Morag: Yeah.

Scat: Yeah you're happy or yeah you're not happy?

Morag: Happy.

Scat: Hmm. That 'happy' is sitting there on my screen like an empty pill bottle on a hotel bed.

[Time passes.]

Hello?

Morag: I'm thinking I might move back to London.

Scat: Really? But you love Brighton.

How come?

Morag: I know, but it's like, what am I doing here?

I need to start thinking about my career.

A career.

Something.

I need to start thinking about the rest of my life.

Scat: Shit, man. Sounds serious.

Morag: Well, it should be serious, shouldn't it?

Scat: I don't know. Should it?

Morag: Of course it fucking should!

Jesus.

Scat: OK, OK.

So move to London.

Morag: Well what about you?

Scat: I already live in London.

Morag: That's not what I mean.

I mean, what are you going to do with your life?

You're not getting any younger, you know.

Scat: You're rather inquisitive for a fuck buddy.

Morag: Cock.

I care about you, for fuck's sake!

I care about you and I hate to see you wasting your life!

Scat: I didn't know I was wasting my life!

I thought I was having more fun than I've ever had before.

I thought I was having The Time Of My Life, in fact.

At least I was before this conversation started.

[Time passes.]

Hello?

[Time passes.]

Are you ignoring me now?

Morag: *I thought you were supposed to be looking for love?*

Scat: *Sigh.*

I am looking for love.

Morag: *Oh all right then. So you're looking for love, but you're perfectly happy with us carrying on the way we are.*

It doesn't make sense.

Scat: *But that's like saying, OK, I really want to go to Mauritius but I can't afford it this year, therefore I'm going to stay at home, even though I'm being offered this fantastic trip to Torremolinos. Of course I'm not – I'm going to go to Torremolinos and have myself a helluva time.*

Morag: *So I'm just a second-rate Spanish holiday to you, am I?*

Scat: *I could've picked Blackpool. You should think yourself lucky. And you're deliberately missing the point.*

I have a great time with you. That's what I was saying.

Look, I don't know what's going on here.

If you want to end it, you should just say so.

I don't know why I'm suddenly in a big flap here trying to defend myself.

I don't know what I've done wrong.

Morag: *You're the lucky one you didn't pick Blackpool.*

I think you're the one missing the point too.

I don't want to end it. That's not what I'm saying.

Scat: *What are you saying? Help me out here.*

Morag: *I'm saying that I've started to feel recently that our 'relationship' as it stands is not really enough for me.*

Scat: *Well, I offered you 'more' months ago.*

Morag: *But I didn't want it then.*

Scat: *Oh well.*

Morag: *Oh well what?*

Scat: *Timing.*

Morag: *That's all you've got to say, is it? 'Timing'?*

Scat: Well, what do you want me to say?

Morag: If I have to spell it out, I'm not so sure I even want you to say it any more.

So?

Scat: Well, is that all you've got to say?

I've got my pride, you know.

Morag: What's that got to do with anything?

Scat: Well, I'm just saying, when we first met, I wanted to be with you, to go out with you, whatever, and you turned me down. Now you're saying you want more – I presume you mean with me but you're not really being explicit enough for me to be sure – and I don't know how you expect me to feel.

I don't know how I do feel.

You can't just pick me up and put me down like a cat playing with a crisp bag.

It's not fair.

Morag: Oh fair schmair. You're like a fucking child sometimes. I tell you what, I'll make it easy for you.

Fuck your childish pride and fuck you. OK? Done.

At which point she goes offline, storming out of the virtual room and slamming the virtual door in my very real, very sad face. I telephone her. She does not answer. I leave messages. She does not return them. I don't really know what's happening, but I do not want to lose her. When finally she comes back online, I try hard to get back to where we were, but suddenly it doesn't seem possible.

Scat: Look, it's more that I want the person I want to want me back and to know it. Oh God, I don't know. Let's talk about it this weekend.

Morag: No, let's not.

Scat: And I'm the child.

Morag: Excuse me?

Scat: Cat and mouse, cat and mouse.

Morag: WTF?

Scat: Why can't we talk about it this weekend?

Morag: Because I'm not going to see you this weekend. I'm going away with a friend.

Scat: Anyone I know?

Morag: That's not likely, is it? You don't know any of my friends.

Scat: Anyone I know of, I mean.

Morag: You mean is it Ollie?

Scat: I suppose so, yes.

Morag: Of course it's not.

You don't know me at all, do you?

Scat: I suppose not, no.

Morag: Right. Any more questions?

Scat: So when was that decided?

Morag: Hold on a sec …

[Time passes.]

Here we are – 'You're rather inquisitive for a fuck buddy.'

Scat: Touché. Right. OK, Morag. Well, do have a great weekend and maybe I'll see you around.

Then, as Morag is typing her response, I close the window on our conversation, storming out of the virtual room and slamming the virtual door in her virtual face. Is this what I'm like? Am I a door-slammer? Is this what I'm like in relationships? Am I in a relationship?

Later the same day, I creep back online feeling ashamed and Morag launches herself at me …

Morag: The thing is, though, your blog is supposed to be about your quest for true love, I just thought your readers should know that here you are being offered love and you've turned it down.

Scat: What? Really? I had no idea.

Was I being offered true love?

When did that happen?

Morag: Don't be a smartarse, please.

I made it perfectly clear that I was offering to take our relationship on to the next level – on to a firmer footing, and you threw it back in my face.

Scat: NO no no nonono. No!

I did not throw anything anywhere. I just didn't see why I should roll over and let you lick my face after you'd already – quite coldly – rejected me.

I didn't think you'd give up so easily, to be honest. I thought maybe you might try and persuade me, buy me Sugar Puffs, make me realise that maybe I could believe in what you were half-saying, that maybe you really did want to be with me, but instead at the first, tiniest setback you're fucking off on weekends and trying to make me jealous.

Morag: It was NOT cold.

Scat: Whatever.

Morag: Are you jealous?

Scat: Whatever.

Morag: You child.

Scat: YOU fucking child. How DARE you?

Morag: This is starting to get a little tedious now.

CAPITALS and all.

You know what I meant …

Scat: I love you.

Morag: Excuse me?

Scat: Nothing. I didn't say anything.

Morag: You're the weirdest person I've ever met.

Scat: Are you sure you don't want to spend the weekend with me? I really want to spend the weekend with you.

Morag: Oh, Stan I can't now. I've promised my friend we'd do something.

Scat: OK, OK.

Morag: I'll see you next week, though, if you're up for it. I want to see Somers Town with you.

Scat: OK, that'll be great.

Morag: Have a good weekend then. I'll speak to you on Monday.

Scat: OK, have fun.

Morag: I'm sorry I was such a cow earlier.

Scat: I'm sorry too.

Bye bye.

xxx

Morag: Bye Stan.

Next week arrives and things stubbornly refuse to get easier ...

Scat: So did you have a nice weekend?

Morag: Hey.

Yeah, it was OK.

Scat: Where did you go?

Morag: Just stayed here in the end.

Scat: What, you didn't go anywhere?

Morag: Nah.

Scat: So what did you do?

Morag: My friend came to see me here.

Scat: Ah. OK.

You're not making this very easy.

Morag: ?

Scat: OK. So be it. So this friend, was it a lady friend or a gentleman caller?

Morag: His name is Christ. I used to work with him. I've known him for a while.

Scat: His name is Christ?

Morag: Oops. I mean Chris. Sorry. I always put an extra 't' on the end of Christ when I'm typing it.

See?

It's like a finger-tick.

Scat: So did you fuck him?

Did you fuck Christ?

Morag: You sure you want to know?

Scat: I think I already do, don't I?

Morag: Yeah, we had sex.

Scat: Cool. I'm happy for you.

Morag: Thanks.

Scat: Was it any good?

Morag: Yeah, I enjoyed it. Thanks.

Scat: Not at all. I'm pleased for you.

That's excellent.

Morag: How was your weekend?

Scat: Shit, thanks.

Utter shit.

Morag: I'm sorry, Stan.

Scat: Hey, no worries. Is he good-looking, this Christ fellow?

Morag: Yeah, he's quite good-looking.

Scat: Brilliant. Very pleased. Smiling all over my face for you now.

Morag: Oh come on. You're not even that ugly yourself.

All this ugly stuff is such an overblown pile of shite.

Scat: I'VE BEEN SPAT ON!

Morag: AND I'VE BEEN HEADBUTTED! AND IT DOESN'T MEAN A FUCKING THING!!!

All it means is there are some arseholes in this world.

Get over it.

Scat: You get over it.

Morag: Oh, don't be childish.

Scat: You don't be childish.

Morag: Right, OK, Stan. I think I better go.

Scat: Wait wait wait don't go.

Morag: What?

Scat: Are you going to see me again?

Morag: I'm not sure that's such a good idea at the moment.

Scat: OK.

Cool.

Morag: Let's just see how things pan out.

Scat: *What about Christ? Will you be seeing a bit more of Christ?*
Morag: *I don't know, Stan.*
Scat: *Look, I don't know how this is, like, suddenly a big deal. It's really not, you know. We're just fuck buddies. We WERE just fuck buddies, whatever, I'm over it. Just be straight with me, I can take it.*
Morag: *Yes then. I think we're going to give it a go. He's been interested in me for a while.*
Scat: *Cunt.*
Sorry sorry sorry.
That just slipped out of my fingers.
Morag: *Stan.*
Scat: *Fucking shit.*
Morag: *Look, I'd better go.*
Scat: *Let's still chat a bit. I promise I'll be OK. You can still teach me French. Hm?*
Morag: *OK, we'll see. I got to go.*
Scat: *OK. Have fun.*
Morag: *Seeya.*
Scat: *Seeya.*
Bye.
Don't become a stranger.
x

Hours later:

Scat: *So when can we have our first French lesson?*
'Allo?
'Allo?
Morag: *Stan, I think we should stop being in touch for now.*
Scat: *Mais non!*
Morag: *Oui. I'm sorry.*
Scat: *But why? I thought we were going to be just good friends.*
Morag: *I don't think it's a good idea.*

At least not for now.

Scat: *You don't think I can handle it?*

Morag: *I don't think it's particularly healthy for you. Or me for that matter.*

For either of us.

Scat: *But it's not like we were going out together in the first place.*

Morag: *Isn't it? I think it's exactly like that.*

Scat: *So why did we stop?*

I really liked it, Morag.

I don't understand how we got from there to here.

I don't really know what happened.

Morag: *I just don't think we were singing from the same hymn sheet, Stan.*

Scat: *Ugh. God. Not the hymn sheet.*

Anything but the hymn sheet.

Morag: *Sorry.*

Scat: *I think we were, though, that's the thing.*

You just ran off before we could start on a new hymn.

[Time passes.]

Are you sure you know what you're doing?

Morag: *God no.*

Scat: *I really miss you already.*

Morag: *This is why I think we should stop communicating for a while.*

Scat: *For a while? What does that even mean?*

Morag: *It means let's see how it goes.*

Scat: *Let's see how singing hymns with Christ goes, you mean?*
I bet Christ's great at singing hymns.

Morag: *You're just going to have to give me some time to figure out what I want. And I want to give you time to figure out what you want.*

Scat: *I know what I want.*

Morag: *Do you? Are you sure?*

Scat: *Absolutely.*

Morag: Well, I'm not. I'm sorry.

[Time passes.]

Scat: I feel sick.

Morag: I'm going to block you on chat for a while, OK?

Scat: Oh Jesus Christ, please don't do that.

Morag: I have to, Stan, otherwise we're just going to carry on getting embroiled in these conversations and it's not going to help either of us.

[Time passes.]

Morag: Stan?

Scat: OK.

OK.

OK.

Fair enough.

[Time passes.]

I'll miss you, Morag.

Morag: I'll miss you too.

Scat: OK. I'm ready.

Block me.

Morag: Bye, Stan.

Scat: Do it.

Morag: xxx

[Time passes.]

Morag is offline.

CHAPTER TWENTY-EIGHT

LONDON TO BRIGHTON

Eyes thick with pity and knuckles sore with impotent rage, I am driving to Brighton to set things straight once and for all. Fantasising as I drive. *I am rooted in the me who is on this adventure. What took you so long? You had me at hello.*

I am upset about Morag. I'm upset at how it came about. I'm upset at how easily it could have been averted, how if I'd been less of an impulsive dick, I could be with her now, wrapped up in her, just the two of us. I'm upset at what's going to happen next. I'm upset at all the upheaval. I mean, I know that change is what life is all about, but I really wouldn't mind a tiny bit of stability for once; just a soupçon of constancy. Emotional constancy, if nothing else. At the moment, however, there is none. Even my family, which I thought was something long dead to me, has come back to haunt me. But for the moment I cannot think about that. For the moment that's the last thing I can think about.

I smoked half a joint I found under my bed before I left the house. That on top of two and a half glasses of wine. I am over the limit. I'm drunk. I'm stoned. And I couldn't care less. Let me lose control and steam into a brick wall. Let me veer off the motorway and careen into a bus full of pregnant women. I am awful. I am self-centred in the extreme. I do not care.

I am halfway there. I text as I drive. 'Are you at home?'

No reply.

I am outside her house. I turn off the ignition and I phone her.

No reply.

I start to feel paranoid. Has she blocked me?

I groan. I curse. I hit my forehead against the top of the steering wheel.

It's Saturday night. It's 8 o'clock. Why isn't she at home watching *The X Factor*? Fuck, why aren't I?

Then it occurs to me. Maybe she is.

I steel myself, get out of the car, walk stiffly, silently, slightly insanely to her front door and knock upon it twice. Then I wait.

No reply.

Then – quite suddenly – it hits me. Keith was right all along. I am out of my fucking mind.

I back away from Morag's house like it's on fire and clamber back into my car, slightly breathless.

'What on earth are you doing here?'

That is the question I put to the me that is rooted in this undignified adventure, the me that is cowering in the rear-view mirror, eyes acidic, ablaze, astringent. His forehead shrugs. He does not know. He does not want to know. I press him: 'Are you a proper looney now, is that it?' A shiny little girl holding her mother's hand walks past the car, catches sight of me frantically hissing at my own reflection, and looks away, confused and alarmed.

I start the car, point it at London and drive. Fifteen minutes later I change my mind and turn around. I find a Chinese restaurant three streets away from Morag's and order some food. I send another text message.

'I'm not a looney, you know. I just miss you. I want to see you. Just for coffee maybe. Just to talk. xxx'

Why is it only when you press send that you realise that you have sent a message that only a *bona fide* looney would send? Why don't you get at least thirty seconds after sending in order to reconsider and cancel if necessary? A silent scream freezes itself to my face as I wait for my message to be delivered.

Then I get a reprieve. 'Message not sent. Retry?'

Thank God for that.

For reasons known to no one, I press 'Retry' and this time it goes through immediately.

I am a looney.

Minutes pass.

No reply.

She's ignoring me.

'Unbelievable,' I spit. 'Fucking cow.'

Someone at the next table looks over at me, then looks away. I am well aware that I am behaving strangely. I pour myself another cup of green tea.

Then my phone beeps and I almost pull a muscle reaching for it.

It's Keith. The shit.

'You about?' it says. I start texting back then get frustrated and give him a ring.

I tell him I'm in a Chinese restaurant waiting for dim sum.

'Are you with Morag?' he wants to know. I groan. 'No, I'm not,' I say. 'I'm alone.' I realise I am behaving very melodramatically, the height of self-pity. I know this is not good but I simply cannot stop myself. Not now.

'Good,' he says. 'Well, I'm starving. I'll join you if you don't mind. Are you round the corner?' He's referring to the Chinese restaurant which is ninety seconds' walk from where we live.

'I'm outside London actually,' I say.

'Oh, where are you?'

I explain where I am and what I've done.

'Fucking hell,' says Keith. 'You're not having a breakdown, are you?'

'No, no, no,' I say, because that's what you say when someone asks you that, especially if you are having a breakdown. 'I'm fine.'

'Why don't you come home and get wrecked?' he says. 'I'll pop over to Quinn's.'

I pause for a moment and suddenly feel like I'm going to burst into tears. 'All right,' I whimper. 'God, that sounds like a good idea. Let's get some crack.'

Another look from the table next door.

'Crack it is.' Keith replies. 'Get your arse in gear then.'

Suddenly galvanised, I call to the waitress and ask her to put my food – which is now ready – in some bags. Then I pay for it, get in the car and drive directly back to Morag's house. I park outside, get out and knock abruptly on her front door. No reply. Thank God.

But I'd tried. No one can say I hadn't tried. I came, I tried, I failed.

Now it's time to go.

Then – naturally, because life is hilarious like that – as I turn to get back in the car, there she is. Off in the distance. Walking towards me. Drifting towards me through lovers' lamplight, her and someone else. Someone who isn't me. Two of them, arms wrapped like scarves against the miserable drizzle, two happy people lazily clumping home for sex. They've just rounded the corner, ten or so houses away. I inch across the pavement and slowly open the car door. But it is too late. I have been spotted. Morag stops walking, disentangles herself. In my mind, I hear her curse. Then she starts up again, slowly walking towards me.

I close the car door, wait, trying desperately to think of a reason to be there that might not sound completely unhinged.

'Hi,' I say, as she gets within speaking distance.

'What are you doing here, Stan?' She doesn't sound angry. She sounds concerned, which is so much worse.

'No, nothing, no,' I shout, far too jovially. 'No, I just popped by on the off chance, to see what you were up to, you know. I'll be off now ... You must be Christ,' I assume.

'Chris,' said Christ. I lean towards him with my outstretched hand. He leans over Morag and shakes it. He is tall. Young. Handsome. Firm handshake.

'Nice to meet you,' I say. Then to Morag. 'I'm really sorry, OK? Have a good night.'

'Stan,' she says.

'No, no, it's fine,' I insist, nodding, smiling, moving quickly, gurning from the driver's seat, taking control, driving away. Bish bash bosh, I am gone and on the London Road in what seems like minutes. All the way home, I play 'Wish' by Nine Inch Nails on repeat, window-rattlingly loud.

I'm home by 10.15 p.m. By eleven I've drunk three bottles of San Miguel, smoked a couple of joints and convinced myself that it was all a terrible, terrible dream.

Unfortunately, there is no crack because Keith assumed I was joking.

At ten minutes past midnight I receive a text from Morag. 'Are you OK?' it says.

I ignore it. Better still, I delete it.

Ha!

I am triumphant! I am victorious!

Now I'm in bed, drunk and fucked up and miserable, bashing away at my brand-new laptop. I have disconnected myself from the internet, just to make sure I don't do anything stupid. I am writing a blog post about how I am done with love. It's true too. I am.

I know that was the reason that I started the blog in the first place, to find love. I know that that's what the last nine months have been all about, but I've changed my mind. All this nonsense with Morag has taught me that love is simply not for me. In fact, as far as I'm concerned, love can go fuck itself. Ziplessly.

I'm done with it.

I used to read Catullus to her in bed some nights. That's how fucking stupid I was.

Well, no more.

This is the new me. The upgrade. Cattermole 2.1. Code optimised. Bugs fixed. Heart totally reformatted.

My heart was a moron. It was braindead. It was like an overripe, pitiful plum, all tender and vulnerable, weeping with aimless emotion. No more.

I've always been too emotional. And it's really not necessary. Life could be so much more enjoyable without emotion.

This year, for example. If I think about it in terms of emotion, it's been a total fuck-up. If I think about it in purely physical terms, I'm actually averaging one vagina every twelve weeks. Compare that to the rest of my life – one vagina every fifteen years – and it's plain to see that things are looking up and life is going in very much the right direction. It's clear to me that I need to concentrate on the physical. With the physical, you know where you stand. It's like science.

Emotions, on the other hand, are mired in dishonesty.

Patricia was damaged and needy, fingers of fire and teeth eager to cut and cry out. She was the best thing that had happened to me in years, but all she really wanted was to get back at Keith.

Then there was Sally. Sometimes when Sally would stare into my eyes, stroke my face and slowly lick her silver lips, I would actually feel mentally ill with desire, my insides tumbling like arcade asteroids. It was divine while it lasted, but all she really wanted was a decent exhibition.

And then there was Morag. I had real hope for Morag. Right up till the end. Right up till this weekend, in fact, but all Morag wanted was – actually, God knows what Morag was in it for. The sport, I guess.

I've got nothing against Morag, however. I should make that clear. I think Morag was straight with me throughout our brief whatever-it-was, or at least as straight as she could be, and that was good enough for me. I'm no paragon of straight talking myself, after all, when I get all braindead, heart-heavy and cockless insecure. But then it's tough to talk straight when you're terrified both of losing what you have and jeopardising what you want.

So I've got nothing against Morag. Everything against love.

After all, there's only so long you can chase a wild goose. I reckon thirty years is about the limit. If you don't give up after thirty years, then it shows a distinct lack of respect for the goose.

After thirty years, it's time to face facts. That goose is not for catching. Let it go. Chase something else.

So I'm refocusing my attention. I've always been too cerebral anyway. I read the preface to *The Picture of Dorian Gray* when I was a teenager and I convinced myself I admired it. I reread it just now and hate it. Seriously. It's barely comprehensible pretentious garbage written by a hypocritical phoney who lived his whole life as a lie.

Done with Wilde.

Done with Art.

Done with Beauty.

Done with Truth.

Done with That Sort of Thing.

Done with Love.

No more pining and moping and yearning and sighing. No more putting the spiritual ahead of the physical. No more putting the brain ahead of the body.

And what better time to make that shift than now that I'm under sixteen stone for the first time in God knows how many years. Now I need to consolidate with bananas and weights.

And another thing: no more intimacy.

No more talking before sex, or indeed afterwards. No more getting to know potential sex partners. No more meeting anyone who reads my blog because people who read my blog know too much. Or think they do. And if they do, they know the old me, the big soppy pushover that would fall in love with them at the drop of a stocking. Tomorrow's women shall revel in their ignorance. They shall know only what they see when they meet me cold: they will know my large elbow-heavy head, my dead-eyed gaze, and my increasingly impressive musculature.

No more confusing emotional need with physical lust.

I'm not done with lust. Just love. Which is a shame really, because for a moment there I feel I got pretty damn close. I got a sniff, a backstairs whisper of what love might be like. Or what we talk about when we talk about love – the hormonal tick that tricks us into staying together and raising children; the genetically modified chemical blindfold we wear gladly; the evolutionary imperative hardwired into our skulls. And I could see, clearly, why other people get so worked up about it.

Not me though. I'm done with it.

So what I'm currently thinking is, now that love no longer exists, I'm thinking I might run away to Paris like Henry Miller and whore myself into an early grave. Or a late grave, as it was in his case. The idea frightens me but I feel I should do it; take a whore quickly while I'm still in the mood, and who knows, maybe I'll take to money-fucking like a zipless duck to water.

Maybe that's all people like me are cut out for.

I blame the parents.

CHAPTER TWENTY-NINE

ALL THAT DAVID COPPERFIELD KIND OF CRAP

When I was nine or ten, a local kid who lived just up the street punched me in the face for no good reason. I was walking home from school. He approached me, told me to stand still, told me to put down my bag, told me to lift my head just a little, then, when the position of my head was just right, he punched me as hard as he could in the mouth. He had two friends with him. They found this deliciously droll.

When I got home I tried to sneak upstairs to wash my face, but Father was on his way downstairs after one of his hideous, shameless evacuations. He saw the blood oozing from the throbbing cut on my upper lip. 'What happened to you?' he demanded angrily.

'Nothing,' I said.

He grabbed hold of my arm and dragged me into the living room. Mother was sitting, smoking, watching TV. 'Look at this,' he said, some semblance of mockery slinking into his voice.

'What happened to you?' demanded Mother, angrily.

'I got punched,' I admitted.

'Who punched you?'

I didn't want to say. Father took hold of one of my shoulders and shook me like a Polaroid picture. After a short exchange, which included more angry demands and a couple of idle threats, I admitted that it was Kenny Ellis who had punched me in the face.

'Kenny Ellis?!' Father was shocked. 'Jim Ellis's boy?'

I nodded.

'Well, I hope you kicked the shit out of him,' he said. 'Scrawny little bastard.'

I stayed silent, made no eye contact, waited for them to talk about something else so I could get out of their sight.

'Oy! Shit-for-brains. I'm talking to you.'

Shit-for-brains was Father's special name for me.

Then Father did something which counts as one of the four or five things for which I will never forgive him.

When he had ascertained that I had in no way avenged myself for Kenny Ellis's unprovoked attack, he grabbed me by the arm again and dragged me out of the front door. Muttering about family shame, about people laughing at him behind his back and about refusing to let me drag the Cattermole name through the mud, he marched me to the other end of our street, where the Ellis family lived.

Kenny Ellis was in the front street with his mini-entourage. They were kicking a crushed can backwards and forwards. I tried to wriggle free from Father, so he tightened his grip. 'No fucking about,' he said. 'Walk straight up to him and headbutt the little cunt. Then punch him in the belly and start kicking.'

'I don't want to,' I whined. 'Let me *go*.' There were tears coming into my eyes. 'Please let me go.'

At which point he stopped, crouched down to my height and pulled me to him like he'd had quite enough and was one word away from punching me himself. 'What are you trying to do?' he said. 'You trying to make me look like a fucking idiot? Eh?' All I could think was that I wanted to be somewhere else. Kenny Ellis and his friends had probably seen us coming towards them by now. They might even have figured out what was going on. 'You're fucking doing this,' said Father. 'If I have to grab your fist and move it myself, you're not letting that little cunt get away with this. Come on!' he hissed. 'Be a man.'

Then he grabbed hold of me again and marched me up to Kenny Ellis and his mates. When we were within ten metres or so, they stopped kicking the can and stared at us. My father shouted Kenny's name. Then he said, 'Stanley wants a word with you,' released his grip on my school blazer and pushed me towards my tormentor. 'Go on,' he said. 'Like I told you.'

Then I don't really know what came over me. I guess it was a combination of obligation, anger and maybe even a part of me that wanted to please my father and make him proud of me.

So what I did was this: I looked up at Kenny Ellis, who was now three metres away from me, and I charged him. Father's instructions went out of my head and instead I ran straight at him, screaming and swinging my arms wildly.

It was my first ever attempt to hit back.

Kenny Ellis moved casually to one side, ducked my pudgy fists with insouciance and gave me a gentle push which, added to my own momentum, sent me scraping across the middle of the street on my face.

As pain and heat began to sear through my face, I heard a couple of stilted giggles.

My eyes were closed. I didn't want to move. I didn't want to face the shame of standing up and having my father force me to fight like a man.

'There's a car coming.'

The voice belonged to Kenny Ellis.

I looked up and saw a car coming towards me in the distance. I stood up slowly and hobbled to the side of the road. I'd grazed my knee in my fall too. I looked for my father but he was gone. I saw him stomping off back down the street to our house. I looked at Kenny Ellis. He had pity in his eyes. Also embarrassment.

The car passed by and then I heard the noise of the crushed can scraping along the street. Kenny Ellis rejoined his friends.

I limped home.

When I got there, I opened and closed the front door as quietly and quickly as I could and I ran upstairs to my room. Father shot out of the living room and shouted after me from the bottom of the stairs, 'Yeah, go on, run. Run away, you useless little bastard. You're fucking useless!' he bellowed. There was hatred in his voice. So much hatred, which I never, ever understood. 'You're a disgrace! Do you hear me? You're no son of mine!'

That night I cried furious tears of hideous humiliation, and as I rammed my fist into my pillow over and over and over again, it was my father's face I imagined.

It was not long after that that the physical stuff – the pushing, the leg-slapping, the public humiliation, the plate-throwing – dropped off, and my relationship with my parents became a predominantly wordless one, with occasional explosions, which gradually decreased in frequency and impact. Until the last one, when I was fifteen and ended up having to move in with Keith.

After that, although I stayed in the same town for another four or five years, and I saw them around every once in a while, we never spoke.

I never spoke to Mother again. But I spoke to Father.

When I was twenty-five, my drunken father swallowed the entire contents of a bottle of painkillers. Mother discovered him slumped in his chair and called an ambulance. The ambulance arrived in time, Father had his stomach pumped and survived. He was then taken to a local nursing home-cum-looney bin where he tried again, a couple of times, to take his own life.

I didn't know anything about any of this until two weeks later, when I got a call from Keith's mum. I was living with Keith in London Bridge at the time. Keith answered the phone, and when he passed the receiver to me and told me it was his mum, I knew something was up.

'Hi, Stan,' said Sheila. 'Um ... are you sitting down?'

'No,' I replied. 'Has one of them died?'

'No,' she said. 'Not exactly.'

Three months later, one of them died.

Mother died of a heart attack. Which surprised me almost as much as it did her. A *heart* attack? How?

Meanwhile, Father was still in hospital recovering from or otherwise ploughing full steam ahead with his breakdown.

Suddenly I felt under pressure to care.

I felt guilty. I felt guilty when I entertained the idea of not attending Mother's funeral. I felt guilty when I considered that I hadn't spoken to her for the last ten years of her life. I felt guilty, I guess, because I knew that's not how things are supposed to be. Just as a mother is not supposed to stand her son in the corner of the room and throw plates at him. Just as a mother is not supposed to tie her son to a chair to stop him scratching his eczema. Just as a mother is not supposed to recoil from her son's affection and do everything in her power to make him feel utterly unlovable. These things are not supposed to happen. This is not how families are supposed to work.

I felt guilty about Father too.

I decided to kill two birds with one stone, so the day before Mother's funeral, I went to see Father in his mental-home hideaway.

When I explained who I was, the receptionist was surprised. 'There's no record of him having a son,' she said, perplexed.

I shrugged. 'We're not very close,' I told her.

She told me I could see him anyway, even though, according to hospital records, I did not exist.

So I saw him, and bizarrely, it seemed that I really did not exist, as Father had no idea who I was.

The nursing home was a thoroughly depressing place. It was visiting time, but few of the patients had visitors. I stood at the end of my father's ward, stalling. I glanced at each of the patients in turn. They were all damaged. All had eyes that were either dead, sedated, or fizzing with fear of things either real or imagined.

There were six beds between me and my father, and from that

distance, he seemed strangely alert. He was sitting up, propped against fat pillows like sick people in films. He was staring straight ahead, in the direction of the bed opposite, which he couldn't see for the curtain which had been drawn around it.

I took a deep breath and began to walk towards him. As I got closer, I was assailed by the strange feeling that the man I was about to visit was not actually my father at all. This would explain the receptionist's earlier confusion. The closer I got, the less it looked like the man who told me throughout my childhood that he was only slapping my legs because he didn't want to touch my ugly face with his hands. This man had a short spiky beard and large square glasses perched precariously on his bony nose. Father – when I knew him – had neither of those things.

I reached his bed. It was him. In the decade I hadn't seen him, he had aged about thirty years.

I was standing by the side of his bed. Nothing happened. He continued to stare at the curtain opposite. I watched him. He had lost a lot of weight. The glasses were far too big for his face. He didn't even wear glasses. It didn't make sense.

The silence continued. I wasn't sure what to say to break the deadlock. He still didn't even seem to know I was there.

I cleared my throat. Nothing. Eventually I swallowed my pride and said the word that I didn't want to say, because it smacked of affection and I had no affection for this man, broken or not.

'Dad,' I said.

Nothing.

I waited a moment, then repeated it, a little louder. 'Dad!'

Nothing. He just kept on sitting, staring.

'Oy!' I tried.

He jerked his head towards me and stared at me, looking into my eyes.

His own eyes were grey, cloudy, and even if I'd seen the eyes and nothing else, I would still know that something had gone wrong with his brain. His eyes were devoid of emotion. There was no recognition, but also, for the first time that I could remember, there was no enmity.

We stared at one another for what was probably no more than ten or fifteen seconds, then finally Father spoke. And thus began a conversation which, although very short, was probably the strangest I have ever had.

'What do you want?'

That was how he broke the ice after ten years.

He was still sitting bolt upright. His hands were resting idly in his lap. His voice was like an ice pick.

And it was a good question. I wasn't really sure.

'I've come to see you,' I said.

He didn't answer for a while, then suddenly he narrowed his eyes. 'I know you,' he said.

I nodded slowly. 'Yes,' I said. 'So you should.'

'Pybus,' he said. 'You are Pybus.'

And with that he turned his head away from me and resumed his staring at the curtain opposite.

My face had taken on a confused expression. Why had my father just told me I was Pybus? What the hell is Pybus? Then it dawned on me. Pybus was the name of a solicitor, one of the partners in a law firm round the corner from where we lived in Dartford. I shook my head. I'd never spoken to a mad person before. I wanted to hear more.

'I'm not Pybus,' I said. 'I'm your son.'

He'd gone back into silent mode.

'Dad,' I tried again. 'Dad!' I wondered whether to shake him, but frankly, I didn't want to touch him. Then I became a little angry. 'I know you can hear me,' I said. 'Why don't you answer me? Eh? What's wrong with you?'

Nothing.

His huge comedy glasses, which made him look ridiculous, had crept down his nose to the point where they were beginning to look uncomfortable, or even in danger of slipping off his face altogether.

I wondered whether he would have the wherewithal to push them back up like a proper glasses-wearer. Time passed. It appeared not.

I suddenly felt overwhelmed with sadness, which again turned quickly to anger. I hated that he made me feel things. And, above all, I hated that there was this bond, something in me – something deep down in my harddrive which couldn't be erased – which forced me to feel something for this man. Something that he never deserved. And something that he never reciprocated. I hated the fact that I was such a fucking pushover.

I cry at films too easily too. I know I do. It stems from a faulty emotional motherboard. I dismiss films such as *Stepmom* as schmaltzy manipulative hogwash, yet still they leave me gasping for breath in a tsunami of tears. Once I wept at an advert. I am such a pussy. Fuck him.

'So that's it, is it?' I hissed. 'Ten years and that's all you can come up with? Fucking *Pybus*?' I crossed my arms petulantly.

He continued to stare straight ahead. I looked down at his hands. They weren't moving. I expected them to be flapping about like the hands of a mentally ill cliché. But they were still. Then I noticed that on the wrist of his left hand was a fairly fresh, half-healed laceration about two inches in length. It was horizontal, which is to say it went around the wrist like a watch, as opposed to up the arm, following the vein.

I winced when I saw it, and despite myself, my heart went out to him.

Fucker. Why did it hurt? Why did this man's pain hurt me? Fuck him. I hated him.

I lifted my hand to his face and pushed his glasses up his nose. He didn't appear even to notice.

I sat there, watching him staring at nothing for another two or three minutes, then I said, 'Right then. I'll be off.'

No response.

So I got up from the bed and walked away.

And that was that. That was five years ago.

Apparently, the medication wasn't working. He kept trying to harm himself, and he wasn't awfully lucid. So finally, as a last resort, they gave him ECT for a few weeks. Short sharp shock therapy. And apparently, it actually did him some good.

Father is now living in a small flat in Dartford. He has a part-time job working in a supermarket and is more or less a fully functioning, ordinary member of society. Not a particularly high achiever, but thankfully, no longer an arch-shit.

I've had his number, and I've known that he asked about me, for about four years. And it wasn't petty revenge or sour grapes that stopped me running to him when he said my name. It was damage limitation. I didn't want to go through anything like the same feelings I'd been through with him before. I'd had enough. That was it in a nutshell, actually. I'd had enough. Father was lost. Mother was dead. It was time to wash my hands of them and get on with my life.

But still the fucker haunts me. And still there is that bond.

So yesterday, I phoned. And with surprising ease and in very few words, I find myself knocking on the front door of my father's tiny flat, giving him, giving *family*, one last chance.

And here he is, shuffling towards me, turning a key, opening up.

The beard is gone. The comedy glasses have been replaced by slightly smaller frames. Plus, the eyes have some life in them. Not much, but some.

When our eyes meet, however, something amazing happens.

My father smiles at me.

It sounds ridiculous I know. It sounds utterly ridiculous and wholly unbelievable, but this, I swear, is a first.

He smiles at me and he offers me his hand to shake. Another first.

As we shake hands, he says, 'Hello, Stanley,' and although his voice is weak and slightly hoarse, there is warmth in it.

'Hello,' I say.

Inside the flat, I sit on a large armchair in the tiny living room while Father makes me some tea. (Another first. Let's just take it as read that everything else from this point on is also a first.)

'So how've you been?' he asks me, sitting opposite in another large armchair, close enough that our feet are almost touching.

I tell him. I talk to my father. I tell him about my life. He is interested. He tells me about his. He works in a local Morrisons, stacking shelves three nights a week, a bit of warehouse work at the weekends, but nothing too strenuous. He has friends: a couple of blokes from the shop, a neighbour or two in this block of flats, a few people from the day centre he still regularly attends.

There are still remnants of his old personality, but none of the particularly horrible stuff. He still watches a lot of football, for example. He still likes bad films: martial arts and horror.

But apart from that, this man bears no relation to the man who would lock me in the back garden in the middle of winter or make me sing 'Gold' by Spandau Ballet for the nasty amusement of his drunken friends.

'I wasn't very nice to you, was I?' he says. 'When you were little.'

I shake my head automatically. 'Not really,' I reply.

'I'm sorry, Stanley,' he says. He shakes his head and looks away from me.

Meanwhile, I am amazed at the emotion I feel. It's like that one simple apology has made all those years of unhappiness melt away. 'That's all right,' I say. And I mean it. It is all right. I'm sure he didn't do it on purpose. He didn't really know what he was doing. His brain was wrong. Or else he was in a bad mood for twenty years. I don't know, and I don't care. The important thing is, he's sorry. And he's making me tea now, and talking to me about my life, and looking into my eyes and saying to me, 'Are you happy now, Stanley?'

There are tears in my eyes as I answer, 'Yes. Yes, I really am.'

It's odd, but it took my new father asking me that question to realise how happy I actually am. Sure, I'm lonely and a bit sad at times, but on the whole, I'm very happy.

Half an hour into our reunion, I mention Mother. 'I want to ask you about … my mother,' I say, pausing, because I've never really known how to say those words. I don't want them to sound loving, but also, under the circumstances, I don't particularly want them to sound bitter.

My dad nods his head sadly. 'I thought you might,' he says.

I am about to ask how she died, when my dad says something quite confusing.

He says: 'I'm sorry we never told you the truth. It just seemed easier at the time.'

There is a pause.

In *Fight Club* Tyler Durden works as a projectionist and splices pornographic images into children's movies. Just single frames, however, so that no one really knows what they've seen, but subliminally something inside of them has been altered, scarred. That's kind of what I feel when my dad says what he says. Only I'm not forced to carry on watching the rest of the film and pretend it never happened. Rather I sit there for a moment, profoundly bewildered, then I seek clarification.

'What?' I ask.

Then it's his turn to look confused.

'Your mother,' he says.

'Never told me what though?' I ask.

He looks like he's put his foot in something, like he wants to backtrack. 'About her,' he says.

'What about her?' I persist.

His mouth is a little way open. He looks a little simple. He shakes his head. 'Your mother,' he says again.

'Yes?' I say slowly, not losing patience exactly, but becoming weary.

'Do you still not know?' he asks.

My stomach suddenly feels conspicuously empty, and is somersaulting inside of me.

'I don't know,' I reply. 'Not know what? Tell me now and I'll let you know if I knew or not.'

He looks panicked, like he's walked into the middle of something he can't control. I feel bad for him. I almost want to tell him not to worry about it.

He clears his throat and forces a small smile. Finally, he says, 'You're not ...' then he stops. 'I ain't your real dad,' he says.

I laugh. That's my initial reaction. A short breathy laugh, the kind of laugh you might give to a joke you don't really think is funny but maybe you appreciate the mechanics of it.

'And your mum ain't your real mum,' he continues.

'Don't be ridiculous,' I say.

He furrows his brow sadly.

'It's true, Stanley,' he insists. 'I'm sorry.'

This is only the second time my father – if that's what he is – has ever apologised to me.

'That's OK,' I say, and as it sinks in, I swear, I feel like I've been pushed head first out of an open plane ...

CHAPTER THIRTY

TURN AND FACE THE STRANGE

Keith pushed open my bedroom door and plonked a cup of twice-spiced chai on my bedside table. 'Time to wake up,' he said. 'Wake up and smell the chai.' I relinquished sleep with all the grace and dignity of a starving man relinquishing a golden doughnut, and slowly, almost painfully, I focused.

Keith was sitting in the leather armchair in the corner of my room, staring and smoking a joint. 'Jesus,' I said. 'It's a bit early, isn't it?'

'It is a bit, yes,' he agreed. 'But I've had some distressing news and I'm using it as an excuse to smoke skunk at 7.30 in the morning.'

I sat up and accepted the ashtray. 'What's happened?' I said, wary, on edge. The smoke waltzed through me like a muffling phantom, leaving me nauseous, woozy, instantly befuddled of both bowel and brain.

'My dad's had a heart attack,' he said.

I stopped.

Like a machine that's had its plug pulled, every part of me just stopped.

'Is he OK?' I said.

'No,' said Keith. Then, slowly, 'He's had a heart attack.'

'How serious is it?' I asked.

'It's quite serious,' said Keith. 'It's his heart.'

'How serious?' I persisted. 'Is he going to die?'

'I don't think so. He's stabilised since it happened last night. I'm going to go and see him.'

A heart attack is a serious thing, but as far as I can tell, just the very fact that he's survived it means that the chances are he's out of the woods for now, or at least out of the dangerous epicentre of the woods, where the Evil Dead lurk. Now he's kind of scrambling on the edge of the woods, dipping in and out of sunlight, tripping over roots and sweating, panicking slightly, desperate to get home.

'I'm coming too,' I said. 'Is that all right?'

Keith nodded.

So for the next couple of weeks, I accompany Keith up and down the country to Burnley, where we stand around worrying, drinking tea and telling Gordon – who is, as they say, a shadow of his former self – that he's going to be fine.

Gordon and Sylvia moved to Burnley from the north-east for reasons of work. On the whole, apart from the fact that, within the first couple of months, it nearly killed Gordon, they seem to like it. I however do not. In fact, I dislike Burnley so intensely that once again I begin to suspect I may have been a little too hard on Dartford. Burnley has – as far as I can see – only three things going for it: football, racism, and battered foodstuffs.

Gordon, however, is going to be OK. He's just going to have to live more carefully from now on.

Back in London I am offered a job writing the year-book of the most tedious government department in existence. It's extraordinarily dull work. I know because I did it last year too. However, it is well paid and I do get a bit of a kick out of being able to say for a few weeks that I work for the government. I'm like a kind of copywriting James Bond. Without the gadgets. Or the girls. In fact, thinking about it, outside of the fact that we're both paid by the taxpayer, there is very little to connect James Bond and me.

Actually, there is one thing. As of last month, I have a nemesis.

I have my very own Scaramanga. It kicked off during the week I blogged about Morag and I splitting up. Someone thought it would be a hoot to leave comments pretending to be Morag. The first time it happened, I believed it *was* Morag and part of me – my heart, I believe – leapt up inside me like an electrocuted salmon. Standing in front of the large mirror in the hallway, I called her. Her voice was wary, weary, not at all what I was expecting. 'You left a comment,' I said.

There was a pause.

'No, I didn't,' she replied, not cold exactly, but far from warm, like she wondered what I was up to, suspected I was up to something, telling strange lies to get back in her favour.

'So you didn't just leave comments on my blog telling me you loved me and calling me a self-pitying snob?'

There was another pause.

'Er ... no, Stan.'

It pissed me off that she had to make the possibility sound quite so utterly ridiculous.

'Oh,' I said. 'OK, sorry. Someone is fucking about then. Great. OK, sorry to have bothered you. You take care, OK.'

'OK, you too.'

'OK, bye.'

'Bye.'

Then I guess I must have felt a destructive combination of furious anger, hideous humiliation, and overwhelming self-loathing, because as soon as the line went dead I rammed my phone with the palm of my hand repeatedly into the centre of the mirror. The mirror cracked. Half of the glass fell to the floor and shattered. My hand was bleeding.

I stared into the mess of the glass that remained in the frame. Oh, no. Damn it. Is that who I am? Am I someone who smashes mirrors? And I thought I'd told my father I was happy. Is this what happy people do? Jesus. What do sad people do?

The person pretending to be Morag stopped pretending to be

Morag but continued to comment on my blog until I had to enable comment moderation, which made me sad, because it took away from some of the spontaneity and camaraderie of inter-commentary chat. It pissed me off so much, in fact, that I thought about packing the whole thing in. But I was overreacting. I was just sore about Morag. I did say I was only going to blog for one year, but that was nonsense. I'll be blogging for the rest of my life, in one capacity or another. I really don't know how I ever managed without it.

However, this lunatic, this troll, this comment stalker, continues to pipe up unabated – at a rate of one or two comments a day – despite the fact that none of those comments are appearing online.

It's getting disturbing. 'I'm scared of myself and who I am.' This was yesterday. Aside from the overall freaky tone of the comments, what worries me is that I'm starting to understand what this person is going through. I'm scared of *myself* too, and I haven't a clue who I am.

The stalking reached a peak when veiled references to books I've read recently began to appear. A shiver shimmied down my spine. I realised that, as well as commenting on my blog, this person must actually be following me in real life. They must know where I live. They must have followed me in the street and on to public transport, noticed me with my nose in certain books and then got hold of the same books. I thought about calling the police, alarming the house, getting hold of a knife. As I realised what was happening, I felt my heart rate increasing. I was scared.

Then I remembered that, a couple of weeks previously, I'd actually blogged about the books I was reading, so probably I didn't actually have a real-life physical stalker. I only had a slightly deranged reader.

The relief I felt was considerable. But it made me realise that I was becoming paranoid.

Perhaps with good reason. I've blogged quite openly about where I live. I've published photographs taken from my bedroom window. It wouldn't take a genius to locate my flat. Just a looney.

Then I realised afresh: *I am paranoid*. Jesus, who the hell would want to stalk me?

If I'm not careful, I'll have an emotional aneurysm and my life will segue into a complicated but ultimately unsatisfactory serial-killer film in which I discover that I've been having dizzy spells and blackouts, and I've been logging in as someone else and ... My God! I've been stalking myself!

So I need to be careful. Something obviously has to change. Life is full of turning points, and teeming with fresh starts. Here comes another one.

I have decided to stop blogging about deeply personal stuff. There shall be no more blow-by-blow analysis, no more recounting personal conversations.

It was all right when I first started blogging, because no one knew who I was and no one cared what I said. All I blogged about was stuff that was long past, stuff that had no impact on the present. Then people came into my life as a direct result of the blog. It was at this point perhaps that I should have stopped. But it's difficult. Once you're writing publicly about your life, it's difficult to know where to draw the line.

Conversations I had with Morag towards the end mirrored conversations I had with Sally. What was particularly difficult was reading personal comments made by strangers. Both Morag and Sally got really quite angry about that.

And I have to say, I do understand. For example, in the week I blogged about the end of our relationship – if that's what it was – Morag was described variously as 'a jerk', 'an anus', 'high maintenance', 'mental', 'a typical woman', 'right up herself', 'a game player' and, cuttingly, 'no good'.

I could of course disable comments altogether, but discourse is essential. I'd rather not blog at all than not have people's feedback. When I was at my lowest ebb recently after the break-up with Morag, the comments on my blog made all the difference to me.

'Don't you *dare* give up on love,' they said. 'Keep hope alive,' they said.

And I am. For one thing, I'm still on the lookout for a happy ending. Actually, any kind of ending. But I don't really know where to start. Then I see that it's obvious. If you're looking for an ending, you start at the beginning.

CHAPTER THIRTY-ONE

MY PARENTS AND OTHER ANOMALIES

Mother only threw plates at me twice. She lost her temper a lot but not once did I see her cry. Father neither. Isn't it a little strange to live with someone for fifteen years and never to see them cry? I think it is. I barely ever saw them laugh either, at least not warmly. Rather, when they laughed, it was bitter, hollow laughter, always at someone's expense. That's how it seems. Maybe I remember them through shit-tinted glasses. If so, I apologise.

Mother had a scowl, a permanent scowl that seemed to have been sewn into her face as a young girl. I could imagine her as a young girl, spiteful and bullying, terrified of emotion, and cruelly contemptuous of anyone who showed any.

She was in a lot of pain.

Mother suffered from very bad rheumatism. Or it may have been arthritis. Or even rheumatoid arthritis. Whatever it was, I believe it was fairly crippling. She used to cry out a lot and break things when it got really bad. She had copper bracelets, bandages, and pills, but I don't believe that they actually did any good.

When I was eight or nine, Mother snapped.

I was at the kitchen table, sitting, idling, minding my own business. My mother was washing up loudly at the sink, banging crockery with unusual violence. Then quite suddenly she screamed. The scream was so sudden that it caused me somehow to lose control of my body and knock a glass to the tiled floor, where it shattered and shot in all directions.

It was at this point that Mother really let go of herself. She wanted to know what was the point. What was the point of her working to keep the house tidy if I was just going to sit there breaking glasses? How would I feel if I did all the work and she went round breaking things whenever she got the urge? How would I feel if she broke something right now? And with that she picked up a cup from the draining board and lobbed it on to the floor, where it broke into four or five pieces with ceramic abandon.

All this happened fairly quickly, with the above exchange quite violently expressed. Lots of shouting and swearing and repeating of the word 'useless', then suddenly there was a plate spinning towards me like a psychotic clay pigeon. Unable to shoot it out of the sky, I cried out and lifted my arms to protect myself. The plate bounced off my forearms and crashed to the floor, where it smashed.

'See how useless you are!' Mother shouted, and then threw another one, then another, then another.

Dodging plates, genuinely frightened, I ran cowering from the kitchen and dashed upstairs to my room. Minutes later, Mother was in my room too, ordering me back downstairs.

'Clean it!' she snapped, back in the kitchen, and tossed a dustpan and brush at me. 'Put it in there,' she said, gesturing at the kitchen bin. I did as I was told.

From then on I did pretty much all of the cleaning at home. The dusting, the vacuuming, the washing up, the bathroom. At first I did it bitterly, resentfully, angrily, as this was time I could have escaped into books, but after time, I began to take pride in it. Naturally, the moment I began to take pride in it, Mother began to complain that I was always cleaning and would snap at me to stop cleaning and go to my room. This was fine too.

When I was twelve or thirteen, Mother made me stand in the corner of the kitchen. 'Stand still,' she said. And she threw plates at me again.

I have no idea why. I can't remember.

I turned my back and took it. Only three or four plates, I think, then it stopped.

'Clean that up,' she snapped, stomping out of the kitchen, out of the house and on to the bus that took her to the hospital where she cleaned floors for money. She cleaned floors for money until shortly before everything blew up and I left home at fifteen. She stopped cleaning floors for money because her arthritis got too bad. I remember wondering, around that time, how much of Mother's aggression and perpetual grousing was down to the pain she was feeling. And I remember thinking that, however much pain she was feeling, it was absolutely no excuse.

I wonder also if the pain in her hands and feet was what caused her to drink quite so much.

The only time she really got close enough for me to smell the booze on her breath was when she tied me up. She used to tie me up a lot. It was for my own good. It was for my eczema.

My eczema came and went, but for much of my childhood was horribly virulent and at one stage or another covered pretty much all my body. From a very early age, in order to stop me scratching, Mother and Father, but mainly Mother – for some reason she saw it as her job – tied me to a wooden chair in the living room.

This happened regularly – for a long time on a daily basis. It was – and I don't think I exaggerate when I say this – torture. I quickly learned, however, that it was all so much better if I didn't resist. When I resisted, it hurt more. Also, Father joined in and it sometimes got quite violent.

Plus part of me believed Mother when she said that if I carried on scratching, I'd make myself even uglier.

Sometimes I actually went further than not resisting. Sometimes I would encourage it. Sometimes I would sit on the eczema chair and hold my hands behind my back ready to be tied.

You see, the strange thing is, Mother tying me to a chair was the closest I actually got to receiving affection from her. I decided she was tying me to a chair to stop me scratching, because it was bad for me. If I was allowed to scratch, the eczema would weep and crust and bleed and scar. Mother didn't want that for me. Because she cared.

Sometimes I would volunteer to be tied up even when my eczema wasn't playing up at all.

There were four ties involved. One at each wrist, one at each ankle.

The worst thing about it was that while I was tied, I couldn't read. If they had placed a book on my lap and turned the page every couple of minutes, I would have been able to bear it, but instead I was placed at the back of the living room and forced to watch ITV. *Coronation Street. Heartbeat. The Bill. The A-Team. Bullseye.*

It really was torture.

I received very little medical attention for my eczema. Mother would stock up on medicated moisturiser every once in a while, but it wasn't always around. When it was, and whenever I used it, I was expressly told not to waste it. As far as I could tell, wasting it meant using it.

My own method for treating my eczema was to lie in a cold bath. I spent a lot of time lying in cold baths as a child. The relief that came with that moment of immersion, when the burning stopped in an instant, was astonishing, the most pleasurable feeling I ever experienced. It was like religion. The relief was such a release. It was how I imagined I was supposed to feel in church. But in church I felt the opposite. In church I felt trapped.

Mother and Father went to church every Sunday, dragging me with them in order, I assumed, to torture me. They were model heathens in every other way – they blasphemed, they drank, they smoked, they swore, they were vile, violent, self-centred, and hateful – and yet, every Sunday without fail, they pretended to be something they clearly weren't. It always fascinated and repulsed me in equal measure.

I'd watch Father shaking hands with people at the end of the service, smiling, and I'd always think, 'Who is he trying to fool?'

I never figured it out.

What I now believe is that both Mother and Father were – at least to a certain extent – mentally ill.

Sometimes I would use my eczema to get out of going to church. Better to be tied to a chair than trapped in a pew. Sometimes. But sometimes I'd enjoy the church service for the irony. I particularly enjoyed it when it was a heavily love-themed service.

The fact that neither Mother nor Father loved me was, I must admit, tempered by the fact that they clearly didn't love one another either.

They fought a lot. They were like a low-rent, uneducated version of Martha and George in *Who's Afraid of Virginia Woolf?* Constant bitching and sniping and drinking and hating. The only time they seemed to make a truce was when they joined forces and took sides against me.

I had a very tedious childhood.

It killed me that my parents never cared for me. And it bothered me that I grew up to hate them. But now all that has changed. Now I have to deal with the fact that they weren't even mine in the first place.

Actually, it's surprisingly easy to deal with. Probably because it makes perfect sense and is every sad child's dream. Every child who ever felt that their parents never loved them must have fantasised many times that they're not actually in any way related to the monsters causing them so much pain on a daily basis. Because if the people making you feel wholly unlovable are not actually your parents, not actually biologically predisposed to love you, then maybe, just maybe, there's nothing wrong with you after all.

I didn't hang around much longer when Father told me he wasn't actually my father.

I was freaked out, frankly. I needed some air. I told him I'd visit again soon. He said I was welcome, any time. It was ironic that, now that he was no longer my dad, he was suddenly being friendly.

Before I left of course, I asked him: 'So who are my real

parents?' followed – before he could answer – by: 'Did you adopt me?'

The idea of my parents adopting me was … it just didn't make any sense. My parents hated me. That much I could handle. That much I could accept. But if I'd then have to consider the fact that they chose me, that they actually picked me out of their own accord, then … my brain would begin to hiss and fart, before capsizing entirely. It didn't make any sense. Why would they choose me and then lavish on me nothing but degradation? Were they sadists?

'Not exactly,' Father said. 'Your mum couldn't keep you.'

My head was swimming. This was highly surreal. 'Why not?' I asked.

'She was really young. She was only fifteen when she fell pregnant. When she had you, she couldn't keep you.'

'So you *did* adopt me?' I persisted.

My father shook his head. 'Well, we just sort of *took* you really.'

'You took me? How could you just take me? You mean you stole me?'

I had images of being snatched from a pram outside of Mothercare.

'We just did what we thought was best,' he said.

I was confused. 'What did you do?'

Father looked in pain. I felt sorry for him.

'My sister,' he began. He stopped. 'Your mother was my sister. That was it.'

I drove home slowly through Vaseline, my head spinning with all this new information. I didn't even know my father had a sister. She would have been my aunt. But she wasn't. She was my mum. I didn't know what to do with the information. I felt giddy, even slightly afraid. When I got home, I went straight up to my bedroom and lay down on my bed in the dark.

I'm still there now. And, still, I haven't the faintest idea what I'm going to do.

I think I might need to see a psychotherapist.

CHAPTER THIRTY-TWO

THERE IS NO SANITY CLAUSE

I really think I might need to see a psychotherapist because, basically, I don't know who I am.

I always suspected that I never knew who I was. In fact, I was almost certain of it, but then I got to the point where I thought, hold on – nobody knows who they are. That's just the way it is. It's the human condition. Who am I? Why am I here? Why do I eat so many pies and weep and whine for company?

But I was wrong. I really didn't know who I was.

I've been sitting on this information for weeks now. And I'm scared.

I haven't been back to see Father – or whoever he is.

I've been in limbo. Not knowing who I am is freaking me out. I look at myself in the mirror and I don't know what it is I see. Not exactly. I see a large asymmetrical face, like a sack of aubergines, which I recognise, certainly, but the expression has changed and the eyes looking back at me are looking back at me like someone else's eyes.

I oscillate wildly between an indescribably unbearable lightness of being and a horrible rain of furious anger.

Morag can go to hell. My virtual friends were right about her. That sweet-faced Christ can go to hell too, and the both of them can rot there. No more internet romance. I make this vow to myself right now.

I'm lonely.

Keith is concerned about his father, which is understandable, but it kind of steals my thunder, which is annoying. He's actually thinking of moving out of London and going to live with his father in Burnley. I'm afraid he's just reacting to the fact that he and Tilly have broken down too. But Keith says: 'I hate my job and I'm sick of London. Plus, what if my dad dies?'

He has a point. Family is important.

I was supposed to meet up with Ange this week, but she weirdly pushed it back to next week and then cancelled on me altogether. Plus she won't talk to me on the telephone. I think she's avoiding me and I don't know why. I presume she's just got round to reading something I wrote on my blog in the summer about her sex life.

Fucking blog.

I really want to blog about losing my mind, but no one will believe me.

I don't even believe myself half the time.

Life is insane.

Frank sees a therapist. His name is David. David gives up his Saturday mornings on a regular basis so that he can get together with Frank and reduce him to tears.

'Saturday is sanity day,' says Frank.

Frank is insane.

'He's fierce,' he says, of David. 'He doesn't let me get away with anything.'

He says that, after a session with David, he needs the rest of the weekend to recover.

'What does he do? What do you talk about?'

Frank smiles, as if to say, 'That's for Frank to know, and Frank to find out.' For one who's very generous with his learning and perceived wisdom, Frank keeps his inner self very closely guarded. He's teased me with the odd mention of family strife, but not in any depth. He certainly doesn't splash his splintered psyche across the table on first meeting like some do. Like I tend to.

He saves that for David.

'I'd like to see him,' I say. 'Can I see him too?'

The guard comes up. I assure him of my sincerity. I splash some of my splintered psyche across the table and swear to him with emotion abruptly boiling up in my eyes that I really genuinely do not know who I am.

Frank promises to pass on my details, warning me as he does that David is 'outstandingly full-on'.

'That's what I need,' I tell him. 'That's exactly what I need.'

A couple of days later, Frank emails me David's details and says I should drop him a line. I do so, then David suggests I pop by for an initial chat. We make an appointment. The next day I receive the following email:

> *I am sorry, Stan, but I need to cancel our appt. On second thoughts I think it is best if I refer you to another therapist, as I usually don't work with friends or partners of existing clients. I don't make an assumption that there will be a problem, but I think it best to err on the side of caution.*

Fucker! What an absolute shit.

I take this email quite badly, turning into a man who breaks computer mice in the process. Thick with ire, I write the following email in reply:

> *What do you mean, "on second thoughts"? Presumably this is something of which you were aware when we made the initial appointment? Why the fuck didn't you err on the side of caution then instead of getting my hopes up that you could save me? Eh? What's wrong with you? Are you mad? I tell you what, I'm glad you won't see me. I don't want to see you. I could never trust my mental health to a man who doesn't have the gumption to write out the word "appointment" in full.*

But I don't send it. Instead I drink a bottle of red wine and my gummy head fizzes with atavistic despair. I don't know where to turn. So far this year, in times of despair I've been turning to the readers of my blog. I have the urge now. Indeed, it is almost overwhelming. I need their help. I want input, dialogue. But I can't bring myself to be quite that open. Or can I?

Am I an emotional exhibitionist? Is that it? Maybe. But if I am an emotional exhibitionist, it isn't titillation I seek. Rather, it's the education of other people. Their personalities, their experiences, their *voodoo*.

Blogging, and the blogging community, offers alarmingly high returns on emotional investment. All I have to do is remember and write and be true to myself and it comes back at me tenfold. A hundredfold. And it's spellbinding. It's awesome.

Since I started writing the blog, people have contacted me and offered their friendship. These are perfect virtual strangers who through my blog already know me intimately. They know all my secrets; secrets previously known to only a tiny, withered handful of real-life friends. Keith, mostly. The truth is, these people know me. You can disguise it all you want, hide behind as many ridiculous pseudonyms as you like, but when you tell your life stories online, it's still you. Whoever you are.

What I'm skirting around – because frankly I'm having difficulty framing it for fear of sounding saccharine or otherwise ghastly and irksome – is love.

Not that myth-kitty shagpenny bullshit romantic nonsense that I'm still most definitely done with, but a more heartfelt, less genital-based love. The love of human community. And now I miss it. I miss the conversation I should be having about my mum and my dad. I miss my virtual friends. I don't think I realised before how important they have become. The sharing of secrets and stories and shame, that intricate, intimate mixing with other people, is all-important. Being, after all, is other people. Spare me your groans. It's true. Life experience is great but only once it's been shared does it become truly fulfilling, enriching, and energising. Monologue is mundane and one-dimensional; dialogue is deeply gratifying.

So I leave clues. I tell them something cataclysmic has happened but that I can't talk about it. They show no interest. I tell them I need to track down a long-lost family member. They give me tips but don't force me to confess, which I know I would at the tiniest bit of prodding. I'm desperate to talk about it, and to talk about where my mind is, but then again, online intimacy has its limits.

How do I say that I think I might be having a nervous breakdown, that I might be emotionally retarded, that I might have 'issues', that I might be mad, have been mad all my life? These things are more difficult to say. To say them seriously. It's tough.

My clues are pathetic. I need to shit or get off the pot.

I get off the pot and remind myself that patience is a virtue and deferred gratification is the most gratifying gratification of all.

I drink more wine and lick at my stained teeth in the mirror. I stare at myself hard, tapping at my reflection with a glass in my hand, and I smile at myself like a serpent. 'Who the fuck are *you*?' I ask with self-mocking passion. 'You dark horse in the grass, you. You voiceless saccharine twerp. *Are you talking to me? You talking to me? Well there ain't no one else here. Who the hell else are you talking to? Are you talking to me?* I'm talking to you, fruitcake. And I'm asking you this: who in God's good name are you? *Who am I? Who am I? Who are* you *is the question you should be asking, my friend.*' And so I ask myself.

But I don't know the answer.

I miss Pablo.

Pablo knew me. Voodoo and all.

I feel like I'm about to explode. All I seem to do all day is sit around shaking my head, thinking alternately, 'I can't believe it,' and 'I knew it. I just fucking *knew* it.'

I swear though, I did. I knew I couldn't possibly have come from those ... people. We have nothing in common. Nothing. Physically, spiritually, intellectually, there is not one single thing which binds us. In fact, so wildly different are we that I keep finding myself now wondering how the hell I didn't realise sooner. I should have known. I feel like an idiot. But then, even if you suspect, you can never bring yourself to believe it. It's like a fairy tale. And even when I lay awake at night despising my parents and dreaming that I was different somehow, of different stock, stolen from my rightful parents, a changeling, I never really allowed myself to believe it, because it was ridiculous. It was a fairy tale. And life is not a fairy tale.

Life really isn't a fairy tale.

When I asked in my blog for advice on tracking down a family member, one of the commenters advised that I ask myself why. 'Is it for your benefit, their benefit, someone else's benefit?' I thought about this. It was for my benefit. And also, potentially, for their benefit. Other people's benefit could also come into it somewhere down the line, but that isn't really my concern at the moment. My concern at the moment is finding out who I am.

But, of course, life isn't a fairy tale. What if my real mother is so awful that she makes my adoptive parents look like the Bradys? (As in the sitcom. Not the child killer.)

She did give me up, after all, and leave me in the hands of people she must have known were unfit for parenting. She was dumb enough to get pregnant at fifteen, dumb enough to have the baby, and weak enough not to be able to cope with it. She was probably a monster, another Dartford housing-estate, hopeless, mindless chav-scum baby-mum.

But then what do I know?

Nothing.

And I have to find out.

So I go back to see Father – or whoever he is – and I ask for more information.

Turns out his sister left Dartford when she'd just turned sixteen. She handed over the baby – me – and left town under an ignominious cloud. The father – my real father – was just some local type, older than she was, making me the product of a statutory rape – nice – who removed himself from the scene as soon as his seed had borne fruit.

After which, my father and his sister failed to stay in regular contact, but he does know that she married. The last he heard, she was living in North London with a man named Hale.

So I come home, and I begin my search.

Fay Hale.

The name sounds otherworldly to me. I ask Google what it thinks. Google recognises her but offers too many alternatives.

So I go to the Salvation Army site, as recommended by some of the blog readers. Apparently, part of their charitable remit is to help find missing people. I don't like the Salvation Army, with all their unpleasant, coffer-rattling, proselytising Blood and Fire bullshit, so I'm pleased when I realise that, in order to have them help me find my mum, they must first charge me a £45 registration fee, then a further £150 to carry out the actual search. I bite my thumbs at them and move on.

Next stop is *192.com*, the directory-enquiries people. They boast over 630 million people, businesses, and places on their books. I key in Fay Hale, London, and up she pops.

I have to register in order to see her details. It is free of charge so I do so.

Within minutes, I have an address, and a telephone number.

I steel myself.

I call.

A man answers the telephone. Gruff voice. Ugly. "Ello,' he barks.

'Oh, hello. Um, can I speak to Fay, please?' I am using my calm, charming telephone voice. It is greeted with silence. Followed by, seconds later, a woman's voice.

'Hello?'

It's a nice voice. It's warm. Young. But then if she had me when she was only fifteen, she'd still only be forty-five. She *would* still be young.

'Hello,' I repeat, concentrating on keeping my voice still. 'Is that Fay Hale?'

'Yeah, who's this?'

Her voice is immediately suspicious. I suspect she already knows who I am. I intuit a connection.

'Formerly Fay Cattermole?' I continue.

'What?'

Oh. Suddenly her voice is wholly alien to me, as it should be.

'Oh,' I say. 'I'm trying to track down a Fay Cattermole,' I say slowly.

'A what? I dunno what you're talkin' about, mate. I think you've got the wrong number.'

I apologise and get off the line, feeling stupid. All at once the whole enterprise seems quite absurd. I consider the fact that my father is most probably making the whole thing up. Not out of malevolence, as in the old days, but out of insanity. You can't fire electricity into an old man's brain and expect him still to be able to cut the mustard. He's lucky if he can lick the knife. The man's a simpleton, with a head full of cauterised haemorrhoids.

I potter around on the internet for a while longer, following up a few more Google results. Then it occurs to me that it might not be 'Hale' after all. I return to directory enquiries and type in Fay Hayle, London.

Up pops a different set of results.

Unfortunately, her details are not on the free list. I need to buy credits. One credit, £1.99. I pay, begrudgingly.

She lives in Archway.

I call the number.

A woman answers the phone. My heart moves.

'Oh, hello there,' I begin, my voice so mellifluous as to be almost creepy. 'I wonder if you can help me. I'm trying to track down a Mrs Fay Hayle, formerly Fay Cattermole.'

There is a silence. A long silence. I break it. 'Hello?'

'Yes,' she says. 'Who is this?'

It's her. I know it. I know I thought I knew it ten minutes ago, but I was wrong. I didn't know it ten minutes ago. I merely thought I knew it. Now I know it. I *know* it.

'Um ...' My voice shakes. 'I'm ... My name is Stan Cattermole. I'm calling to—'

There is a gasp. A voiced gasp like this woman has been punched in the stomach. I stop talking and wait. My eyes are watering.

'Stanley,' she says, her voice a whisper. And then she starts to cry. She tries to stop herself, but she can't. She says my name again. She says, 'Oh God,' four or five times. She says she's sorry. She is crying, sobbing. 'I'm so sorry,' she sobs.

'It's all right,' I say. I am crying too. Tears quite suddenly gushing out of my eyes. I am weeping with this woman I do not know, have never met, but *feel*, distinctly, profoundly, right there in the core of me.

This is my mother all right. And she's an emotional train-wreck. Just like me.

Time, I think, for a little distance.

CHAPTER THIRTY-THREE

HIS NAME IS STANLEY CATTERMOLE

Stately, plump Stan Cattermole was conceived in 1977, on the eve of April Fool's Day, in a garden shed. It was an uncomfortable, painful coupling which fifteen-year-old Fay Cattermole had no intention of repeating. Unfortunately, for her at least, once was enough.

Stan's father was Doug Dinsdale, a nineteen-year-old labourer who at the time of the coupling was working on the construction of the second Dartford Tunnel.

It wasn't rape. Fay wanted to make that quite clear.

Technically, it was rape. Yes. But for a while there, Fay thought she might actually love him. Which is why, on 31 March 1977 – Doug's nineteenth birthday – she let him take her virginity.

'I didn't enjoy it at all,' she told Stan in the French restaurant he had chosen for their first face-to-face meeting. Actually, they'd met in a pub round the corner first and had a couple of drinks to steady their nerves. And prior to that, they'd spoken on the telephone three times. 'I told him it was a one-off, a treat for his birthday. I thought we'd get married when I was sixteen.'

But then of course she fell pregnant. And Doug disappeared.

'Literally,' she insisted. 'The last time I saw him, I told him I was pregnant and asked him what he was going to do about it. He said we'd get married. He actually asked me to marry him, and I said yes, and for a day, I was happy. We made love again that night.

I still didn't enjoy it. The next day he went to work and I went home. The next night I tried to find him, and he'd moved out of his digs, packed his job in and disappeared.' She shrugged. 'What a pig, eh?' She smiled. 'You have to stop crying, you know.'

Stan wiped at his eyes with his serviette. 'I know,' he said. 'I know. I will. I'm sure I will, at some stage.'

'You're so emotional,' she said. 'You're worse than me.'

Stan smiled. He had his mother's smile. Also her eyes. Stan's mother was ever so slightly plump. If she married a royal, the press would call her dowdy, but she was actually far more confident and vivacious than that would imply. She had freshly dyed ash-blonde hair and freshly applied lipstick. She had high cheekbones and a tender mouth.

She told Stan that, when his father had deserted her, she turned to her mother for help. And her mother just told her to get rid of it.

So she got rid of it. Her mother filled a bath hot salty water and forced as much of a bottle of gin into her daughter as possible. Then her daughter vomited and the baby was dead. 'I could tell,' she said. 'I could feel it dying.'

Then she smiled across the table and wiped her own eyes with a tissue.

'A couple of weeks later you came back to life,' she laughed. 'You were a determined little bugger.'

'I'm sorry,' said Stan.

'No!' Fay reached across the table and stroked her son's face. 'Don't say that. Don't ever say that.'

'I just mean I'm sorry that you felt you had to do that, you know. I'm sorry you were in such a terrible position, and then you failed. It must have been devastating.'

'It was devastating,' she said. 'I was going crazy with it. That's why I couldn't keep you. I lost it, started having … bad thoughts.' She looked away from her son, ashamed. 'I was a danger to myself, and to you. I didn't know what I was doing.'

Which is where her brother came in. Jack was nine years older than Fay and had recently married a woman called Maggie.

Maggie had fallen pregnant a year previously but had lost the baby. It was the summer of '76. There was a big drought, an interminable heatwave, and complications set in. Fay can't remember exactly, but she thinks the baby was strangled by the umbilical cord.

Although they hadn't been trying for a baby in the first place, after nine months they were used to the idea, and when the baby died, they too were devastated.

Fay thinks her brother changed then, when their baby died. Changed from a decent bloke into something of a heel. Which is why she resisted when he said he'd take the baby. She resisted because she didn't trust him. She trusted Maggie still less.

She'd never really got on with Maggie and tended to keep her distance. Then, after Maggie lost the baby, she became an unbearable monster.

Maggie was happy to take the baby, but she wanted Fay to sign a contract. A pre-natal.

She wanted Fay to sign away the baby. So that she'd have no rights. She wouldn't be able to see it, wouldn't be able to send birthday cards, wouldn't be able to acknowledge that she was the mother.

Naturally, Fay refused.

'I was just a kid,' she said, 'but I wasn't stupid. I agreed that they could adopt you, though. I didn't feel like I had a choice really. And I felt bad for Jack. I always felt bad for Jack. I thought maybe having a baby would sort him out.'

Stan was a difficult birth. A long, difficult labour. And by the time she was returned home with her baby, Maggie and Jack were waiting to take him away.

Fay resisted but was reminded that it was for the best.

Stan was taken away on his first night out of hospital.

Fay was wracked with remorse.

The next day when she went to visit, Maggie refused to let her past the front door. She produced the typed contract which Fay had apparently signed during her labour.

Fay was distraught.

'I know now that it was meaningless and would never stand up, legally, but at the time I thought that was it, I was convinced I had signed you away.' Fay shook her head sadly. 'I'm so sorry,' she said.

'Please don't be sorry,' said Stan. 'You were just a child. You did everything you could, and you didn't do anything to be ashamed of.'

'I knew what my brother was like,' she said. 'I should have given you up for proper adoption.'

'Don't,' said Stan. 'Really. This is great. Just ... this. This is perfect.'

'I came back for you,' she said. 'I waited till you were sixteen, then I came looking for you. Jack didn't know where you were. He said you'd gone to Scotland.'

'What? Why would he say that? I was half a mile away in Dartford when I was sixteen.'

She shook her head scornfully. 'So he lied. I was wondering. He always was a liar.' Fay paused and drank from her glass of wine. 'How is he?' she asked.

Stan shrugged and smiled. 'Great,' he said, laughing. 'Genuinely better than ever. I think they should've given him ECT when he was twenty-five, and life would have been great.'

A cloud of sadness moved over Fay's face.

'Don't,' said Stan, pre-empting her renewed apology. 'I'm so happy to have met you, I could cry.'

'But you are crying,' said Fay.

'Happy tears,' he said. 'Happy tears.'

CHAPTER THIRTY-FOUR

GLAD ALL OVER

I wrote a beautifully nauseating blog post yesterday about how happy I am at the moment. Inspired by watching *Pollyanna* on TV a week ago, I decided to play 'The Glad Game' and list fifteen things that made me feel glad. I was kind of bluffing, to be honest, but not entirely. The one thing I am particularly genuinely glad about at the moment I didn't really mention. Instead I wrote, 'Change is a remarkable thing.' Amen to that.

'I'm glad you're glad,' read one of the comments, left by Fermina. Fermina is a character in *Love in the Time of Cholera* by Gabriel García Márquez. Fermina is Morag's online moniker. It was definitely really her. I ignored it. Comment moderation had been in place since the stalker turned up and started leaving messages like this one: 'Hi- it's- M- here- I'll- be- c- to- G. M, I's- y and is - c -home -b of- l. lol.xx' and 'Why don't you get an "ASSHOLE" tattoo?'. So I binned Morag. Not out of spite or malice or any kind of bad feeling. I just thought it was best to draw a line. Plus, just seeing her fake name and feeling her presence dredged up all kinds of stuff for me and made me feel less glad. I decided it was better to cut that off at the knees.

That night I received a text message. It read: 'I miss you.'

To say that this message left me feeling conflicted would be an understatement. On the one hand I was furious that this woman felt she could just dip in and out of my life as and when it pleased her, riding roughshod all over my emotions like a ten-stone fly on an eggshell chandelier. On the other hand, part of me soared.

Then I had to decide whether or not to reply.

Of *course* I replied. Not only because I feel like a giant cauldron of semen bubbling away on an enormous purple fire, but also, quite simply, because I love her.

I love her.

I know I might have rather devalued the love coin in the past by claiming to feel it at the drop of an aitch, but for that I can only apologise and be reassured by the power of the pain in my heart that, this time, it's real.

'Not as much as I miss you.'

That's what I wrote in reply. I'd like to pretend it was something wittier, more sophisticated and urbane, but the truth would only come back and bite me on the arse.

She called me. We spoke for a short while. She said, 'Why don't you come up and see me some time?'

I said, 'What about tomorrow?'

She said, 'OK then. Tomorrow.'

And here I am. In Brighton. With Morag. We're having a pizza. And catching up.

'So how are things going with Christ?' I ask.

Morag frowns like it's not something she particularly wants to talk about, then she frowns as if to say, *Comme ci, comme ça*. '*Comme ci, comme ça*,' she says.

I wonder what I'm doing here. 'So it is still going then?' I ask.

'Not really,' she says.

It's my turn to frown. 'You still don't know what you want, do you, Morag?'

'Is that a crime?' she asks.

'No,' I reply. 'Of course it isn't a crime.' I drink. She drinks.

'I miss you, Stan,' she says, 'because you make me laugh, and we have fun together, and do stuff, but mostly,' she says, 'most of all ...'

'You like the way I move?'

'No,' she says. 'No. You offer me love. And it's difficult to turn down.'

'You've turned it down before,' I point out.

'I know,' she agrees. 'Maybe I wasn't ready before.'

Suddenly it occurs to me that I'm only here because Christ has dumped her. This paranoid scenario assails me, complete, spinning, and perfect. I'm the fallback guy.

'Actually, that's not it,' she says. 'I was ready. I don't think *you* were ready before. I've been keeping up with your blog and I think you've changed. Something's happened,' she said.

My fallback-guy scenario falls away as swiftly as it assailed me. The fact is, Morag and I were meant to be together. She is the only one with insight enough to see that something has happened to me. She is the only one who knows me at all.

I tell her about the revelations, about my mum.

Morag is shocked.

'No. Way,' she says, enunciating each word like a spell.

'Way,' I say, predictably.

'I knew it,' she says. 'I knew something wasn't right.' Morag always said that there was something weird about my parents. When I told her how they treated me, she couldn't quite get her head around it. 'I don't mean any disrespect,' she used to say, 'but that's not normal parenting. By any standards.'

She puts her hand over mine. I soar.

'I'm so happy for you,' she says.

'I'd like you to meet her,' I say.

'I'd love to meet her,' she says.

The waiter arrives with the bill. I pay it. I insist. 'So what should we do now?' I say.

Morag smiles. 'Take me dancing,' she says.

I laugh. We've had this conversation before. She knows I have all the grace and rhythm of a fridge full of bats thrashing down the side of a mountain. But of course, this is the new me.

'I would be honoured to take you dancing,' I say.

So Morag takes me to a club where they play the Smiths and the Propellerheads and a song I've only ever heard once before about prehistoric animals and parthenogenesis, and I dance like I've never danced before, not like a fridge full of bats, but like a silk sack full of sweetly greased monkeys. We dance together. We laugh. We kiss.

After the club we get a cab back to Morag's and we go to bed. The joy I feel is beyond words. I'm glad we split up. If we hadn't split up, I'd never be feeling this, and this is all I've ever wanted to feel, I swear.

'You'd better put a condom on,' she says. Of course, she's right. I do so quickly and move back inside.

The next day I can't stop myself wondering where we stand now. Over an afternoon breakfast I ask. 'Where do we stand now?'

'Give me a while to sort things out,' she says.

'OK,' I say, pretending for a moment that that is enough of an answer. Pretending to be that cool.

The moment passes.

'And then what?'

Two days later we meet in London and it is decided. We are back together. But this time we are actually going out with one another. None of that fuck-buddies nonsense. Fuck buddies! I mean, come *on*. Who were we trying to fool? What were we thinking? This time round we're having serious fun. Grown-up, going out and forsaking all others fun, with no messing about, no mind games, and no nonsense. This time we have made a commitment to one another. We've even started talking about Christmas. And about the new year in London.

I bluster through the rest of the month like a man made of biscuits and clouds.

I finish the copywriting job for the government with gusto and I find myself somewhere to move to in December. It's a terraced house in North London with a spare room to write books in and a back garden for a cat. The moving date is the same weekend as my thirty-first birthday, the same weekend I started writing the blog that changed my life in so many ways.

It feels like my life really is starting afresh.

CHAPTER THIRTY-FIVE

WEE TIMOROUS BEASTIES

Morag tells me we're starting afresh and says it's time to meet her friends. I cheer inside. *This is how it's supposed to be*, I tell myself, and we drive to Brighton, Heathcote handling like a dream, his wheels dancing across the tarmac with 'The Blue Danube' on the stereo, and there's nothing at all can touch us.

And everything goes swimmingly. On Saturday we meet Jack and Kelly and Nat and Roy and we have a whale of a time and stay at Nat's house. On Sunday we meet Amy and Sean and we spend the night in a hotel. And then on Monday we go to Beth's house for dinner. In attendance, apart from the obvious, are Nat and Roy, Amy and Sean, and Jane. Also, Beth has a four-year-old son called Jamie. Jamie takes rather a shine to me, and frankly I to him, so he's crawling all over me, and I'm being a bit silly, making him laugh, tickling him and showing him my excessively brilliant magic tricks. All good innocent fun, and obviously a great little brownie-point earner as far as Morag and her friends are concerned.

But then it all goes horribly, hideously wrong and I'm cursed with a memory which I know will leave me cringing and crying out in horror for years to come.

The adults are in the kitchen, talking adult talk. I am in the living room, visible from the kitchen, but separate, playing childish games. I have hold of Jamie under the arms and I'm throwing him up in the air and catching him. I barely let go of him at all, of course, as he's really rather heavy and probably a little too old to be tossed about like a baby. He's airborne for a second maybe, but it's enough to amuse him, which in turn amuses me. 'More!' he cries, chortling and gurgling.

'Careful, Stan,' says Morag from the kitchen.

'I know,' I reply, slightly fractious. 'Don't worry,' I say. 'I don't work for Haringey council.' Topical. And I faux-toss Jamie in the air again, walking slowly around Beth's large living room as I go, tossing and catching. 'More!' he cries, amidst wild giggles. His mother doesn't seem to mind at all, and I am perfectly in control so I continue. 'I'm going to throw you away!' I say, and I toss him up in the air again.

It is *hilarious*.

'More!' he cries.

And then it happens. In the blink of an eye, Jamie's giggles turn to the most ear-piercing screams I think I've ever heard as his head cracks loudly against the concrete ceiling.

Basically, the wall between Beth's living room and dining area has at some stage been removed to make one large room ... except for one column in the centre of where the wall used to be, and maybe a metre of wall hanging down from the ceiling all the way across. I'm sure there's an architectural term for what I'm making a pig's arse of describing here, but obviously I don't know what it is. Basically, there's a bit of the wall left, above, and I didn't see it, didn't even know it was there until I smashed a small child's head against it.

When I realise what has happened, I instinctively squeeze Jamie close to me, start rubbing the top of his head and saying things like, 'There, there.' I don't even know what 'There, there' means, but I am desperate. With his face bright red, soaking wet, and contorted in agony, he pulls away from me and reaches out to his mum, who is there in seconds. I try to explain what happened as she takes her son away from me.

I feel horrendous.

I feel like a monster.

This really is one of the worst moments of my life.

The fact that he is still conscious and able to scream at all I am sure is working in my favour, and probably means that no lasting harm has been done. But then what do I know? Brain damage is probably painful.

Beth is fine about it. She takes control and begins soothing the boy immediately, like the professional mother she is. Morag, meanwhile, is giving me evils from the kitchen, while the rest of her friends look on in a combination of amusement, concern, and pity.

My mouth is still hanging open and my arms are still somewhere between the memory of tossing the boy and covering my face in shock and shame.

In the end, Jamie is fine, and Beth is really nice about it, much nicer, I fear, than I might have been if some stupid fucker had bashed my son's head against the ceiling.

But of course I don't have a son.

Or do I?

A week ago, Morag was a couple of days late.

Now, she's over a week late.

'It doesn't mean anything,' she says. 'I'm not massively regular anyway.'

Plus she'd just come off the pill over the summer after fears of thrombosis, embolism, and stroke.

'I've been a month late in the past,' she says.

I am shocked. A month seems like an awful long time to imagine you might be about to start a family. At two weeks, I'm already making lists of names.

I actually quite like the idea of being a dad. I think I might be ready. I'm mature enough, I reckon. I can get fairly lucrative work when there isn't a recession looming, and I'm constantly learning important lessons about child-rearing. Don't give them away to heartless, plate-wielding lunatics without a discernible conscience. Don't dash their brains out on low ceilings.

Oh God. I still can't believe I did that. What if he'd just died?

I ... it doesn't bear thinking about.

We drive back to London after dinner, and I again bring up the possibility of us having a child.

'But if you are pregnant,' I say. 'What would you like to do?'

'I don't know,' Morag replies. 'I haven't really thought about it.'

'Well, really think about it,' I insist. 'What does your gut tell you?'

'My gut tells me that I'm not ready to have a kid.'

'Oh.'

We drive in silence for a moment. Not exactly silence. We are listening to Dave Brubeck.

Then Morag says, 'What does your gut tell you?'

'Being considerably more capacious,' I reply, 'my gut has a lot to say on the subject.' I explain that although I would prefer for us to have more than a couple of months of relationship under our belts, I am actually genuinely excited by the idea of becoming a father. 'I didn't really realise before how much I want it,' I tell her. 'I reckon I'd be pretty good at it too,' I add.

'When you're not inflicting brain damage,' says Morag.

This is going to take some time to live down.

'No, I think you would too,' she adds, stroking my gear-stick arm and giving it a squeeze.

It is appreciated.

As we hit heavy late-night traffic coming into London, Morag drops a bombshell.

'Stan,' she says.

She says it in that way too. That way that says, 'I am about to say something you will not like.'

'I don't know if this has occurred to you, but if I am pregnant – and I really don't think I am – but if I am, has it occurred to you that it might not actually be yours?'

Instinctively I jab my palm against Heathcote's horn and anger the guy stuck in traffic ahead of me. He glares at me in his rear view and I give him an apologetic wave which he doubtless misinterprets.

'Why did you do that?' Morag asks.

'I have no idea,' I reply. 'I didn't do it deliberately. It was like physical Tourette's. So what are you saying?'

'Isn't it obvious?'

'Spell it out for me, though, please. If you wouldn't mind.'

'I'm just saying, if I am pregnant, there's every chance that the child could be Chris's. Probably more chance, in fact, if you think about the timing.'

Despite the inherent sense in what she's saying, I am baffled by what I'm hearing.

'But how could it be his? I don't ...' I run out of words.

'Well,' says Morag, in a deliberately condescending tone, 'you know when two people like each other.' She stops, apparently feeling like she has made sense.

'Yeah, go on,' I say.

She sighs, exasperated. 'You do know we were having sex, right?'

'Well, *yeah*,' I cry, 'but I kind of assumed that you were using some kind of protection!'

'Do you want to calm down, please?' A beep from behind alerts me to the sudden flow of traffic. I move off and Morag continues. 'Of course we were using protection. But, you know how it is, sometimes you ...'

She has stopped again.

'Sometimes you what?'

'You get a bit carried away. You know how it is.'

'So hold on a minute,' I say, driving with my forearms, two forefingers pointing skyward as if in order to realign things in my mind. 'You're telling me you had sex with him *without* a condom.'

'Sometimes,' she says. 'Just for a little while,' she clarifies. 'Yes.'

'You allowed an unsheathed penis—' I begin.

'Oh, shut up,' she says. 'Don't even think of finishing that sentence.'

We stop at some lights, my mouth still open on the word 'penis', and I sit staring at her as if to say, 'What?'

'What?' I say.

Suddenly she explodes. 'You've done the same thing! Don't you *dare* try and take the moral high ground over this.'

'But that's *me*!' I yell back.

'*What?* So what?'

I shake my head. I don't know.

'Lights have changed,' she says.

I drive. We drift into silence. Whether it's a childish sulky silence or a mature contemplative silence I cannot tell. Even for my own part. I do tend to sulk, though, no matter how much I deny it afterwards. Morag tends to sulk too. That's probably a bad sign. Probably a relationship should have – at the very most – one sulker. Two sulkers and you could be losing one week out of every four to grumpy, simmering silence. To her credit, Morag has two methods of expressing discontent: sulking, and flying into a rage. I find it difficult to deal with either. And I know she finds me difficult. Sometimes I wonder what on earth we're playing at. Sometimes I think we haven't got a chance.

As I drive, I imagine that Morag really is pregnant. I try to picture what it would mean, how our lives would change if we decided to keep the baby. I try to imagine the sudden stress we'd both feel at the thought of having a child together. I shake my head and sigh. We wouldn't last five minutes.

For the next twenty minutes, I become increasingly tense as I imagine us squabbling and scowling our way through the pregnancy, tearing each other to pieces and regretting the day that we ever laid eyes on one another. By the time we're parking the car outside my flat, I feel utterly miserable. And hopeless. Plus, I remember that my living room is piled high with half-empty boxes and piles of books and unused exercise equipment, because I started packing a few days ago, in preparation for my move in a fortnight's time. And though I am able to live in squalor and disarray quite comfortably, Morag hates mess. Despises it. By the time we step through my front door and into the mess, I am convinced that we are completely incompatible.

'Why don't you move in with me?'

I think the question has taken Morag almost as much by surprise as it has me. But I'm thinking that, if we are incompatible, then moving in together is probably the best way to find out for sure. And as far as Morag is concerned, she wants to move to London in January anyway, so it makes perfect, wonderfully impulsive sense.

'You mean, apart from the fact that we've only known each other a few months?' she asks, slightly mockingly.

'So what?' I reply, slightly pugnaciously. I know it's soon to be thinking about such things, but fuck it. I want to be with her.

'So it's probably too soon, speaking practically.'

'Oh, practically schmactically. It'll be great. And if it's not great, you can move out.'

Morag isn't convinced, but she says she'll definitely think about it, and she's very flattered and moved by the offer. 'Flattered schmattered,' I say, then I take her upstairs and I flatter her to orgasm.

Afterwards, lying in the dark, the evening's conversation goes round and round my head. Then something occurs to me.

'When did you last have sex with him?' I ask. 'With Christ,' I clarify.

Morag sighs. 'Oh, let's not,' she says.

'No, let's,' I say. 'I just want to know about the timings. I'm curious to know why he's more likely the father than I am. In the unlikely event,' I add, 'of the pitter patter of tiny feet.'

'Patter,' she says. 'Just patter. Pitter patter is rain.'

I grunt. 'Are you sure?'

'Pretty sure,' she says.

I grunt again. I don't like being wrong.

'November the sixteenth,' she says.

I do the math. Then I go cold. 'But that was after we got back together,' I cry.

'Not really,' says Morag. 'It was after we slept together again, but we hadn't definitely decided anything yet.'

'We'd definitely decided that you were going to finish with Christ, though, hadn't we? I mean, we had definitely decided that.' I am now sitting up in bed, turning on lights and preparing for another bedroom scene.

Morag shields her eyes. 'Yes, I know. That's when it was.'

'But you were supposed to be finishing with him, not fucking him! Didn't you understand that bit?'

'It was just break-up sex, Stan. Just a goodbye fuck. It would have been cruel not to have given him that.'

'But ... It was a safe goodbye fuck, though, right?'

Morag screws up her face. 'Mostly,' she says.

I shook my head slowly, mouth open. 'I can't quite believe I'm hearing this. Seriously, Morag, I mean, fuck the man goodbye if you absolutely have to, but don't let his unsheathed cock in your babymaker. That's just rubbing salt into the wounds.'

'I'm sorry, Stan,' she says. 'It's over now,' she says. 'I'm with you now.'

She tried to stroke my face, but I pull away from her.

'Please,' she says. 'Let's not fall out over this.'

'But it hurts!' I cry, and then suddenly I'm storming out of the bedroom like a child.

I recover, return to bed and let bygones be bygones. Morag insists she hasn't done anything wrong. Begrudgingly, I accept this.

'So shouldn't we have a test?' I suggest.

'I was thinking the same thing,' says Morag.

'OK, good. Let's go to the chemist first thing tomorrow morning then. Presuming nothing happens in the night.'

She looks at me like I've just laid an egg. 'No,' she says finally. 'I mean an AIDS test.'

My mouth falls open, rather like the mouth of a naïve child. 'AIDS?' I say. 'But—'

'I'd like to be sure,' says Morag.

'But I haven't had unsafe sex since ... you know.' She says she doesn't know, so I remind her about Sue.

Once reminded, she is surprised. 'Really?' she says.

I agree to have an AIDS test anyway, more to show solidarity than anything else, then I get back to my original point.

'Honestly, Stan,' she says, 'I know my own body. Eight or nine days late is nothing. I'll start worrying after a month.'

'A month?!' I am shocked. 'Jesus, I'd be painting the nursery after a month.'

'That's because you don't really know anything about it,' she explains.

'OK,' I say. 'I'll shut up about it.'

'Please,' says Morag. 'That'd be nice.'

But it's not easy, shutting up about it. Because suddenly, I want to be a dad. I really want to be a dad. I want a kid I can play with like Pablo and love like a child, and the child can love me right back.

'Can we call him Pablo? If he's a boy, come on, let's call him Pablo.'

'Sweetheart,' she smiles, and I soar every time, 'don't get your hopes up.'

I say nothing.

Morag looks at me, and I cannot hold her gaze. I smile, guiltily. She says that she can read me like a book. I laugh and pretend that I really must write that one down. Then I find my latest notebook and write that one down. I speak as I pretend to write: '"I can read you like a book," says Morag. Full stop.' Thinks. '"What kind of book?" I retort wittily. "A baby book?" Morag bursts into gales of uproarious laughter.' Pause for real-life laughs. Continue. '"Oh, I do love you, Stanley. So very much. Even more than Audrey Tautou loves you in your deepest, most pathetic, shoddy fantasies. Plus I admire and respect you. And am in awe of your lovemaking prowess. And do you know what I want more than anything else in this crazy, cockeyed caravan called life? Do ya? I want to have a baby with you."' Stop. Rewind.

No rewind.

Morag glares at me gently, a pitiful smile stroking the corners of her sultry, child-bearing mouth. 'There are other psychiatrists, you know,' she says. 'You know?' She is Mental Health Nurse Morag. It's a role she plays for inappropriate laughs. I flinch from her hand and she laughs and is loving, so loving. 'My poor, wee timorous beastie,' she whispers, creeping up my arm like a reckless sex-goblin. Then she strokes my face and kisses my mouth with those ecstatically forgiving lips and a tidal wave of desire washes me clean off the bed. I want so much to make babies and live my life with this woman that hot shivers molest me everywhere with every touch of her tongue.

We make love.

Fuck it, it's been a fantastic year. Whatever happens.

CHAPTER THIRTY-SIX

POSITIVE MENTAL ATTITUDE

Things are going well for me and I feel blessed. I have a new mum, who I really love, I don't have AIDS and my girlfriend may be pregnant with the Christ child. Everything I touch turns to gold.

'It's been a year,' says Ange in an email I read this morning, 'since the big reunion. We should do it again. I have important news too. Big news.' Karen is copied into the mail, so the three of us meet up at Ange's house the day after my birthday, the day after I move into my new home. I'm pretty sure I know what Ange's news is. The last time we spoke on the phone – in October some time – was on the back of a photo she'd messaged to me. It was a headshot of a bloke I didn't recognise. He was smiling. And he was black. The accompanying message said, 'Racist, my arse!' I called her up. She told me that she'd started seeing this guy. His name was Renoir.

'I thought you didn't like black men!' I cried.

'I don't!' she cried. Renoir, however, made her laugh, and in the end, apparently, that was enough to break down her ridiculous prejudice.

So I get it in my head that she's either pregnant or engaged to be married. My money is on pregnant and I am thrilled, because this might be as close as I get to a happy ending. As I stand at her front door, I find myself excited for her, and suppressing a tiny giggle.

When she opens the door, I'm shocked. I haven't seen her for around three months, but in that time she's lost a lot of weight. And she's wearing a hat. And a not particularly fancy hat at that. I try to hide my surprise, and hug her hello. We swap how-are-yous and good-goods, then I swap some more with Karen, who's also just arrived and is waiting in the kitchen, and we all sit at the table. And breathe.

Then Ange tells me her news. 'So. This is the thing,' she says. 'I got your cancer.'

'*No.*'

She nods, smiling, beatific, tired.

'No, no, no.'

She laughs. 'I'm afraid so, Stanley.'

It seems every time we've met over the last year, I've whined about some niggling pain or other, convinced that nascent tumours were munching at my innards.

'I found a lump,' she says. 'I was so lucky.' I pull a face. I'm in shock.

'Totally by chance,' she continues. 'I never checked myself. I don't know why, but all my life it just never occurred to me, and when it did occur to me, I just didn't bother. Then one day, without me even knowing I was doing it, my hand moved up over my boob and I found the lump. Then I lost it again. I kept trying to find it and I couldn't. So I forgot about it, then the next day, I lifted my arm and I got a shooting sensation across from here to here.' She points from her chest to under her arm. 'It wasn't a pain. It wasn't painful at all. It was more like a tingle. But it freaked me out. So I made an appointment at the doctor for the next afternoon. Then some stuff at school came up. There was an emergency meeting to discuss a bullying situation which was getting out of hand, and I knew both of the kids involved, so I had to be there. I was just about to cancel the doctor's appointment when the social worker phoned to say he'd just been hit by a car and would have to reschedule.' She raises her eyebrows, and her hands, and is nodding appreciatively. 'Makes you think,' she says. 'If that hadn't happened, I probably wouldn't have gone. And, you know, I might not have been so lucky.'

I agree, grudgingly.

'So I went along anyway, but the doctor couldn't feel anything. He was a nice bloke. He'd just started there. He said he was pretty confident there was nothing to worry about, but then he admitted that he didn't really know for sure. All he knew was that he couldn't feel anything, but he said that didn't necessarily mean that there was nothing there. So he booked me in for a mammogram, saying I'd have to wait two weeks. That night I told my dad, and he said, "Fuck that. Pardon my French." That's what he said. He said, "If you're worried, I'm not having you wait two weeks," so he made me an appointment to see his private BUPA people the next day.

'So I went and had the mammogram and I saw the doctor afterwards – they give you the results immediately – and he said it was perfectly fine. He said if there was anything wrong it would have shown up, and there was nothing.

'I was so relieved, but then, and this is the weird bit – I didn't even know what I was going to say until I heard myself saying it. I just shook my head and said, "There's something wrong." He asked me what I meant and I said I didn't know. I said, "I just know something's not right." It was really weird. I swear I didn't know any such thing until I heard myself saying it. But I could feel that there was something there. The doctor was really nice. He said, if it would put my mind at rest, they could book me in for a biopsy.'

Karen and I sit and stare, listening, entranced, horrified.

'Don't ever have a biopsy,' says Ange. 'Unless you need one, of course, but pray you don't need one. The most painful thing I've ever had. It was like being attacked with a staple gun.' She does a brief but violent mime. 'Really, I felt like I was in *American Psycho*. They did two biopsies, one in my boob and one in my armpit. I was crying. I couldn't stop myself. I'm usually good with pain, but this was like nothing I'd ever experienced. The next day I had a huge purple bruise all over here.'

Then, when she went back for the results of the biopsy, the

doctor asked her to sit down and then asked her if she'd like a glass of water. That's when she knew.

'So I've got cancer then?' she said.

'I'm sorry to say that you have, Angela, yes,' the doctor said.

The biopsy located two tumours, one in the top part of the breast, one in a lymph node under the arm. They acted quickly to remove them.

'It all happened within ten days of my first visit to the doctor,' she says. 'Within two weeks of first finding that lump.' She smiles. 'Thank fuck for private medicine.'

Karen and I are devastated, shell-shocked.

'You're so young,' says Karen. 'It's such bad luck.'

'It is and it isn't,' Ange insists. 'I honestly feel really lucky. Unlucky would be not finding the lump when I did or taking the mammogram's word for it and carrying on with my life in ignorance with the cancer spreading. Seriously. I feel blessed.' She smiled. 'Fingers crossed!'

As far as they can tell, the lumpectomy was a success. 'I'm a little lopsided,' Ange says, 'but nothing to get upset about. And the surgery went really, really well. Now I've just got to get the chemo out of the way.' She grins. She's booked in for her first chemo session in just a couple of days. And while she obviously isn't looking forward to it, there is a peculiar kind of excitement about her, like she's embarking on a brave new adventure and can't wait to see what it throws at her. It's like she's thrumming with matter-of-fact, honest-to-goodness, purest PMA.

'How's Harvey handling it?' asks Karen.

'Brilliantly,' says Ange. 'He couldn't be any more supportive. And he's not afraid to talk about it either. Which is a relief. He said that, even if I end up having to lose the breast entirely, he'll just love the other one even more.'

'I thought his name was Renoir,' I interject.

'No, love, this is a new one,' says Ange. 'Keep up.'

'Oh.' I am disappointed. 'I was picturing mixed-race children for you. I was looking forward to seeing how you'd cope. Who's this then?'

'This is Harvey. He's another teacher. He's a carer. He's what I need now.'

'And what colour is Harvey?' I persist.

Ange shrugs. 'Do you know, I haven't even noticed.'

I laugh and say *'Touché'* flamboyantly. But my heart isn't in it. I feel devastated. I feel afraid for the future. For Ange. For myself. As she talks, I imagine how I'd react if I were in her shoes. When she talks about the surgery, for example, I imagine the cut, then the throbbing, searing, ceaseless pain of healing. Or infection. I'm afraid of pain. When she talks about getting tested and retested, I imagine the tyranny of the imagination, the absolute inability to stop imagining ever more frightening scenarios. And then when she talks about the chemo, I am flabbergasted.

Ange has a friend called Sarah, another teacher, who had both breasts removed. Sarah kindly wrote down exactly what Ange has in store for her. It makes for gruesome, vividly distressing reading.

I read it aloud.

'First you get your FEC. That's your fluorouracil, your epirubicin, and your cyclophosphamide. Bright-red liquid. Makes your piss blood-red. Terrifying.

'You get dosed in a big room with all kinds of machines and IV drips, and everyone sits in little areas together, about fifteen of you, women with breast and ovarian cancer, men with prostate cancer, all in there together. Take books and snacks. Knit. It takes hours. My mother-in-law brought knitting.

'You'll be offered a cold cap. This is where they freeze your head a bit before and after the chemo to stop your hair falling out. Don't do it. Your hair will fall out anyway, and it's the most dispiriting, undignified thing ever. I recommend you get it cut beforehand so you can get used to it.'

I look up at Ange and she whips off her beanie hat. 'Ta-daaaaa!' she sings.

'You look amazing!' I cry. She does too. I mean, I loved her hair, but everybody's got hair. Hair is so last Thursday. Now Ange is the chick with the sexy shaved head! 'You look gorgeous,' I tell her. 'You've got a head like a peach!'

Then I get back to the oncological charge sheet:

'I wish I'd cut my own hair. I would definitely have felt more in control. I did the cold cap. It gives you blinding headaches and you have to hang around in the hospital for hours after the chemo. My hair started falling out after the second session anyway.

'Chemo is injected into your veins. First you have a twenty-minute bag of saline, then a twenty-minute anti-nausea bag. Then you get a thirty-minute syringe of red chemical warfare released into you. Then another bag of saline, a couple of bags of epirubicin, and a bag of cyclophosphamide for good luck. All told, it takes about four hours. I promise you, it's a riot. Then you wait another hour to get the drugs you need to take at home. I had to take fifteen different pills every day. Anti-nausea pills for the first three days to stem the tide of severe vomiting, followed by stomach pills to counteract the anti-nausea drugs, anti-inflammatories to counteract the inflammation, painkillers to the kill the pain, antibiotics to counteract the biotics, and so on and so forth.

'On the first day after the chemo, you'll feel more tired than you've ever felt before. For three days after that, you'll feel sicker than you've ever felt before. Then for two days after that, you'll have a bright-red face, brighter and redder than it's ever been before. Also, your immune system's shot because your white blood cells have taken a hit, so you'll have a hideous flu and your entire body – your legs, your arms, your bones, your joints, your skin, your liver, everything – aches and cries out in pain. After two and a half weeks, your strength starts to pick up and you start to feel better. Which is when you get dragged back in for your next session.

'You have three lots of that, then the fourth session is Taxotere, which is *really* nasty. Taxotere hits neurological cells, causing severe short-term memory loss and hammering the immune system. It's like your body just breaks down and everything revolts. I had crippling leg pain and uncontrollable vomiting and had to call the doctor out. He prescribed more anti-sickness, antibiotics, and painkillers. I had to have an immune booster injection in my stomach. Tom said it was like living with Hunter S. Thompson.

'All told, that takes five and a half months of your life. Then there's a month off before the radiation starts. Every day for three weeks.

'You will lose your hair. You may lose finger- and toenails too. They will turn yellow and purple and crack and break but become too hard to cut. Your teeth will become hypersensitive and discoloured. You will have burning red-hot flushes a few times a day. You will lose your nose hair, your eyebrows, and lashes and you will learn to appreciate why these things exist in the first place. You will have no body hair at all and your legs will be smoother than they've ever been before. Score!

'Darling, it's a riot. You're going to love it.

'You will feel worse than you have ever felt in your life before. But you will remember that, like everything else, it will pass, and it's probably doing you good. You will then feel better and you will carry on living a fantastic life and filling the lives of the people around you with pleasure.'

Ange is still smiling. 'Sounds like fun, right?'

Karen has tears in her eyes.

'So you're going to be all right,' I say. 'This time next year you'll be right as rain.'

'That's what the kids say,' she says. 'The kids have been fantastic.' Ange has spent just a couple of afternoons in the school since the op, and some of the kids have been making home visits to check on her. 'One of them,' she says, 'Marlon, he's like, this seven-foot Hackney gangsta, and he says to me, "Miss, you got to own that tumour innit. You got *fuck* it up, Miss."'

'He's right,' I laugh. 'You've got to pop a cap in its arse.'

'I am,' says Ange. 'I'm fighting the fucker.'

'You're young too,' says Karen. 'And strong. That's got to count in your favour.'

'Yeah, but so's the cancer. Me being young counts in the cancer's favour too.'

'Oh,' says Karen.

When Karen pops to the loo, Ange says that she's sorry she didn't see more of me this year. She feels bad because she stayed away because of Keith. 'It got a bit weird,' she said.

'It's my fault too,' I say, when really it's entirely my fault. 'I should have called you more. I'm sorry. I've got no excuse.'

'Well, we can see each other now,' says Ange. 'And next year. I'm going to be all right, you know.'

'Oh, I know, I know!' I reply, really enthusiastically.

Before I leave, I tell Ange about Alright Tit, a beautifully written blog on the day-to-day insanity of beating breast cancer. She smiles.

'You and your blogs,' she says.

Back home, Morag turns up in the evening and is bitching about something which I rather insensitively dismiss as pointless, trivial nonsense. I tell her about Ange. She sympathises but quite rightly points out that there is no need for me to guilt her or demean her tribulations. I apologise. But I am right.

While she is soaking in the bath, I come over all upset and get a bit weepy thinking about Ange, about life and death and living and dying.

It was worrying me a lot even before I found out about Ange.

Now I practically feel an episode coming on.

Life is cruel.

I've got to know someone through the blog who found the man she wanted to spend her life with, travelled halfway round the world to be with him, and then they both found out that he had only a few months to live.

I imagine there's never a good time to die, but that's just too cruel.

Then there was Keith's double whammy of MS and aneurysm.

Then there's his dad's heart attack. Then there was Ange's mum. Now there's Ange. And there are others, people I know less well. Every which way I turn at the moment, someone has died, or been diagnosed with something scary, or been rushed to hospital. It's like there's an epidemic of bad news out there, and it's taking all my concentration not to panic or take it personally. What I try very hard to do instead is to force into my head some sense of perspective; I try to use this litany of personal tragedy to reinforce awareness of infinite possibility and actual reality, and to feel gratitude for my own good fortune and determination to make the most of it. Or – if you prefer – I count my blessings. Because, of course, at the moment, I'm the lucky exception that proves the bad-news rule. At the moment, everything is going swimmingly for me.

Which is precisely why, suddenly, I find myself on the verge of panic.

It's, like, how long can it last?

One in three people will get cancer at some point in their lives.

That's terrifying information, and I'm not really sure what to do with it.

In the end, I do the only thing I can. I vow to stay positive, and to make the most of however much time I have left. And Ange too. And Keith. And Morag. Everyone. When I think about it more closely, I realise that this is what I do. In fact, if I have one innate quality of which I'm actually rather proud, it's my ability to take whatever life throws at me and make of it something positive. I may whinge and moan along the way, but when something truly horrendous happens, my instinct is to learn from it and grow.

Realising this afresh, I feel good about myself and I go into town to spend money I do not have on Christmas presents, including twenty DVDs for Ange – feelgood fare to help her through the chemo months – and something called a graphics tablet for Keith. I may have forgotten his birthday, but I intend to make up for it with Christmas.

CHAPTER THIRTY-SEVEN

THROW YOUR ARMS AROUND THE WORLD

This year, for the first time in my life, Christmas is finally that precious thing that everyone else has always blathered on about: a time – smug, theatrical pause – for *family*.

Fay is excellent. I really like her. She's the otherwise good apple that saves the whole sorry tree from burning. She's the one that got away from the intellectual grime of Dartford, and Father, who I suppose I can stop calling 'Father' now if I like. But I probably won't. It would just seem spiteful. I don't blame him for who he was, and I have no intention of punishing him. In fact, Mum and I are going to see him on Boxing Day. Spread a little happiness. That's what we do.

So I set up the spare room for her, for Fay. I stacked a bedside table and shelf opposite the bed with books I hoped she might like. She reads non-fiction, lots of biographies, and memoirs.

I always knew I was born of a reader.

This Christmas is going to be the opposite of all previous Christmases, the one that stops me hating Christmas.

In the past I hated Christmas because my parents would use it as an excuse to drink themselves even further into oblivion.

I hated Christmas because I had to go to midnight mass and pretend that I believed in the concepts which I invariably heard expressed there, concepts such as love, acceptance, forgiveness, peace, and compassion. Concepts such as God and the family. I hated church. I hated church because my parents would also be pretending, and they would put on a show for the people they knew at church, the people they called friends, and then when we got home they would revert to the scowling, cursing, ruthless vulgarians that deep inside they truly were.

I hated Christmas because I was a child like any other and I wanted Sonic the Hedgehog and a PC, and I wanted videos, hundreds and hundreds of videos, but unfortunately Christmas gifts that were anything other than absolutely necessary were in our house deemed frivolous and irrelevant. One year I received a new school blazer. Another year I received a new carpet for my bedroom. Sometimes, however, if I was lucky and my parents were feeling particularly festive, one of them would bung twenty quid in an envelope. We never had a tree.

I hated Christmas because I had to stay at home for most of it and pretend.

I hated Christmas because the only bit of Christmas I loved was spending time round Keith's house. This caused a real schism within me. On the one hand, it was wonderful to be given the opportunity to be able to understand what Christmas could be and to see why other people enjoyed it so much; on the other hand, it brought home everything that was lacking in my own family. On the whole, though, I cherished the time I spent at Keith's house, or – as I came to know it – The Great Escape.

And then I escaped for good, and was miserable to discover that I had begun to hate Christmas for new reasons.

Primarily, I hated it because I was scarred, and because hating it had become a habit.

As an adult, I spent quite a few Christmases alone, despite protests from people who knew me – to some people there is no greater crime against nature than spending Christmas alone. For the most part I never minded those Christmases, though. I'd tell myself I was going to write, then I'd watch six films back to back instead. It was fun, but it was sad fun. One Christmas I had a tin of meatballs for Christmas lunch. That was very sad, actually. I remember feeling rather unhappy at that point.

Then last year there was change and I had excellent fun. Christmas with kids is a whole new kettle of festive fish, and I hope to spend many more Christmases in future with children. *Inshallah*. Last Christmas seems like a long time ago now, and indeed it was. It marked the beginning though, of a turning point.

This year is even better.

Mum comes over with flowers on Christmas Eve and pops a bunch of presents under the tree. Morag roasts a salmon, and we eat like kings and get to know one another. Morag is on wonderful form and I'm so proud of her. She and Fay really seem to hit it off.

'I love your hair,' says Fay.

'Aww, thank you,' says Morag. 'I need to get it done before New Year,' she adds. 'It's getting a bit out of hand.'

'I'll do it for you,' says Fay. 'I've got scissors.'

Fay dresses hair, by the way, professionally. She has her own salon in Kilburn. My mum is a hairdresser. How cool is that?

'Stylist,' says Fay. 'I'm a stylist.'

'Pardon me,' I say.

So on Christmas Day, in my new house, my new girlfriend is getting her hair styled by my new mum.

Life is insane.

Morag is made up with her new hair. She loves it and tries to insist on paying my mum something. My mum laughs as if there were no way in a million years that she would accept any money, then says, 'As you're my son's girlfriend, let's just call it £90.'

And, for a second, just long enough for Morag and me to believe her, she keeps a straight face.

Then she laughs and tells Morag not to be ridiculous. Her laugh is the most beautiful, heartfelt thing I have ever heard. I love it. Of course she won't take her money. 'It's an honour,' she says. 'I can't believe I'm here,' she says. 'I've thought about this all my life,' she says. 'Christmas was terrible, always terrible, with a big, horrible hole in it.' She looks at me. 'Every Christmas Day I phoned your house, hoping you'd answer so I could just hear your voice. And Maggie always answered.' She stops. 'She never let me speak to you. And then the sixteenth year, on your birthday, I turned up. When you were sixteen, you were an adult and no one could stop you speaking to me. But I was too late. Every Christmas since then has been a little sadder.' Morag is stroking my mum's back gently. 'This is the best Christmas ever,' she says. 'No competition.'

I am aching to hold her in my arms.

'Right,' she says. 'Now you.'

She hops across the rug towards me like a little silver bird, snipping her scissors through the air like a mystical mechanical insect. 'Mummy's going to cut Stanley's hair!' she chirrups.

I laugh like a little boy.

We're in the tiny kitchen, where all the hair can easily be cleaned from the tiled floor. I sit in the wooden chair facing the window of the back door, which serves as a mirror. My mum ties the sheet we're using as a cape around my neck and smoothes it across my shoulders. I think about my old mum, Maggie, tying me up to stop me scratching because the sight of me scratching went through her. That was the real reason. It irritated her. Made her feel itchy herself.

'How would you like it?'

'Just a trim,' I say, and Morag takes some pictures.

As Mum starts to cut, Morag excuses herself to go and take a bath. She thanks Mum again for such a fantastic job.

'She's really lovely, Stan,' Mum tells me. 'I'm so happy for you.'

'Me too,' I say. 'I'm happy for myself too.'

'I guess I need to get back out there,' Mum says absently.

Mum was married to a man for four years, engaged to another she was with for five years, but they all just fizzled out in the end. 'I don't know how people make these things last for ever,' she said.

'You should start a blog,' I say. 'You'll be fighting them off with a shitty stick.'

She smiles. 'I'll think about it,' she says. I told Mum about the blog during our first meeting, when I told her about everything.

She appears to be thinking about it as her fingers massage my scalp and play with my hair.

'I can't believe you think you're ugly,' she says.

I smile. She's so sweet. So nice.

'Yeah, but you're prejudiced,' I say.

'No!' she cries, shaking her head, almost offended at the thought. 'Seriously. Objectively. Well, as objective as I can be. You've got a very striking face.'

I nod, just loving her. We're both looking at my face in the mirror of the back-door glass.

'I love the shape of it.' Her hands are all over my face, and it feels wonderful, like they belong there, like that's where they always should have been. 'And you've got fabulous eyes.'

'Yeah, I like my eyes,' I say. 'I've always liked my eyes.'

'They're the same as mine,' she says.

'I know,' I say.

Then she tops up my glass of cherry brandy and starts to cut my hair.

'The second time I went back to see my dad,' I say, 'Jack,' I add, 'I asked him something. And his answer really intrigued me, really freaked me out a bit.'

'I love the way you talk,' says Mum, cutting, listening. 'Go on,' she adds. 'I'm listening.'

'I asked him why he'd never loved me. Why he'd never shown me any affection, never told me he loved me, and hugged me or tucked me in at night, and do you know what he said?'

Mum shakes her head, snips another lock, waits.

'He told me that they used to, when I was born, and that I wouldn't let them. He reckons I spurned their affections, pushed them away and wouldn't let them love me.'

'But even if that were true,' Mum says, 'you're not just going to accept that, are you? I mean, any parent worth their salt would insist on loving their kid, even if he did try to push them away.' She's quite angry. 'But look at you. I can tell by the way you've responded to me since we met, the way you've opened yourself up to me. I've never met anyone so willing to be loved.'

'I know,' I agree. 'I'm sure you're right. But I do like the idea of me rejecting them because they weren't good enough. Maybe I knew. I reckon somewhere deep inside, I knew something was wrong.'

'You must've,' says Mum.

After a few seconds' silent cutting, Mum asks: 'There's something I wanted to ask you, Stanley. I – I just need to know, did they hurt you at all? I mean, physically, did they hit you?'

I don't want to hurt her, and I don't want her to blame herself, but I don't want to lie to her either, so I tell her that there wasn't much physical abuse outside of leg-slapping, chair-tying and the occasional swift beating with a belt. The real abuse was psychological, though, telling me all my life that I was ugly, for example. Telling me that there was something wrong with me, that I was a freak of nature. Telling me they were sick of the sight of me even at birth.

Mum is trying to carry on with my hair, but there are tears rolling down her cheeks.

I smile and give a little moan of concern. 'Oooh, it's OK. Mum. You're my mum now and all of that is in the past.'

'But it's just so wrong!' she cries, stamping a foot.

'I know,' I say, equally touched and amused. 'But you mustn't let it interfere with my Christmas haircut. Now, come on. You need to concentrate, or I won't tell you any more.'

She laughs and blows her nose and wipes her face and sips her Christmas Baileys and is just about to start snipping again when she says, 'Oh, but it's so infuriating! They weren't *there* when you were born. I was there by myself, and the first time I held you I loved you so much that I couldn't bear that I wasn't going to get to keep you. And you were beautiful! You were the most beautiful baby that had ever been born. Ever. You still are, Stanley. You still are. You have to believe it. It's true.'

The haircut is put on hold while she flings her arms around me and sobs into my chest for a moment. Tears ooze over my fat cheeks too, but I'm smiling and feeling, oddly, more like an indulgent father. I kiss my mother's head and laugh. 'We've got to stop crying!' I cry, laughing, my cheeks shining.

'I know,' she says. 'I know. We will. I think we're just getting it out of our systems.'

A few moments later, we're back on track.

I make her promise that she won't get angry, and I make her swear on the heart of all that is sacred to her that she will not even think of blaming herself, and I tell her about how they used to tie me up.

She breaks her promise immediately and says, 'That's fucking abuse!' It's the first time I have heard her swear and I find it quite shocking.

I tell her about the last time. I was fifteen and proper hefty by then, more than capable of resisting if resistance I felt. Maggie had long fallen out of the habit of tying me up. I wasn't scratching so much any more and I rarely spent any time in their presence, so it never came up.

On this occasion, I was alone in the kitchen, nursing a slice of Marmite on toast and dreaming about Ange, on whom I was still nursing a huge, pulsing crush. Also, obliviously, I was scratching a forearm.

Suddenly Mother was there. She was frail by then, and somehow seemed shrunken from inside, like her bitterness was eating her away. 'Right, I've had enough,' she said. 'Get in the chair.'

I looked up from the kitchen table, surprised.

'Chair,' she said, twitching a thumb in the direction of the living room.

I sighed. I just didn't have it in me any more.

'No,' I said.

At which point my mother flew into one of her rages. She started screaming at me to do as I was fucking told and came storming towards me. I stood up from my chair and faced her down. I was breathing heavily through my nose, like a horse. I was scared, not of my mother but of what I might be about to do. Mother tried to grab me, and I pushed her away from me violently. She staggered back and gasped.

'*Right*,' she hissed. 'Now you've fucking had it. Jack! Jack, get in here!'

Jack was in the living room drinking, watching loud television. He only ever watched television at full blast. As a consequence I hate loud television. I hate all noise.

Maggie swore some more and stomped screaming into the living room to fetch him.

I stood still, staring into the space she had left, shocked. I knew something was happening that would change everything for ever. My heart was roaring like an engine, the noise of it drowning out everything else. My fists were clenched.

Seconds later I heard the pair of them, screaming and swearing and storming back into the kitchen. Maggie had the lengths of ruined skipping rope we used as ties, and Jack had half a hand-rolled fag hanging from his gob. He was all slovenly shirt and unbuttoned cardigan, pulling his belt from his dirty jeans and furious that he had to stop drinking and watching to administer a beating.

'I thought we were fucking done with all this,' he shouts.

Maggie had informed him that I hit her. He was furious because he knew he hadn't brought me up to hit women. He was furious because my first duty as a son was to honour him. 'Honour your mother and father!' he shouted. 'I'll teach you not to hit women,' he shouted.

Despite clear verbal clues and visible cues, the first strike took me by surprise.

With the thick leather of one end wrapped once around his right fist, Jack swung the business end of the belt and snapped the buckle into my forehead, just above my left eye. I sprang backwards, my hands flying up to feel the wound. I knocked over the kitchen chair and fell back against the cooker, the horrible grimy cooker that was only ever used to heat things up and make toast. So much toast.

I was bleeding. I assumed the prong of the buckle had split my eyebrow open. Blood was all over my fingers and slowly gathering in my eye.

As I began to straighten myself, Jack hit me again. This time the buckle ricocheted off my shoulder and on to the back of my head. Then Jack began to readjust his grip on his belt and Maggie came towards me with the rope, still screaming and griping and swearing and calling me names like a nasty little goblin in a children's horror story. She never stopped, on and on and on and on about how I was a bad kid and I was going to do what I was told if it killed her. Then she stopped.

She stopped shouting in the middle of a sentence and collapsed to the floor at my feet.

Jack looked on with an expression of absolute terror plastered to his face, the belt in his hand hanging limply by his side.

Silence.

I looked down at her body, blinking, focusing.

Maggie died of a heart attack. But not for another ten years. On this occasion, she'd merely been knocked out. Daddy had belted Mummy again. But this time Mummy had buckled.

I stepped over her body and moved towards Jack. Simultaneously, Jack let out a noise like a growl, backed away from me and quickly but feebly swung the belt at me again. I grabbed hold of it, jerked it out of his hand and raised my right hand to push past him. Presumably imagining that I was about to hit him, he shrank away, collapsed into himself on the kitchen floor, his head protected by one arm, the other held up towards me in pathetic pleading and self-protection.

I walked past him to the front door, beside which, on a table, we kept the phone. I called for an ambulance, walked through to the living room and turned off the television. Then I sat and waited.

Social services were incredibly nice to me. They assigned wonderful doctors who were kind enough to let me spend a few days in a warm hospital full of smiling nurses and fresh cut flowers. They stitched up my eyebrow and rubbed special creams into my skin, and they talked to me about everything that had happened and they were so, so nice.

They told me I didn't have to go back to my parents if I didn't want to. Which was when Keith and his parents stepped in and said they'd be more than happy for me to live with them. And so that's what I did.

The most surprising thing to me was that, as soon as I moved out of that house, my eczema began to fade dramatically, retreating further into my past with every new day.

As I tell Mum all this, she moves to another chair next to me, gasping and moaning and laughing and sobbing throughout.

'You're amazing,' she says, when I finish. 'You had to go through all of that,' she says. 'And you came through.' She shakes her head. 'And just look what you've done!' she cries. 'Look at who you've become!'

I turn back to the glass door and I look at the reflection of who I've become. I see a man with a large, angular head and a dark, brooding face. But I'm not sure it gives me the information I seek. So I turn back to my mum. She moves her chair closer to mine and takes my hands in hers. Everything she is and everything she does is in her eyes. She's witty and warm and she laughs and she cries and she's happy and sad and she's human. Gloriously, heartbreakingly human.

I look into her eyes. And I see what I've become.

Finally.

I know who I am.

CHAPTER THIRTY-EIGHT

THE SCOTTISH PLAY

I am in Edinburgh with Morag for the latter half of the Festive Perineum, that tender temporal crease which ties Boxing Day to New Year's Eve. It is a peculiarly timeless time in which the normal rules of engagement don't really apply and all flesh seems of its own accord to expand miraculously. The Festive Perineum is enjoyed to its fullest, of course, when massaged gently with the languorous tongue of Free Time and, ideally, intermittently prodded with the well-lubricated fingertip of Sybaritic Indulgence.

I think I've probably stretched the perineum metaphor far enough there. Stretch it too far, of course, and it snaps, and that's something you don't want to happen, for when the Festive Perineum snaps, the guts of the entire year spill out on to the floor, making a terrible, untimely mess.

Let's move on.

It's the last night of a long, eventful year, and we're in a not inexpensive room in an Edinburgh hotel near the centre of town. We've been out for Mexican food, shared a couple of pitchers of frozen Margarita, and we're back at the hotel room waiting for the fireworks to illuminate the limpid black sky. We have the large sash window open, a couple of tumblers of whisky on the sill and I'm standing behind Morag with a sex-hungry boner pressed into the perfect cushion of her buttocks.

This is the first time we've been properly alone since we arrived. Before tonight, we stayed with Morag's family, and, charming though they are, it's great to have some time just the two of us.

We arrived two days ago and were met at the train station by her dad, Ronnie, and the youngest boy, Ant. Ant is twelve and, unless my instinct is way off, is absolutely, without a shadow of a doubt, one hundred per cent, a psychopath in the making. At the moment he's all cricket arms and teeth that his face has yet to grow into, but soon he'll be surrounded by cronies and extorting protection money, you can tell. He's got an evil streak. There's just something about him, the way he's able to twist the knife when his brothers are bad-mouthing one another. He's not as funny as he thinks he is, but it doesn't matter because he's able to make people afraid of him. He has his older brothers – for the most part – eating out of his hands, always ready to gang up on one another to gain his favour. There's something eerie about him. He's small and physically quite harmless, but he exudes power. I can't help feel that he'll go a long way, in one unpleasant direction or another.

The holiday so far has not exactly been the road trip we'd anticipated. We're staying at the family flat in Edinburgh. The first two nights we stayed in Ant's room, which is cramped and full of boxing posters – but enormously appreciated, don't get me wrong. We'll stay there tomorrow too, and then it's back to London, when Morag will move all her stuff into my place and we will set up home together. Tonight, however, as one year moves inexorably into another, we are here, in this mediocre, overpriced, sexy-ass hotel, and my fingers are massaging Morag's neck and my penis is throbbing like a chunk of uranium.

I kiss her neck and she moans softly amidst the anticipatory buzz drifting up to our window from Princes Avenue. I wrap an arm around her waist and pull her closer to me, so that our bodies are squashed hard against one another. She pushes her buttocks against me still harder, and I lift her heavy skirt to ingratiate a hand.

Relationships are funny things. Strange, baffling, bewildering things, every bit as capricious and confusing as life itself. I've never felt for anyone else what I feel for Morag. This is all new to me. And

I'm guessing that this is what it's supposed to be like. This is Love. This is a woman I'm fully prepared to settle down and have children with. I know it's too soon to say that with any degree of certainty, but I want to, so badly. I'm ready to jump in out of my depth and over my head. I want that. I'm guessing I want it too much. And yet still it's complicated.

Yesterday we drove to Fort William for the day, Ronnie, Ant and Greg, Morag and me.

Ronnie is a tall, powerful, proud patriarch. He is also balding, bespectacled, overweight, and incapable of speaking, lest it is in an attempt to say something amusing. He makes gags. Wisecracks. Everything is a joke to him. 'Nah, I'm just playing,' he says, frequently. He is also the kind of man I imagine sits around farting in his vest and Y-fronts all summer long. In the winter he's wrapped up in a puffa jacket like a giant duvet, constantly sucking on a plastic cigarette. He's quite a strange man, all told. Amiable enough, but strange. I wouldn't want to be married to him.

Nettie is married to him. She's a round-faced, shiny-foreheaded woman who smiles a lot but says next to nothing. Indeed the only time you really hear a peep out of her is late at night when Ronnie is riding her like a drunken cowboy buggering a banshee.

At fifteen, Nicholas is the middle one. Thickset and unforgivably indolent, Nicholas does an awful lot of skulking and scowling, escaping for hours at a time inside a baggy black hood and semen-stained, crack-flaunting sweatpants. Actually, it probably isn't semen. Nicholas is constantly plugged into what I suspect is a full collection of Rufus Wainwright albums on his iPod. But I'm saying nothing. He is as tall as I am, but he has the lolloping, shambling gait of a novice hunchback. He has a dense thicket of blond curly hair under his hoody and an unfortunate habit of pushing his lower jaw slowly forwards, and then pulling it slowly backwards, when he thinks. No, not often, but still, it's disconcerting. I am, however, assured he has a good heart. And I'm absolutely certain there's every likelihood that it's true. He's probably just a tad anxious about the idea of inadvertently making a giant arse of himself. Join the club, kidda. It doesn't get any better.

Actually, it does. In some ways at least.

Finally, there's Greg, the eldest at seventeen, who has a ginger pony tail and a complexion so poor that I suspect a spot of eczema. Morag has warned me off the subject, though, lest Greg fall into another depression. At the moment Greg is on a high because he is cheekily cultivating *frisson* with his best friend's girlfriend. While, I hasten to add, his best friend is on festive holiday with his family. The youth of today, eh? I despair. I want to tell him, 'At least wait until they've been split up a week or two,' but Morag has warned me off the subject.

'Just let him be,' she says. 'Dinnae bother him when he's up.' Ah, yes, upon setting foot on her native soil, Morag became transformed into Morag, Queen of Scots. Somewhere between the train and the platform, she picked up her haggis and sceptre and hasn't really been the same since.

When we went to Fort William, Nettie and Nicholas stayed behind in Edinburgh so that, presumably, they could sit in silence together. Ronnie drove the car like it was packed with fully dilated cervices and we made it there in just over two hours.

'Let's conquer Ben Nevis!' I cried as we drove into the small, quaint mountain town.

'Conquer Ben Nevis today and you'll not be coming back down alive in a hurry,' said Ronnie ominously.

'You'll be coming down in a body bag,' added Ant, with a forced glint in his eye.

'Well, let's just go for a walk up there somewhere,' I said, pointing into some nearby hills. 'It looks cool.'

'Go for a walk up there somewhere today and you'll not be coming back down alive in a hurry,' said Ronnie ominously.

'You'll be coming down in a body bag,' added Ant.

At which point Morag jumped in and saved me. 'Yeah, let's go for a walk,' she said. We arranged to meet them again in the

Ben Nevis Inn in a couple of hours. They were going to spend their time putting a tent up and taking it down again. When I asked them why, they seemingly took great pleasure in not telling me. 'The secrets of the tent shall be known only to those that wear the tartan of the Clan McKendall.'

'Right you are,' I chirruped and clambered out of the 4x4 with Morag, Ronnie and Ant snickering in our wake.

It's cold in Scotland – freezing, in fact – and as we made our way up the stony path of a suddenly quite steep hill, the cold seemed exacerbated by the chilliness between Morag and me.

How does an argument start? That's something I don't particularly understand. And I don't know how to avoid it. 'Arguments are healthy,' Morag says. 'It's when you stop arguing that you know you're spent,' she says.

I guess there's some truth in that. I guess a couple that never rows might be seen to have an unthrillingly dispassionate relationship. But surely there has to be a balance between spiky passion and placid harmony.

Morag and I have been arguing a lot recently. Silently, it worries me. Scares me, actually. It scares me that already we could be creeping towards the end. So soon. Or maybe we're just one of those couples that fight a lot. I guess we could be. So be it. As long as we're making up a lot too, then I'm prepared to overlook it. I just don't think I'm as comfortable with constant bickering as Morag is. I don't want to remind myself of the people I grew up with.

Yesterday morning we'd grown frosty over breakfast. I think it may have been my fault. Morag had not made me a cup of tea while she was making everyone else one – something utterly insignificant like that – and I'd allowed it to bring me down.

When we were twenty minutes into our silent mountain climb, I broke the silence and offered an olive branch. I apologised for taking the tea thing to heart. Morag said I was going to have to be less sensitive. I said I would try, and we started talking about something else.

We started talking about her dad and his family. Minutes later, Morag was crying.

There are few things more heartbreaking in this life than the face of the person you love slowly crumpling in the first flush of weeping. I took Morag in my arms and asked her what was wrong. What had I said? What was she thinking? What was going wrong?

It was nothing, she said. She was just being oversensitive.

Was it the baby? I asked.

We found out the morning we caught the train to Edinburgh that there would be no tiny feet in our life any time soon. Morag was almost six weeks late, but finally, she bled. I'd shed a tear or two, but Morag had remained stoic.

She shook her head. She'd be fine, she said.

I dried her cold tears. We went a little further up the mountain.

So I figure this is what happens. This is what relationships are. Hot and cold. Up and down. Good and bad. I mean, I *know* that this is what relationships are. So I need to be cool about it, not panic at the first frost of winter bickering and assume it's all over, but rather hold on tight and love my way through it.

Now, in the hotel room, we brace ourselves against the cold.

'I love you,' I tell her.

Morag has unzipped me without turning round. I have lifted her skirt and lowered her knickers to the hotel floor.

'Good,' she says. 'Now I want you to fuck me,' she says. It's a few minutes to midnight. 'Fuck me into next year.' She gasps at her porn-audacity and laughs.

I don't feel ugly with Morag. I'm not ugly. Not with Morag.

I roll a condom on to myself and push inside her as the countdown begins.

As fireworks fly and I'm fucking her hard and fast from behind at the open window, we both gasp and cry out, staring open-mouthed at the lights, the colours, the flashes, and trails, like awestruck children mesmerised by a skyful of electric fairies.

When the fireworks die, we close the windows, move over to

the bed, strip ourselves naked and get under the duvet. Once underneath we try to get warm, grabbing on to each other and rubbing, shivering against icy bedding, our teeth chattering.

'It's been a really good year,' I say.

Morag kisses me. 'Yeah, it's been all right,' she agrees, smiling. I return her kiss adoringly, ecstatically, burying my plain face in her prolific beauty.

Prolifically beautiful though she may be, Morag is wrong. We're both wrong. It's been a *fantastic* year. It's been four whole seasons of consistent contentment made, some might say, glorious by a deliciously wicked synthesis of chance and striving. I can return to my New Life Resolutions with confidence and considerable pride, noting without irony that even my failures come coated in a not insubstantial cloak of almost outstanding achievement.

My weight loss, for example. Although I'm still far from 'fit and healthy', and have only lost half as much weight as I was really gunning for, I still feel like a different person to the bed-ridden wastrel I was this time last year. These days, when I find myself in the company of people, I'm pleased to report that I'm not necessarily burning with shame.

I have stopped smoking cigarettes, but even though that didn't prove as tough as I'd anticipated, I'm still not going to be rash enough to suggest that it's 'completely and for ever'. One day at a time.

As for falling in fully reciprocated love with the woman of my dreams … sometimes, it feels that way. But, surely, one can never really know about the reciprocated part.

More importantly, love has reared its lovely head in the most unexpected places, gushing forth from friends and family I never even knew I had. The fact is, I feel much less alone this New Year's Eve than I've ever felt before.

Morag moves her body over mine and I feel consumed by possibility. Actually, what I feel consumed by is *the present*. There'll be no resolutions this year. This year I just want to get on with it.

Morag lowers herself on to me, kisses my face and says, 'Happy New Year, Stan. I love you.'

I gasp.

We make love.

Everything is going to be all right.

CHAPTER NINETY-NINE

HIDDEN TRACK: PS I LIED TO YOU

In the preface to this memoir, I mentioned in passing that a couple of crucial facts had been changed. Unfortunately, one of these crucial facts was also stated in that same preface. Namely, that this book would have a happy ending.

Although I didn't know it at the time of writing – if I'm absolutely honest, however, I did suspect it – this book does not in fact have a happy ending.

This book in fact ends now, miserably, the morning before Valentine's Day, with you and me walking through the winter streets of London, giving ourselves space together, letting ourselves off the leash of our sudden seeming inability to get along without fighting. This book ends now, as we pass a dead fox in the street and I lean down to photograph it with my mobile phone. It ends now, with you crying in the street, telling me you knew I'd do that, telling me I'm shamelessly me, telling me sometimes the thought of being with me for ever is unbearable to you, telling me you were overjoyed when you found out you weren't pregnant, telling me I must have known it was never going to be for ever.

This book ends now, as you move out of what I quickly came to think of as *our* house, and into a nicer area, presumably with nicer people, and I begin to suspect that you merely used me to get a foothold in London.

This book ends now, as I stand in my empty back garden, my face turned away from my small, empty house and the French Scrabble set I bought you for Christmas, left behind and still in its cellophane skin.

This book ends now, with a garden fork, a barrelful of compost and a bagful of bulbs, planting for the future and starting again, mourning what I've lost but not to the extent that I don't run with what I do have, loving what I've learned, loving what I've lost, loving whatever's about to happen next.

It ends now, with me buying myself flowers and soppily shopping for a fantastic fluffy new kitten. And something for my mum. And for Jack. And for Keith.

Actually, maybe this is a happy ending after all. Just not the one I was hoping for.

Fuck it, yes it is. I declare this ending well and truly happy. Now, quick, before I change my mind.

This book ends now.

WITHOUT YOU, I'M NOTHING ...

This is just to say a heartfelt thank you to the following people, all of whom helped shape the last year and a half, whether they knew it or not: Pablo, Keith, Di Gallagher, Kitty Kendall, Aiko, Bittersweet, Pearl, Lauren W, Deb Morse, Tim and Jenny, Uncle Did and Biscuits. And not forgetting – deep breath – Alan, AlexB, Alice, Alison Eales, Allenby, Aliss, ·Amb, Amy, Anastasia, Andrea, Anna, Anna Pickard, Ani Smith, Ann Anon, AndrewM, Angela-la-la, A Nightingale, Annie Rhiannon, Annie Slaminsky, anitakrishlee, Antipholus Papps, Antipo Déesse, Aoife B, Ariel, Ari Gold, Artful Kisser, Assassin, Autolycus, Ava Cadell (Dr), Avitable, Barbara Ellen, Barb McMahon, BBP, Beavercreek Community, BE Earl, Beggars, BenefitScroungingScum, Beth, Brett Baldridge – good luck! Boz, Bridget Jones, Canuckian's Evil Twin, Carla A, Carlos Fandango, Caroline, Carrie Myers, Cat, Catherine, Catofstripes, CatsPuke, Chloë, Christ, CK, Clive For Nothing, Coastal Aussie, Claire, Coffee Boy, CommonPeople, Conortje, Courgette, Curiosity Killer, Curly, curlywurly, Dan, Dandelion, Dave2, David McC, Diana B, Delores, DJ Kirkby, Drawn Like A Dream, Duke Orsino, EasyEyes, Egbert, Eileen, Elena, Eloise, EmmaK, emordino, ErnieWeaselFat, E. Von Bertalanffy, Fat Hobbit Girl, Fat Roland, fathorse, Fenz, Frank, French Fancy, Gannet, Garrett H, Geoff (no, not *you*), Geeky Tai-Tai, Giles Hattersley, Ginny, GlamourPuss, Gonzalo Otalora, Good Girl Gone Blog, Gordon, Gorilla Bananas, Grace, Grym, Gullybogan, Gwennie K, handrekja, Hank 'Kennedy' Kingsley, Hannah, Hanspan, Having My Cake, Hayley, Harlowe, Heidi, Heath, Heather, Helen, Helga Hansen, Hendo, Henk Van Vleck, hey, Hg, Hiraeth, Hullaballoo, Ian, Ian Calvert, iLL Man, Innocent Loverboy, Insults, Inwardly Confused, Irina, Iron Fist, Isabella Snow, Isabelle, Isabel W, Jack Pandemian, JanetyJanet, Javaira & Willett, Jessica Rae, Jo, Joanne, Jonny D, Judith Isaac, Julian Meteor, just-thinking, K, Kat, KK, Katie, Killashandra, King Kong, Kirses, Kono, Lady Julia, Lady Lush, La Framéricaine, Lala, Lainey, Lana Chan, Larry Teabag, Laura, Lauren, Laurie, Lauri Shaw, LA Wallace, Lena, Lennie Nash, Le W, Lilithgirl, LiLu, Lily Lane, Lindy, Lisa, Lisa Lynch, Litha, Little Sparra, LizSara, Lizzie Barrett, Looby, Louche, Lucy H, Luka, L Wyndham Jolly, LyleD4D, Lynndie England, Lynne Miles, Mahreen, Mallory, Maria RML, MarkF, Marsha Shandur, Martin, Mary Setrakian, Maureen, MaxGirl, Max Gogarty, Mary T, Maynard, McAsh, Megan, Meep, Melissa, Mellie, Michael, Michael Kimball, Mike, Mike Sizemore, MikeTD, Mina McKay, Miranda, Miss Mohair, misspiggy, Miss Schlegel, Miss Snuffleupagus, Misssy M, Monica H, Monster, Mr Fermata, mrsean, Mrs Hall, Ms Baroque, MsMarmitelover, Mumbo, Musical Midnight, Naughty Eric, Nessy, Newbie, Nick Tann, NJ, Not Ruairi, Oatmeal Girl, Octavia, Offensive Mango, Our Glamorous Heroine, Our Juicy Life, Neil Strauss, nursemyra, nuttycow, Panda, Patricia, Patroclus, Pawpads, Peach, Penelope (it's you!), Peter Griffin, Picto, pinkjellybaby, Pip, pleite, Poppy, Purest Green, Quinquireme, Rachel North, Raven, Rhodri & Jenny, Ringo Starr! Ro, Rob, ropebunny, Rose, Roszs Bif, Rowan, Ryan Lawson & Family, Saffron, Sam, Sam Scott, Sarah, Savannah, scarletts-web, Schoolgirl, Sebastian Horsley, Selena, Semele, Sharon, Sharon O'Quinn, Sherylificus, Shimacat, Silk, Sir Garence, Smudge, Soph, Sophie, StuckintheAlps, Sudders, Sue, Suz B, Surly Girl, Suzi Duke, ~~Swineshead~~ ;-) Tamara, Tanjoska, Tank, Tanya Jones, Tea and Margaritas Lady, Tea-Cantata, TH, The Drinker, The Duloks, The Monkeyman, The Pink Half, The Princess, The Telf, The Ting Tings, The Tombstone, Thomas, Tim Footman, Timorous Beastie, Tina, Todger Talk, Tor, Triplescience, True Lateral, Urbane Spaceman, underdogartco.com, Valerie, Vicky, Vixen, Vonnie, Vulgar Wizard, Vulcan Follower, Walker, Walter, weirdpixie, Wellington: stop whining! Windypops, WiseWebWoman, Woody, Zoe and all my PUA buddies, all of whom mean more to me than they will probably ever believe.

Oh, and finally, with love and a soupçon of sadness, Avril, Sue and Cathy, Patricia, Sally and Morag, Charlie Kaufman, Audrey Tautou, Baudelaire, Belle de Jour and Bamse.

And a big hug for my mum.
x